Cultivating Inner Peace

For
S.N.G.

with lifetimes of gratitude

CULTIVATING INNER PEACE

EXPLORING THE PSYCHOLOGY, WISDOM, AND POETRY OF GANDHI, THOREAU, THE BUDDHA, AND OTHERS

Paul R. Fleischman, M.D.

with a Foreword by William Radice, D.Phil.

Pariyatti Press

Pariyatti Press

an imprint of Pariyatti Publishing
www.pariyatti.org

———————————— 🌳 ————————————

© 1997, 2003 Paul R. Fleischman, M.D.

First Edition, 1997

Second edition, 2004
Reprint: 2017

Print ISBN: 978-1-681723-55-6
ePub ISBN: 978-1-928706-67-0
Mobi ISBN: 978-1-928706-25-0
PDF ISBN: 978-1-928706-66-3

Library of Congress Control Number: 2003112385

Cover photograph and cover design by Julie Schaeffer

Printed in the USA

Permissions

Contents

FOREWORD

WHEN, IN PREPARATION FOR THIS FOREWORD, I had a long telephone conversation with Paul Fleischman, the first thing I told him was that my family and friends were teasing me for reading his book. I'd been rereading it over Christmas, a time when we all ought to cultivate peace. Yet everyone was cheerfully agreeing, with British flippancy, that a world in which all of humanity had successfully cultivated inner peace would be appallingly boring—inhuman, too. To my relief, Paul took this point very well.

He also responded benignly when I told him I was thinking of writing a book called *American Friends,* to explore how Americans think about the world. He said he would gladly be one of my interviewees, and in a follow-up email—with "teasing out peace" in the subject line, and written just before departing for India for six weeks of concentration on Vipassana meditation—he assured me (referring to his son):

> During his high school years Forrest trained us in the ways of Monty Python. So we are now prepared to meet the British invasion head on.

A week or two later, on a beautiful, snowy yet sunny day, I walked with friends along the west side of the Pennines, not far from my Northumberland home. I found myself thinking about Paul's book a lot, as I had just finished it. The day was of a sort that comes to us rarely: perfect weather, perfect company, perfect happiness. We can't live like that all the time, and I don't think most of us would want to. Apart from other drawbacks, how would we fully appreciate such days if there were not other, less happy days to compare them with?

Reflecting on this question, after talking to Paul and finishing his book, I concluded that he had addressed it fully. He is the last person to want everyone to go around in a state of perpetual serenity, with beatific—and intensely irritating!—smiles on their faces. He sounded very calm on the phone, despite the fact he had wrenched his knee badly while skiing, four days before he and Susan were due to leave. Yet I expect, like all of us, he can get ratty and impatient at times; even as a psychiatrist, listening to his patients' sagas of inner pain and turmoil, he might sometimes feel bored, though it would be professional suicide to admit to that.

He told me that Vipassana meditation in fact involves phases of considerable, subjective turbulence before calm and objectivity are achieved. In the chapter of his book where he writes of his personal experience of meditation, he emphasizes the unveiling of "ceaseless change . . . the fluidity and impermanence of every particle of your being." That itself is not peaceful; but direct awareness of it can be.

He is also fond of quoting Robert Louis Stevenson's: "To travel hopefully is better than to arrive." All the figures he writes about in his book—from Juan and Kathleen Mascaró to Scott and Helen Nearing, the Shakers, Walt Whitman, Gandhi, John Muir, Thoreau, and Tagore—were travellers and seekers. They were finders too, to varying degrees, but none of them thought that in our mortal existence the journey can ever entirely cease.

Similarly, with the problems of overpopulation, pollution and environmental degradation that Paul writes about with such passionate eloquence, no one imagines that we shall ever solve all such problems completely. But we can agree that we should commit ourselves to travelling towards a solution, and that the achievement of peace at a personal level can help us greatly towards that end.

As I read the book, I found myself often thinking of a sequence of short poems I wrote from August 1986 to November 1987. They were a sort of diary in verse—all I had time for at a time when I was looking after our two small daughters while attempting to finish my D.Phil thesis. I called the sequence "The Retreat," and put it into a book of that name which was published in 1994 by the University Press Limited in Dhaka, Bangladesh. The book was dedicated to Kathleen Mascaró, and I used as an epigraph an aphorism of Juan's: "The universal is personal." I wrote in a Preface:

> For a while, I regarded the book as a failure of nerve, a retreat from the poetry I really wanted to write. But now I do not see it like that. Sometimes retreats are necessary in order to advance: *reculer pour mieux sauter*, as the French say. And the title has positive as well as negative associations for me, as it is the name of the house near Cambridge where my friend Juan Mascaró lived, and where his widow Kathleen still lives. . . . Looking back, I find it miraculous that during hectic and worrying years I managed to 'retreat' sometimes into my imagination, and come up with poems that may last better than I thought they would.

In many ways, the inner peace that Paul is inviting us to cultivate, in emulation of the thinkers, poets and environmentalists he writes about, is a capacity for "retreat," which does not necessarily mean withdrawal from an active life in a busy world. Looking at my poems again now, I find plenty of irritation—

> *Do you want to hear of the peace*
> *That the Bible says is in store?*
> *No, I say, and slam the door.*

and dismay—

> *Famished war-torn poisoned world,*
> *What is the Word you speak?*
> *Groping for a gloss, I touch*
> *A power huge, yet weak.*

and environmental anxiety—

> *I walk in the Park: the autumn colours are warm*
> *As the sunshine: I have a sudden bad day-dream.*
> *Suppose we become so liable for the world we're in*
> *That it becomes our task to take the leaves off,*
> > *every one,*
> *Each autumn, and then, come spring, stitch them*
> *on again?*
> *Does God intend to leave us more and more on*
> *our own?*

Yet the very act of describing that turmoil in verse was perhaps my way of achieving peace. Certainly, whenever I am writing poetry, now as then, I concentrate totally. I'm not a meditator—I told Paul I'd always been reluctant to pursue anything such as yoga or meditation that required long periods of doing nothing. But perhaps in poetry I've found my way of cultivating inner peace, just as Paul's heroes cultivated it in their respective ways.

I mentioned to Paul how much I admired the style in which he had written his book: the energy, vividness and sophistication of his language. He is a real writer, with an adventurousness in his use of English such as British writers often envy in their American counterparts. It's an adventurousness that is underpinned by his love for the American land—her wildernesses, huge open skies, and endless forests. Land and language are part of who Paul is: no timid quietism there.

Combined with these deeply American qualities is a love-affair with the East. In this he owes something to his New England heritage, for the 'Boston Brahmins' (Emerson,

Thoreau, Bronson Alcott) also looked Eastwards like him. But in his discovery and dedicated practice of Vipassana meditation he also shows an American capacity for composite self-cultivation. 'I went to Mexico recently,' he told me. 'There's an age-old Hispanic and indigenous culture there that we Americans do not have. Here, each individual has to pick and choose and create his or her own culture.'

He was being self-deprecating, as Americans often are when talking to someone from the Old World. But that quality of picking and choosing—'selectivity' as Paul calls it in his book—is precisely what makes Americans like him impressive. They are not hidebound. They are not locked into large joint families, or trapped in nets of social convention. Their vision is as free and open as their landscape.

Perhaps I can indulge myself with one more poem from "The Retreat," written just after my first visit to North America:

> *I have reached North America at last.*
> > *The Fall, the Fall!*
> *Till you've seen it you cannot understand at all*
> > *The American dream.*
> > *If ageing leaves can seem*
> > *So lapidary, so also can*
> > *Post-lapsarian Man*
> > *Triumph over sinfulness,*
> > *Overcome his feebleness!*
> *Red, brown, orange, yellow, gold—*
> *No autumnal sense of a world grown old.*
> *I wander ecstatically in the bright Ontario air:*
> *Adam and Eve saw nothing so passing fair.*

—WILLIAM RADICE, D.PHIL
Northumberland, 29 January 2003

PREFACE

THE CULTIVATION OF INNER PEACE is as rational and orderly as any other aspect of the human condition, and pertains equally to all of us despite our differing starting gates, nervous systems, and life experiences. Out of my own life, and the lives of teachers and friends and those I have been privileged to know professionally, and out of the lives of great souls who left their footprints for us to follow, I would like to provide pragmatic, concrete guidance toward inner peace and radiant harmony. My examples will be drawn from real people, whole lives filled with the dynamic of human suffering and relief. I will tell the stories of people I know (often disguised or overlapped with other people to preserve privacy), or people whose lives are richly documented in historical record.

This book isn't organized to present an argument or exposition, but to animate in readers a myth of possibility, to inspire through captivating biographical images, to evoke sympathetic realignment rather than to convince.

The people whose stories are told in this book don't represent spiritual homogeneity. They can't necessarily be considered on the way to mystical union; nor are most on the direct path to Nibbāna, which was the term the Buddha used for what later came to be called "Nirvana." Representing diverse levels of attainment of inner peace, most aren't perfect examples of the entire process, and are often emblematic of only one or two aspects. As Christians, Hindus, Jews, Buddhists, Transcendentalists, atheists, socialists, and poets, they had different philosophies or theologies and were riding on different conveyances, but all of them camped for a year or a lifetime in the pinewoods of peace. No mere ideology can cup it, because the cultivation of inner peace is the activation of an atmosphere.

A person with the temperament, or yearning, or philosophy, that impels toward peace will find himself or herself confronted with many difficulties. Peace is a form of mastery. It must be won. It is narrow, a "strait gate," yet it is broad in the sense that all of one's life can contribute to the process. Every one of your thoughts and actions can facilitate your growth in peace, so you are always on the verge of parting the veil and entering.

WHEN MY WIFE AND I lived as guests of a poet in Gujarat, western India, a white-haired, retired barber served tea around the house and yard day and night. This small employment enabled him to contribute to the income of his joint family. Though serving, Babubhai wasn't a servant. Literate only to the third grade level, he was a devotee, a man of God, in a household of God. He contributed to the spirit of the place by singing traditional *bhajans*, devotional folk songs, and by accompanying himself on an *ektara*, a goatskin-covered gourd with a stick neck and one twanging string. He poured forth his heart in the artistry of crafted song. He also practiced mantra meditation, the ceaseless repetition of the name of

God, so that his heart and mind were focused on their target in every passing moment. He inwardly recited the name of Rama, one of the incarnations of God in Hinduism. The vegetables for lunch were bought from the market with *Rama nama.* The tea was served with *Rama nama.*

Having been born under the British Raj, Babubhai spoke some English; with that, and cross-cultural charades, and a phrase or two of Gujarati, we communicated. When we were sure enough of each other, I dared to ask him whether he thought God heard him, a retired barber on a planet of billions of people; whether his life was other than a dry leaf falling downward incognito to the sea of dust. He counter-questioned me: "You know how the Poet [in whose house we were] keeps eccentric hours, and may want tea any time day or night? Now suppose you want tea at midnight, and I'm asleep. You'll call out 'Babubhai' but I won't hear. You'll get up, leave your room, come to my door, and yell 'Babubhai!' You'll tap, you'll rattle the doorknob, you'll knock upon my door with all your force. As deeply asleep or tired as I may be, do you think you won't get tea? With every moment of my life I'll knock upon God's door with my whole heart. Do you think I won't get tea?"

Out of his own folk tradition, this orthodox Hindu had spontaneously echoed the New Testament: "Ask, and it shall be given you; seek, and ye shall find; knock, and it shall be opened unto you. . . . he that seeketh findeth; and to him that knocketh it shall be opened."* Babubhai's tradition or personal experience was such that his image had a doorknob and more caffeine, but was equally certain of the outcome.

Inner peace isn't limited to one culture or personality trait, or to a particular brain wave that you can buy from a guru. It's a determined way of life, continuously directed toward its goal, that proceeds through knocking and shouting for each person's own cup of midnight tea. Starting from

---

*For this, and all other references, see Notes.

many different courtyards and doorsteps, it always converges on purity of heart, horizonless perspective, and service to the common cause.

SOME TWENTY-FIVE YEARS AGO, I sought out among the commercial quackery and sugary sales pitches of India a genuine meditation teacher. I was prepared to accept no one unless they met my own criteria. First, they had to teach for free—no scam. If they accepted donations, it should be only for the costs of the food, lodging, and so on. A spiritual meditation teacher teaches for free, and earns his living elsewhere. Second, my teacher would have to be nonsectarian—no attempt to twist me out of my name and culture. Third, I was interested in a teacher whose personal morality was open and clear. Fourth, I needed a rational, comprehensible explanation of meditation that was compatible with my scientific and medical education, and that was free of esoteric secrecy or grandiose claims. At that time, I adopted Vipassana meditation as taught by a nonsectarian layman, Mr. Satya N. Goenka, in which the focus of meditative mindfulness isn't a mantra or mental image, but just the factual reality of mind and body, observed as continuously and objectively as possible. Through this practice, which I will describe in detail in Part IX, and which I have maintained now through the mature decades of my life, I have been provoked to study religion psychologically, seeking its universal essence, and I have reported some of my findings in my books, *The Healing Spirit* and *Spiritual Aspects of Psychiatric Practice,* and in various other writing and teaching. Although many of those discoveries lie outside the topic of this book, I want to report a few facts to you, which aren't based upon the medical textbooks I groaned over once long ago, but upon my systematic, scientific observation of myself. After all, I want to speak with you from the perspective of a physician, who can't preach religion to you, but, I hope, can help you treasure those features of your science or religion that are embossed and affirmed by rational inquiry and objective observation.

A first and great gift I owe to Vipassana is a daily submergence in the law of change directly experienced within my own body. Through my own years of meditation I rediscovered for myself a psychological fact well known to every religious tradition. Deeply felt penetration into ultimate reality, of ceaseless cosmic flux, threatens our self esteem. If I am only a cricket on one summer evening in a world of millions of crickets and eons of circling summers, what value is there in my trembling chirp? Freud said that all experiences of the vastness of nature and the reality of death wound our narcissism. Who wants to be a two-hundred-million-year-old trilobite fossilized in Albany County shale? Who wants to confront our personal transience and insignificance? Can the old religious metaphors really slake the nihilism implied by scientific time?

But in my meditation I rediscovered another old law of religious psychology as well. As soon as we surrender our egotism, our vanity, our overly personalized perspective, we not only can digest scientific-religious truths, we can embrace them as the source of deep inner peace. A vision of our personal dissolution within the glacial epochs of time will crush our egos, true. But, if overwhelming evidence, and commitment to the truth, leads us to relinquish our myopic, narcissistic, parochial worldview, peace will flood into us like songbirds into springtime woods. My self-aggrandizing, cardboard-box universe needs to be opened and removed so that I can unwrap the gift within. Peace is based on experiencing yourself outside of your old frame.

The obstructionistic role of vanity is an ancient observation of all religions. You may know the story of the old Jew who went to visit his teacher, not to hear his lectures on the Torah or to ask his advice, but just to see how the Master tied his shoelaces. Spiritual realization in a genuinely receptive and modest soul is manifested by practical canny—like shoelace tying—combined with sublime sense of proportion. This is the fusion of adaptation with transcendence. Religion that blooms peace is earthy in both senses of the word: skillful, and bowed over to the ground. So you may also know the reason, given by the Hasidic Jews, why today the sense of the "holy" sounds preachy and archaic, but in the old days, prophets and wise people actually encountered God face to face. The answer is that today everybody has a bad back, and nobody can bend down that low.

Peace pervades personality in proportion to the shrinking of self-importance. Peace is faith in "other." If there were a simple synonym for it, that would be "humbling." Only the very small know how to peek through the tiny hole that looks out into the expanse of the "yes."

ACKNOWLEDGMENTS

I OWE MY OWN nature education to an elder who devoted his life to sharing his knowledge with children. Such people are scattered here and there, like golden leaves, among high school teachers, professors, camp directors, and in other disguises.

Lloyd Bridges Sharp devoted his life to creating outdoor experiences for city children like myself. He was director of Life Camps, and later his own Pole-Bridge Camp, where he spread his social and environmental attitudes under the motto, "Living and learning in the outdoors." He created a sense of membership in small, self-reflective communities among pines, mosquitos, folk songs, and stars. His doctoral thesis at the School of Education, Columbia University, documented the educational advantages of such a setting, and was the first formally footnoted study of outdoor education. He lived six months a year in a tepee that he heated by chestnut-wood fire, and he constantly interrupted his own conversation, gesticulating toward a treetop and exclaiming. "Hear that redstart!?" "L.B." believed that education was *characterological* rather than conceptual: "When personality changes take place as the result of desirable experiences, we call this education."

He provided me and thousands of others a sanctuary that exceeded location, a memory and guiding image of what it is to teach about life, to give the gift of harmony. He taught us:

—to take the time to be quiet . . . still . . . and hear the woodland symphonies . . .

—to make the forest, with all its beauty and mystery, our friend and teacher . . .

—to come closer to the meaning of time and space . . .

L.B. felt special reverence for the blight-decimated American chestnut tree, and for views of the horizon. Fire was a sacrament that drew the small community together in reflection, appreciation, song, and planning nightly; a presence, the energy of past lives released to warm the hearts of the new generation. L.B. realized that a pendant oriole's nest swinging from a hickory limb was a visitation; human eyes and minds naturally looked up.

To this long-dead forest teacher I still bow down in gratitude: I hope your peaceful, nature-loving spirit will enter and spread through these words.

I HAVE KNOWN SATYA NARAYAN GOENKA, to whom I refer by the formal Hindi equivalent of Mr. Goenka, "Goenkaji," over a period of nearly thirty years. I have listened to his discourses as one of many students, and have had intimate conversations with him about myself, or about other students whose cases merited extra concern. In his beautiful lectures I heard the voice I had sought all my life, and I often marveled, "Why doesn't anyone else acknowledge the primacy of these things?" I have practiced Vipassana meditation as he has taught it, without modification. I have treasured a sentence he spoke to me. But I remember him best walking away from the meditation hall at the Center in Shelburne, Massachusetts, an old man side by side with his wife, half a world from home, eyes focused inward, chanting his *dohas* of "mettā," loving-kindness, magnificent in the reach of his teaching, poignant in the paired devotion that his wife's and his rhythmically matching steps revealed, and yet alone, gray, stooped. It is only through mortality that the truth is revealed.

THE VIPASSANA MEDITATION COMMUNITY in Shelburne and around the world has provided me shelter and companionship. A whole prairie of humanity has conspired to speed me on my way. That I woke up healthy and free and could meditate this morning puts me in debt to hordes of devas and angels who've disguised themselves as people and peas in my world.

Mike O'Brien hovered above through serial word processing, beaming inaudible sonatas back at me. Sean Williams, Mark Gosnell, Jill Cooper, Laura Bruggeman and Alex Williams combed the text of this second edition for all the small errors introduced in the reformatting.

My wife, Susan, and my son, Forrest, have lived all of this with me and are the deepest source of my conviction that I can commune with the universe, from which they were born. Together, we have left our tracks side by side on many a planet and star, and in gravel beside the Great River, where we divvied up our last freeze-dried enchilada.

INTRODUCTION
TO THE SECOND EDITION

SINCE I COMPLETED WRITING *Cultivating Inner Peace* in 1997 the world has moved left and right, shaking in its eternal ambiguity, instability, vitality and freedom, careening in danger like a sphere losing its upright axis, while simultaneously catalyzing the opening of human consciousness like a flower and like a whirlwind.

For the individual seeking inner peace, the age-old paradoxical tension between involvement and remove that I had written about remains. On the one hand, self-absorbed complacency is callous and in any case never yields true purity of heart, because it is built on a defensive fortress mentality. Inner peace cannot be found behind walls of smugness and isolation. An uncaring human being seeking inner peace finds only desert islands and dismissive querulousness. On the other hand, the world's problems are overwhelming, and our access to expanded information makes us aware of more problems than any individual can keep in mind, let alone solve. We need our privacy, our solitude, our right to shut out the clamor and grow our garden. How can we cultivate inner peace, find and dispense our harmony and love, within the confines of our own confused, wounded, incomplete and limited lives? We are afloat among resource depletion, terrorism, war, religious psychosis, population expansion, totalitarianism, and nuclear arms.

To be true cultivators of peace, we have to stare into the maw of the problems that intrude over the borders into our mind. Then we have to grow joy and resilience in the soil of inner peace so that, as citizens of the world, we contribute the age-old balm of peace, but in new potions and with new pungency.

In recent years, intrusion and threat have poured in upon us with heightened fervor. We have also heard enticing whispers, and seen auras gilding the ancient mountains that rim our sense of possibility.

Thoughts of Increasing Threat

Every day, something seemingly unheralded and increasingly ugly confronts us. September 11th awakened us to more than violence. The perpetrators' cunning, patience, and skill, their abandon with their own lives and the lives of others, made them seem both more and less than human. They presaged not just increasing violent crime or warfare, but absolute destruction. Victory does not exist for nameless automatons of surrender, whose goal is retaliatory annihilation. In a world of nuclear weapons, September 11th foreshadowed combat in which political or territorial conquest would be replaced by theologically driven extermination. September 11th was threatening to constructive people of any country or religion, because no city or region is exempt from its precedent in which revenge exceeds any affirmation, and even triumph is suicidal. Yet there were people who danced in the street to welcome this shadow harbinger.

Religious fundamentalism, which was once thought to have been in recession since the Renaissance, surges forward in Islamic, Jewish, Christian, and Hindu leadership. India and Pakistan, in conflict over Kashmir, contain significant nuclear arsenals, and Pakistan overtly threatens a first strike policy, while India openly flaunts its capacity for extreme response. The Middle East teeters on the brink of a religious nuclear war. The political peace process seems endless and ineffectual.

Electorally driven rhetoric has crippled the process of constructive and restorative dialogue. The concept of statesman has vanished. Self-righteousness is mistaken as the insignia of concern. New rage-filled accusations and fawning compliance congeal into P-C orthodoxy; the fundamentalism that captured democracy and enlightenment as religious fundamentalism has commandeered the holding together that religion is intended to facilitate.

Population growth continues. Governments are afraid to confront the religious, ethnic, political, and short-term economic forces that undergird population growth, most of which occurs at the expense of hundreds of millions of disempowered and choiceless individual women. A blind eye is turned towards this overwhelming problem because of the belief that, "growth rate has declined and will soon level off." But a declining rate of a massively ballooned base number is still an absolute increase. Furthermore, the problem is uneven and regional, crushing hope in the poorest barrios and the most subdivided farmlands.

American dominance, unchecked by balance of power politics, has led to unrestrained resource predation and to facile militarism. The possibility of worldwide consensus and alliance building around issues of terrorism and totalitarianism has been shortchanged. A meaningful United Nations, with both antecedent ethical positions of religious tolerance, elected governments, rule by law—and with efficacious alliances and interventions—remains unborn.

The will of nations to constrain corporate power—a battle allegedly fought and won in the late nineteenth century—has crumbled. Short-term profit taking without an eye to future generations threatens the way we harvest food, field and forests, the way we manage soils or prevent diseases. Corporate employment patterns, wages, and benefits, not government legislation, form the *de facto* laws that regulate most people's lives in both the developing and developed countries.

The planet is febrile, its temperature rising due to unmodulated human numbers and activity. How long will shrinking forest products house growing populations? How long will soils feed and oceans bathe us in health? How long until governments decide that this is not an issue to be studied, but a fact that requires rectifying adjustments?

Close in, ill temper more frequently invades the outmoded courtesies. Anger is the modern badge of strength, where once restraint was worn. Lawsuits and divorces replace limits and listening. Armed violence and hostage taking stalks the overflowing metropolises of many Latin and Asian countries. And even our spiritual intentions are polluted by New Age Spirituality, which withers authentic quest by substituting convenient, brief sale of ego-boosting exercises, where once the enduring human spirit heaved and vaulted.

All of these terrifying prognosticators crystallize into thoughts that drag us away from optimism and equanimity. Are they real? Are they accurate? Is my mind a reliable tool with which to discern reality, or is it another phenomenon that requires dispassionate observation?

I observe my thoughts and find they are impersonal.
They arise and fade in me, they pass through me, the common
                              thoughts, the same thoughts all
                              people think.
Thoughts are pilgrims traversing the empty spaces of the world
And our minds are trails that record the footprints
                              of their having passed.

The night thinks its own thoughts and they pass through us.
Will life on earth endure? Will humankind ever relinquish
                              their delusional frothing gods,
                              their tribal and aggregating hates,
                              their drumming frenzy to destroy?
Will the gardening and singing girls live out their days in dresses;
                              creased sheets in enfolding afternoons,
                              babies racing back towards their knees?
Will the scraped and clawed earth continue to bequeath to us
                              our life that we rape it for,
                              our breath of trees, our liquid lakes?

The night thinks these black thoughts.
The day does not, and never answers them.
I watch them pass like a shepherd with a flock of black sheep.

We Bond Through Our Common Base

What hope do I find?

A new worldwide culture calls out for the cultivation of inner peace, and for its transpiration into the breath of common humanity, as the primary imperative of our lives. There is no city or country where the call of this aspiration and opportunity has not been heard.

Mexicans and Mongolians, Americans and Moldavians, click on the same web, and would be scorched by the same nuclear cloud. College students in Moscow, Boston, or

Buenos Aires are thinking about environmental sustainability, and the limits of a fossil fuel economy. Policemen and prelates can no longer constrain access to ideas that leap the old national or religious boundaries, and that address the living planet as our shared household.

Meditation has stepped out from its Asian sequestration and has spread to every continent. In Tel Aviv, Lima, and Teheran old and young people fall silent for ten days to practice Vipassana meditation intensely. Hundreds of thousands of people of varying backgrounds meditate at hundreds of courses. Not just new information or ideas emerge. Around the globe serious meditation is awakening new conformation of realization.

We look back down into the future with a far-flung team standing on the heights in recognition that peace transcends beliefs and boundaries.

> *Tell me that you, too, realize*
> *That our human eyes are signal fires*
> *Flashing messages of hard-won tranquility*
> *Backward into the oncoming hordes.*

Why then does the world seem so much more threatening and dangerous?

As a tolerant, non-sectarian, interlocking planet evolves, all that is antithetical to it becomes apparent. No longer dominant and subterranean, the ancient hatreds, superstitions and divisions rise up and stand out as stark black lines lingering in a clear backdrop.

When I fly to Mumbai or Oaxaca, I step off the airplane that I boarded locally, and I enter a city that is simultaneously one step from my door, curiously exotic, and peopled with instant friends of mine who share similar concerns, hopes, and language. We recognize in each other that we have shed worship of our projected fantasies. We delight in our ability to immediately connect across colors, cuisines, and customs.

We bond through our common base in birth, death, and suffering, rather than claiming for ourselves some political, racial, or divine exemption.

> *Because I have suffered in distress, pain, loneliness*
>   *and fear,*
> *I can open the door of a timeless room*
> *And join in meditation inspiring peace, rest,*
>   *companionship*
> *And common boundless universal life.*

A Return to Reverence

It appears we are destroying the world, for its temperature is rising, the oceans are depleted, the forests are being cut down, the air is polluted, and soil is eroding and disappearing. But for the first time humanity pervasively recognizes that it is riding a ball. For the first time there is widespread awareness and agreement that our insights and actions—and not some fantasy men in the sky—will determine our wellbeing and our future. We know we share our pan-human cultural heritage. We know all people of all races and genders share equal responsibilities and rights. We know we inhabit a biosphere, a single breathing planetary life. Are we on the verge of extinction, or of a renewal that will turn us over to reveal a new side to our dilemma? We ourselves may be washed to new shores.

> *No, even love is not enough,*
> *Without access to the tides of renewal*
> *Washing over us, drowning us,*
> *Replacing us like seashells.*

Most people who have relinquished fairy tale religions understand that the kingdom of heaven referred to by prophets and seers is in our hearts in the here and now.

To love without attachment
To transmit the mountain light
Is the exquisite alleviation
Under whose influence we ask:

If there is no heaven
Then where am I now?

Science has done a journeyman's work informing humanity about the conditions of our sustenance and survival. Superstitious and fundamentalist thought seems to be surging, but is that surge its desperate last stand? Along with science, the completion of our renewal may require a return to reverence and beauty—poetry in the generic sense.

Amidst the primal terrors that grip and rend mankind
                —war, violence,
                delusion, disease, and death—
The poet, like a redemptive ray of sunlight,
                pierces each and every person,
                more or less,
Transmitting from generation to generation,
                fundamental truths and feelings
                that instill a degree of harmony and faith.

Her topic is compassion: life itself like a May-born robin
                fallen onto the grass.
His context is cosmic, every person suspended in a cat's cradle
                hung over corners
                of the galaxies.
Her chorus is selfless detachment amidst eternal change.

The poet is a force of nature that never dies . . .

In *Cultivating Inner Peace* I have tried to reemphasize that visions and poets—in the big sense of the word, and not versifiers—are intrinsic to the path.

Complexity and Possibilty

Inner peace derives from purity of heart coupled to multiplicity of perspective. Complex thought without purity is merely Machiavellian strategizing. Thoughtless purity of heart engenders passivity and dependence. To live vitally and with hope within the welter of the world's degradation and strife, one needs an inner glow of goodness—proof that within one's self, ideals and affiliations continue to thrive—and one needs discernment of both the real and the possible. *When I listen to upset people I hear preconceptions and foreclosures limiting information and options.*

When terrorism or war strikes, naïve people deny its dangers and its roots, thereby contributing to its spread; and cynical people exaggerate its impact, expecting pervasive negative consequences. The cultivators of inner peace balance their inner wellbeing with competent participation that neither turns a blind eye nor strikes back wildly.

Most events are only relatively good or evil, and have multiple causes and diverse effluents. Strident speech and linear conclusions rarely match the woven and layered textures of reality, and are less effective and less soothing than perspective and possibilities. All conclusions are tentative; all events morph into futures; something else is possible. Our world is an anthill among galaxies, and people who cultivate peace position themselves within long foregrounds, long consequences, an awareness of amplitude. All of history is our womb. Reality is an expanding motile field.

Yet there is a tendency in humanity to simplify and dogmatize. As the old orthodoxies recede, new constructions of thought replace them, bringing comfort of false convictions along with the stress of rigidity and defensiveness.

Fresh, malleable, hopeful perspective springs from a tutored realism that listens to the deeper meanings below the world's surface events. *The two laws of the universe are change and continuity of causality.*

The silence found throughout the world in evening ponds,
*   unbroken forests, mountain-enfolded ravines,*
*   hilltops at dusk,*
Is not an absence of noise, but a presence.
In the company of silence, people hear more clearly the passage
*   of eternity,*
*   rustling between the lattice of the cells*
*   of their own mind,*
*   like wind through a screen.*
In the calm of silence . . .
People hear the common tongue of love, the universal language
*   of mortal things, soft, like a baby's voice,*
*   passing from person to person, pulsing from*
*   trees and grass and animals, connecting*
*   existence with existence.*
Through the universal silent sound of mortal joy, individual life
*   becomes bonded, tolerable, and touched.*
Aware of this,
You can never speak up too often with the love of all things.

The Community of Love and Reason

In times of turmoil and violence, concerned people often cast aspersions on the cultivation of inner peace, as if it were a self-absorbed luxury. A good proportion of this book is spent rejecting the myth that inner peace is a selfish pursuit. I have tried to show how the cultivation of inner peace rises up from a long nurturance within the human community, and in turn amplifies itself at both the personal and cultural level. Throughout the body of this book I have tried to show the web of interactions that connects history, people, literature, lifestyle, and meditation, to inner peace. For the purpose of this introduction, and to further debunk the archaic, cynical myth, I have invented a new phrasing: inner peace is a product of, and the root to, the community of love and reason. Cultivation of inner peace results in an expanding social enlightenment, the community of love and reason. We are mammals who can respond to the geo-bio-anthro potential of inner peace the way that birds fulfill a latent potential of air by their flight. The earth itself dictates how human beings can and must evolve towards an inner peace that informs our social and ecological relationship. The new world culture, the new common humanity, is responding to the innuendos of earth.

The earth has given us three imperatives.

The first is to reproduce with foresight. Our planet is a sphere. Space and materials are finite. Freedom, health, and breath cannot coexist with a limitless surge of fleshy billions, doubling in decades to decabillions and doubling again. Protoplasm is a participant in cycles of nutriment, respiration, and interrelation.

The second is to consume with pleasure and consideration. We can only take as much as earth can give. How long can we desecrate the air of our lungs, the water of our blood, the soil whose molecules are our food, and the green forests who breathe out to us the oxygen that fires our life?

The third is to build a community of love and reason—a community of love, in which compassionate, affectionate identification of any one life with all living things is the

*arterial magma of cohesion and wellbeing—and reason, the
effort to find the actual cause of the intended effect, to solve
problems with observation, investigation, logic and dialogue.*

Three steps build the community of love and reason:

*The first step is to augment everywhere and continuously
all ideas and actions that recognize, expand and implement
the right to dignity and life: the liberty of feet and minds in
each locale; our shared existence and fate with our
zoological and botanical coinhabitants; and those
conversations by which we address, redress, and rebalance
the conflicts and confusions within the quilled and
multiplex expression of those rights; and access to the
essence and the source: books and ideas; health and homes;
freedom from intimidation and violence via the creation of
judicious and enforced law.*

*The second step is to challenge everywhere and
continuously all ideas and actions based on separation,
superstition, exclusive revelation, and hoarded dominance;
to speak up clearly against reproductive anarchy and for
women's freedom and the well-parented child; to form a
wave of thought and evidence against theocracy, divine
exemption, holy wars; to underfund economic oligarchy that
uses penury to crush participation; to animate voices
against coercion by armies, police, red or black books; to
outvote any governments of gods or generals; to corral
corporations away from resource rape into returning
nature's services unspoiled; to conduct a hubbub of any and
only those cultures that extend the hand of tolerance and
touch a common human thread.*

*The third step is to beat the drum of the human spirit,
limited and constrained by love and reason, unlimited and
unconstrained in its dazzling haberdashery, its effulgent
music making and poem speaking; its creative probing of
atoms, genes and stars; its myths and symbols unbound
from authority and literalism; its amplification and
expression of the iridescent joy inherent in the open iris; its
life-giving question, the transmission from teacher to pupil,
parent to child; and its quiet, peaceful meditation, aware, at
ease with reality as it is, removed, at one, seeking nothing
more.*

*Political correctness is the attempt to expand the human
collective by asserting the relativity of knowledge and of the
values that underlie culture. Enlightenment is the
unabashed propagation of love and reason.*

*The community of love and reason is an ancestor, an
adolescent, a springtime, an earthforce like greening rain.*

*Community of love and reason, I reach out to you between
the bars that hold me; in a daydream I hear beyond the black
iron voices of fanatics and apologists, your ruby throated
song. You are only an anticipation, a shoreline of an
undiscovered continent, a memory of a numinous dream.
As elusive as the wind, your promise effervesces like salt
air, miles from the seminal sea.*

*I hold you in my hand like a fluttering bird, like a geode.
I dig for you, ancient buried king.*

*Amidst my despair for this sweaty planet, premonitions of
the community of love and reason flash across my vision
like electrodes of the sun.*

Original Equanimity

The main thing I want to say is that we do not create inner peace. We discover it. It is in fact present and available. We touch down into it by being its good listeners, diligent followers, keen discerners, and energized practitioners. We cultivate inner peace first by transforming ourselves rather than by hyperfocusing on strategies and schemes to control the world; by permitting our perspective to keep expanding to trans-historical eternal insight; by attending to what is universal rather than to what is exclusive or parochial; and by dipping into realizations of our own impermanence, which creates kinship rather than boundaries with all mortal things.

Black gneiss of Guilford
Your ancient crusted carapace
Sets a measure to all my human efforts.
Against the backdrop of your subterranean convolutions
The wars and poems of people are like the jerking
Of shadow puppets silhouetted upon a tattered negligee.

Your endurance and immobility contain a calm
That makes all prayers of peace little more
Than Spring freshets that stream down your creases
Season after season disappearing into your nether womb.
All my anguish is to you less
Than the lisp of falling things like leaves and rain
Upon your unbreakable black armor.

Yet a child approaches your gnarled outcrop
And sees in the frozen fluid mosaic of your skin
Lockets of garnets,
Scintillating flecks of mica
Sewn like a brocade across your infinitely absorbing bosom.

Into the panoply of tiny mica mirrors
The sun is touching its eager fingers
And you sparkle with fertility like a bride.

I have found in dead rock an ecstasy, a relationship
Of love that is older than the human or the leaf.
When I rise up and hold in the cup of my heart
A burning passion to restore the world
To its original echoing equanimity,
I am only like the mica, like the gneiss and sun
Obedient to the original and fundamental thrust.

—Guilford, Vermont
& Amherst, Massachusetts,
March, 2003

PART I

Chapter 1

THE QUEST FOR
INNER PEACE

INNER PEACE CAN BE STUDIED the way the naturalist George Schaller likes to study pandas and snow leopards—as an endangered species. How can I stalk this elusive species of human emotional life, track it to its lair, and then, like a modern environmental naturalist rather than an old-fashioned safari hunter, not merely capture it, but instead meet it upon trusting and intimate terms, proclaim its territory a sacred preserve, and so ensure its continuity and vigor as a free spirit in the world for years to come? If my hunting of this legendary mood were successful, I could return to America and write an article for *National Geographic*, promoting the Inner Peace International Wildlife Refuge and illustrating with Kodachrome photographs its exotic and enchanted terrain.

In fact, I have made many such expeditions to the last hideouts of wild peace, but my slides are all blank. The cat wasn't in the viewfinder. Like all psychological phenomena, inner peace is rare, intermittent, developmental, like a friendship patiently cultivated with a lynx. You will find it impossible to merely saunter up and pet it, for your subject will simply vanish at your approach. Before you can befriend inner peace, you have to shed your old ways and enter its ground on its own terms. It will take tenacity, faith, and maybe even years of observation before you find yourself face to face. At your first glimpse of this wonderful manifestation of creation, you will chuck your camera. The only way to know whether you have captured it will be whether any change flashes into your demeanor.

Although inner peace is so cautious in letting you approach, everyone has had the glimpse. Inner peace is a universal experience, filed in memory among the mother-breath of soil and living grass, which were so close to us when we were toddlers, yet which faded from our familiar touch.

At some young, innocent hour, when you and I were only ingenuous inhabitants of the green world without corners, we passed inner peace in the sunlight. Our memory of this fleeting encounter has continued to animate our hopes for a deeper union. In the same way that sexual feelings disrupt the cozy sanctuary of childhood, rupture our satisfaction with our parents' homes, and scatter us into the world to seek that magic Other who will complete the preamble and initiate the great middle chapter of our lives, similarly, peace has a deep claim on our hearts and drives us toward consummation. There is nothing I desire more than the development of inner peace.

Inner peace is much more than a nostalgic cloud. It's an adult concern, an urgent yearning that can motivate mature lives, a potent life force. Without peace, we feel our days and years haven't brought to fruit the truest, deepest seed in us. It is a call from the center of ourselves, from the place behind the waterfall.

If inner peace is really as I have described it, a natural phenomenon, a sweet memory, and a provocative force, then why does it remain furtive behind the hubbub of our ordinary days? Something is in the way. A conflict in human nature blocks us.

Human life has two directions: survival and transcendence. In the *best* lives these opposites come full circle and complement each other, but more often they stimulate antithesis. Let me describe first our survival-oriented nature.

As mammals, we are impelled to eat, to provide, to earn, to build, to create warm, safe homes, neighborhoods, societies for ourselves and for those with whom we identify, our families and fellows. Our bodies scream for necessities. Every day hunger stalks us—at least three times a day, and for grazers like myself, continuously. And we still inhabit jungles of violence, in which our flesh right down to the hair follicles rises with outraged fury against those who threaten us on the street, in schools, or in our kinsmen's countries. Based on millions of years of evolution, every human being is an animal adapted for vigilance and survival. Such an animal as we are in our adaptational mode has no room for inner peace. Not only would that drain time and energy away from the tasks of safety, but is in itself an opening, an unlocked window, over the sill of which danger can intrude its eerie hand.

This mode occupies most of our waking hours, and it should. Every one of us carries memories of the terror that can befall us. In my psychiatric practice located in pastoral, collegiate New England, survivors of every war of this century have walked wounded into my office. Many people have faced the maximum horrors, and those who haven't all know that someday they might.

People don't focus on success and safety alone. As the human mammal evolved, another inspiration came to the fore to rival security, so that people are pulled along by two mighty horses competing in the same harness. I believe that the most human trait isn't language, intelligence, or knowledge, but awareness of death. From the consciousness of the reality of dissolution, cessation, nonbeing, derives the impetus for spiritual life, for transcendence and peace.

In childhood we transiently cross paths with peace; at the earliest stages of life we also receive glimmerings of mortality. Even as children we begin to realize that we will die, lose everything, face final and ultimate extinction. Unlike other mammals with whom we share our survival focus, humans have a spiritual life because we understand time, change, death, and our own proportion. We are very, very small, a vapor, a drop of dew, a part of something bigger, nothing by ourselves.

Human lives, like middle-aged eyes, are always bifocal. In the most desperate times, or in the most humdrum hours, we adapt by thinking, planning, saving, spending, moving, or fighting, but we also relinquish adaptation to yield, to accept, to turn away from our own fate and open to something bigger. Since I'm going to die, and everyone and everything around me will pass away and millions of years will pass and they will also vanish . . . why not live my life *now* with peace?

Inner peace is an aspect of spiritual life that derives from the awareness of our own insubstantiality. Inner peace isn't a single emotion, but a felt relation to the vast project of finding meaning and purpose within the context of incomprehensible infinitude. Like any relationship, peace has its moods, ascents, nadirs, eclipses, and laws.

Inner peace is like marriage. It isn't a one-mood state, but a particular context for all of them, reflected in one endlessly beloved face.

You can now understand that when I write about inner peace, I am not referring to an object, a fixed, blissful glee, but to a dimension of existence that is complex, variable, and multifaceted, which nevertheless leaves only its own footprints, has exactly its own visage. We have all known it, lost it, found it, thrown it away, wanted it again. But don't you find, as I do, that the longer you live, the more value you place upon it? How can you turn your life toward the peaceful transcendence of your own limited time without becoming foolhardy or inept, remaining worldly and skillful, yet focused more and more on peace?

INNER PEACE WILL GROW in your life in proportion to its importance to you.

No one could imagine an entrepreneur who devoted twenty minutes twice a day to his business and expected it to prosper. No one could imagine a mother who took care of her children one day a week and expected them to thrive. Like a business, like a child, inner peace will flower only from the sunshine of your focalizing effort.

But realistically, how much time can you spend pursuing inner peace? If twenty minutes twice a day isn't enough; if one whole day a week isn't enough, will you have to give up everything in order to pursue this course?

Over the years that I have studied people who obtained *deep, recurrent, long-abiding, life-transforming and outward-reaching* experiences of inner peace, I have found one salient common bond they all share. Inner peace is found by an intensity of devotion to the goal so relentless and powerful that it bursts through the bidirectionality of life, and suffuses the survival-oriented, adaptational daily tasks with the transcendental, all-permitting light.

The first rule on the quest for inner peace is to make it the number one priority without disrupting or devaluing the spectrum of daily life. Twenty minutes twice a day, or one day a week isn't enough, because inner peace has no separate time or place. It is the infusion of mundane savvy with transcendental fervor that marks "wisdom"—a psychological truth to be found in every culture, religion, and era. Peace comes from the holy fire of concentrated intention. Still engaged, the man or woman truly on the path seeks every moment as *the one* in which to activate life's highest blessing.

This intentional concentration translates best into contemporary phrasing as the word "pace": appreciating what you have or do, and not having or doing more than you can appreciate. I'm using the word "pace" in contrast to "distraction," which presages dissatisfaction. Our lives are our feelings, and feelings unfold slowly, cued by their invisible tempo. The most obdurate obstacle to peace in the lives of many people today is the rate at which they move and think, without allowing time for the glow of peace to filter up and pervade their pauses. The punctuationless, run-on sentence of modern life derives not only from obligations in work and family, but ironically from the harried pursuit of pleasure too.

It's important to appreciate at the outset that peace is a dynamic product of the way you live, and not a mere parenthesis or vacation from who you really are. This way, your whole being can become entrained behind it, and can contribute to your momentum. Don't look for a safe platform, but for a direction recurrently renewed, until your friendships, your diet, your work, your reading all add to your downhill, first-class, express train of peace. Another way of describing "dynamic" is: committed, forgiving, patient.

If you want to find inner peace, you will need a new criterion for all your life choices, and that is the criterion of emotional tone. You will need to initiate decisions based not upon convenience, success, or conformity, but upon how the outcome will affect your peace of mind. Inner peace will have to become the rudder by which you navigate the straits of great and small decisions.

It is often said that the Psalms contain the greatest nature poems ever written. Many passages are replete with the authors' direct encounters with stars, mountains, and deserts. The words feel deeper because we know that they have sprung from lived experience. For the authors of the Bible, as for us today, the planet, the cosmos, provide metaphors for lofty attitudes and states of mind. All seekers of peace familiarize themselves with wind, water, and dawn.

Every person not only wanders through, but is a manifestation of, nature. This is both a spiritual and scientific principle. People are nature, and observation of external nature is an entry to internal self-observation. Appreciation of the cosmogonical grandeur of the planet is only the vestibule to understanding our own nature, which opens out into even greater vistas. When we turn inward, to observe the nature of ourselves, on the quest for inner peace, we will make discoveries peculiar to our own personalities, and we will also confront universal truths that pertain to all people, all nature, all phenomena.

I'll illustrate this point with an example. Please stand beside me on the bank of a river, where we can begin, like the ancient psalmists, to look for the laws of our own being mirrored in the riverine regularities.

Water flowing over river rocks holds a shape into which the submerged stones have molded its yielding fluidity. If you stare at a section of river, you'll see the same dynamic yet apparently constant forms of flow, like a sculpture garden, containing shoulders, buttocks, and elongated body-shapes looking as if they were designed by the sculptor Henry Moore. The smooth, watery, anatomical curves are a momentary illusion: one fleeting, glittering expression of sunlight, water, mineral, and earth-form in endless geomorphic play. The apparent solidity of shape is a temporary appearance over the ceaseless flux of nature. The river will be visibly transformed after the thundershower, after the heat wave, or next spring, as it is in fact invisibly changing every second.

Similarly, each moment is a river that is temporarily shaping matter into human and earth forms. All of the mountains, oceans, shoulders, and buttocks are molded by the millionfold contemporary conjunctions into their momentary form. Our bodies are exactly like the river. The shoulders and hands, thoughts and feelings, are sinuous shapes, matter rolling in the river of time. We are being born, living, and dissolving all at the same time, always. The whole world around us and inside us is part of this ceaseless process of transformation. Regardless of your age, as you read this page, you are still being born. Inner peace is predicated on the insight that the world is always an embryo.

In every molecule, every cell, every body, every river, every planet, every galaxy, the fundamental law of the material universe is change. The atoms themselves are not solid or elemental, but vibrating energy fields, rivulets, inconstant, changing. All scriptures tell us that mountains are washed to the sea and that life is temporary. Inside of us is the continuous tremble of awareness of our own pending death, because it is already in process. This law of change, decay, disappearance is part of our guts and bones. All temporary security or success at the worldly level will certainly dissolve in the river of time, so that inner peace can derive only from gripping, convincing answers to the question about what individual life means in the context of personality-obliterating time, death, and eternal change. Realization of peace at this depth is like obtaining an anchor that can stabilize you throughout surface storms. Deep peace that is affirmed rather than negated by awareness of ceaseless change can become yours, as these unfolding pages will clarify.

Arrival at this transcendent perspective doesn't justify neglect of your circumstances. The distant horizon and the foreground both contribute to the picture of your life. The skill that I hope the unfolding chapters of this book will help you cultivate is how to keep all of the components of the picture harmoniously related within the same frame. We human mammals are caught with two agendas we must fold into one: maintenance of our earthly life, and realization of its true proportion. Inner peace is the product of competence illuminated by ultimate reality.

I HAVE DESCRIBED how concentrated intention on peace leads to a pace of appreciation. And I have described how appreciation of inner and outer nature leads to a liberating perspective. To keep both of these attributes of the path of inner peace well toned in your life, there are exercises. Disciplined interiority, sustained reflection, meditation are the only ways by which your peace can remain vibrant and not just the occasional product of serendipity. *Practicing* peace is the way toward confident strides in its company. I have emphasized so far how your whole life can join your quest for peace, but it's also true that you need a sacred time and place, an enclosure, where your intention can bask. Every day you might well close your gate and contemplate your garden.

To develop inner peace in your life, you need to place it on your agenda ceaselessly, not compartmentalized to a ritualized time or place, but also with its own bower. Skill and inspiration must marry and walk down the center aisle together every day. You need to observe nature, joining the men and women of old under the stars, observing within your human nature the whirling, fluid embryogenesis of eons. Let yourself dissolve into the real dimensions, whose limitless horizons will hurtle you beyond chronological conceit into awe and devotion. The incense that arises from this sort of worship is peace.

Over the years that I've studied people who obtained deep, recurrent, long-abiding, life-transforming, and outward-reaching experiences of inner peace, I have found that they share a second common feature: surrender and reverence. Peace is peaceful. The struggle for peace is a paradox: accepting, observing, letting go. We are animals born and made to be flooded from beyond ourselves by all-pervading peace.

The experiences of cosmic dissolution and of reverential beholdenness sound like they might leave you depressed, cynical, disengaged. Actually, the opposite happens. When you experience your life in its true dimension, many fears and frustrations fade into insignificance, and you can at last live out your inwardly inspired vocation. Your life choices will derive from the deep cave of calling. You ask yourself, "What will I do here on the shore of eternity, at the meeting of life and death?" Your decision won't be hapless, but unencumbered. If you continuously base your decisions upon peace-permitting perspective, you will find yourself living out what you always wanted to do anyway. This happens when you cease to live as if the totality of the world is encased inside your own time and place, and you can allow yourself to become suffused.

We are made with the capacity for inner peace. It can flow into us, and that primes the pump. Then it begins to flow out of us, coming back day after day. Like rays passing through storm clouds, your peace won't remain "inner," but will descend to light upon family, community, shade trees, and pets.

Personal relationships are the theater in which peace has its validation. Its interpersonal qualities include clarity, because it enables greater distance from personally driven needs and distortions. Clarity and objectivity catalyze appreciation and concern. Peace facilitates love without urgency. Every near person is a treasure, an old, old friend. Seen in the light of true proportion, spouse or child provides companionship crystallized from the universe itself. Loving people are local manifestations of a greater love. Not just people but all life will seem closer and friendlier.

Peace gives birth to righteousness and to the ethics that spring from communion with all lives, coincidentally manifesting now out of the endless foment of time. Peace is a social activity, a product of human civilization, a form of communication. It is passed on, radiated, and dies without fertilization. It has already left its golden dust on your windowsill in many previous springtimes.

If you are seeking inner peace, it must be planted and bloom at home. Do your spouse and children ever receive your unalloyed attention? Are you accessible? I wish you would remember from this book at least this one fact: the big and little people at your kitchen table are all couriers from the kingdom. If you listen accurately to them, they will guide you to the other shore. The people you live with will direct you to love if you let them.

As I understand it, the story of Noah and the flood is a metaphor for the same truths I have talked about so far. All the individual Noahs who permit ultimate reality to rain down on them will find their naïve sense of self dissolved and, setting forth on the waters of scientific and religious time, they will drift on the egoless ocean. How lonely, how frightening—yet Noahs sail on with determined faith. If you do that, the dove will alight. That's the bird we're talking about. If you travel this far from your isolated personal self you will be opening and sojourning in kinship with everyone cohabiting your contemporary ark. You will also be floated free of conventions and institutions that may have previously blinded you to what you have now discovered. The dove will lead you to a new world, emergent. Peace is intrinsically contextual, ecological, a membrane, an eardrum attuned to what harms and heals the infinite multitude of neighbors, furry and green.

IN THE RAREST GENIUSES OF EMOTIONAL LIFE, peace may, after years of intense effort, attain such deep saturation that it not only absorbs all assaults upon it like an ocean, but it spreads its own essence, as evaporated oceans spread rain to soak the surrounding continents. In some august people, peace at last becomes absolute, and radiant. Peace pollinates its neighbors, like corn. It becomes unbreakably yielding, like its mother, time.

For most people, inner peace is increasingly possible, a continuing project that will grow if you feed it, so that it can be expected to put on muscle and take up more of your house—like a teenaged son. Inner peace, like a teenager, is always in love with and chasing after possibilities. Peace is a lecture you are writing over ample time, and with each rewrite, the language harbors more residue of your life's wisdom. Peace matures during courageous confrontation with suffering. Ill-ease and fear are its antitheses. An unblinking examination of the pervasiveness, origin, and cessation of suffering is the only way out of a life of furtive, cautious repression. Honesty is the crucible of peace.

Your own quest for peace may not cure the world, but neither will it fail you if you are its devotee, its congregant, its loyal friend. Peace pays dividends on your policy, and willingly names all your cousins, friends, and acquaintances as beneficiaries.

The modern world, governed by a cathode-ray-tube eyeball that flickers breakfast cereal ads and erotic gestures into every home, has nothing to offer you on the path to inner peace. No one on the street corner is planning to waylay you with wisdom. In Albany, Jerusalem, Phnom Penh, and Sarajevo, the ancient conditions pertain. Even in your office, or your home—maybe even in your church or synagogue—a restless, frantic, self-alienated, electronically stimulated confusion dominates life.

The implications for inner peace in the modern world are exactly the same as they were in the ancient world. We will always have the same problems. It is always the morning of the flood. It is always the same day.

The universe is filled with secret messengers. They arrive instantaneously anywhere through the cosmic ray of gratitude. They enter our homes at night through doorways in galaxies that open when we forgive someone. Raindrops carry to our roof the same poetry of surcease and patience that Noah must have heard. If we prepare for it, our bodies may open at the right moment like the Red Sea, to make way for the incomprehensible magnitude beyond the material world. The rocks themselves will break open, and every molecule will speak the same truth to you in your native tongue.

Peace is always present, hovering, invisible. Occasionally, we dare to divest ourselves of personal worry and turn to peace, so that it momentarily blinds and pierces us. Peace is when your brain makes way for the color of eternity. Then each cricket, your spouse, child, every leaf calls out for your very personal hand.

Chapter 2

Peace is a Personal Encounter: Juan and Kathleen Mascaró

THE POSSIBILITY OF A LIFE devoted to personal peacefulness that then atomizes outward to others is *conveyed from
one person to another.* For a sustaining image of such a life, I
am indebted to Juan and Kathleen Mascaró. They drew me
like a magnet into their world. This is how I met them.

When I was twenty, in imitation of Thoreau, I set up camp
alone in the woods and pursued reading and solitary wandering, trying to answer the question about the future of my life.
What was *worth* doing; what *could* I do? I was already interested in psychology and biology. I read Ernest Jones's thick
biography of Freud, and was deeply impressed with the great
psychiatrist's awesome inquiry, his relentless quest for the
truth, his spirit of "conquistador," as he referred to his determination to find answers for himself. But the atmosphere of
Freud's world, with its stuffy European drawing rooms and
its mechanistic model of mental life, seemed suffocating to
a young man inspired by poetry and owls.

Under the influence of Thoreau, I tried to read the Bhaga-vad Gita, of which he had written: "In the morning I bathe my intellect in the stupendous and cosmogonical philosophy of the Bhagvat Geeta . . . in comparison with which our modern world and its literature seem puny and trivial." Inspired by this extreme praise, I had bought a paperback copy of this ancient Indian religious-psychological poem, translated from Sanskrit into English by J. Mascaró. To my disappointment, I found the old poem superstitious and opaque. I focused on what was exotic and unacceptable to me—such as the description of birth in the next life being determined by the phase of the moon in which the person dies—and quit reading it.

I rebounded into something rigorously scientific: E. Odum's textbook, *Ecology*, which, along with technical discussions of seed dispersal and plant succession patterns in old fields, gave me a sense of the integrated interdependence of individual living things with their surroundings.

In an idle moment, I flipped open the Bhagavad Gita to a random page, and this time the text was clear: along with some archaic religious passages, it contained an intuitive, poetic restatement of Odum's text.

> *See now the whole universe with all things that move and move not, and whatever thy soul may yearn to see. See it all as One . . .*
>
> *Even as mighty winds rest in the vastness of ethe-real space, all beings have their rest in me . . .*
>
> *Through my nature I bring forth all creation, and this rolls round in the circles of time.*

Science and religion have a deeper, shared substrate. I realized that I would not be able to find what I was seeking by being a student either of religion or of science. I would have to live directly, trusting only those texts that thrust me out beyond themselves and carried me directly to an encounter with ultimate reality.

That summer helped me set my compass toward an integration with deeper realities, such as I imagined I'd found in Thoreau and the Gita. Over the years, however, I collected numerous translations in English of the Gita, of which there are said to be several hundred. I found to my amazement that the poem had no appeal to me as a religious-philosophical text, except in that first poetic translation I had read. About twelve years later I began to tackle the Gita in Sanskrit. The flavor unmistakably was the same as J. Mascaró's translation. Other translations attempted to impose a religious orthodoxy or a philosophical consistency on a fundamentally intuitive vision. I was not a believer in the Hindu Gita but a disciple of its poetic affinities.

While visiting a friend who was living in a Zen Buddhist monastery, I picked up a small paperback edition of the Dhammapada, a 2,500-year-old Indian Buddhist text. The Dhammapada previously impressed me as a boring list of dry injunctions, but as I skimmed through the new paperback translation, it seemed to sparkle as never before. The translator was Juan Mascaró.

I had always assumed that the translator of my inspired edition of the Bhagavad Gita was a long-dead Victorian from the era when Sanskrit was originally being translated into English. I was following the old belief, "That man is so great he must be dead." But this new translation of the Dhammapada was only a few years old.

On a hunch, seated in a canvas chair next to the woodstove in our Vermont cabin, I wrote to J. Mascaró, explaining how his translation had set me on a quest years ago, how I had poked into the Sanskrit and found the spirit of his words true, and how I had woven the study of psychiatry and religion into a profession I continued to pursue. I wrote that through his translation I imagined I had heard scientific ecology break forth into rhythmic poetic couplets of reverence and love. I sent the letter care of the publisher in London and, knowing it was a long shot, pushed it from my mind.

Some months later, an answer arrived in a shaky, small hand. Over the next seven years, letters continued to cross the Atlantic. Juan Mascaró was in his eighties, slowly declining with Parkinson's disease. He and his wife, Kathleen, used their letters to speak of personal things as one does to a psychiatrist; I replied in kind. They described two birds singing at the end of a raw English winter.

In the winter of 1986 I made a mad dash across England to meet Juan and Kathleen Mascaró. I was changing planes in London on my way to India and so, with no time to wait for trains, I spent an absurd sum on a long distance taxi ride. The driver, with mannerly British reserve, carefully interviewed me. I was spending a lot of money; these friends I was going to visit must be very well known to me?

"I've never met them!"

It was snowing. White lined the iron gate to the small, shrub-bounded garden, and white lay on the steep thatched roof of a cottage. Thatched roof! Kathleen opened the door and we hugged; as soon as I saw Juan I began to weep profusely. He was tiny; his whole body trembled within the precinct of a three-legged walker; he put his palms together and said, "Namaste," the ancient, traditional Indian greeting. He could barely speak. He gestured for me to sit down; there was a copy of the Dhammapada there. I read out loud from the page and verse he indicated:

> "—*Oh let us live in joy, in love amongst those who hate! Among men who hate, let us live in love.*

*"—Oh let us live in joy, in peace amongst those
who struggle. Among men who struggle, let us live
in peace.*

*"—Oh let us live in joy, although having nothing!
In joy let us live like spirits of light."*

There was only one fully furnished and heated room in
the house—furnished mostly with bookshelves. Heat was
a fireplace, wood hauled by Kathleen. They spent their last
years together as they had spent the rest, studying over and
over the great texts of humanity: the New Testament, the
poetry of Rabindranath Tagore, the Gita. A few years earlier
Juan had written to me with irony and earnestness, "I have
not yet read the Gita or the Upanishads or the Dhammapada
or the Gospels." Juan also had extensive, careful notebooks
of his own words, which were clearly not intended to be
published in his lifetime. The Mascarós' existence was trim,
yet lush with personal love; concentrated, yet world-scanning,
for Juan's translations had brought international acclaim;
relentlessly serious yet sweet and welcoming. It bubbled like
a fountain with poetry, flowering plants, and days of quiet.

In the obituary notice for Juan Mascaró in the London
Times, British poet and translator William Radice wrote:

> His model was the Bible . . . he believed that the poetic
> and spiritual were one . . . . He found examples in all
> the major religions and literature of the world . . . .
> All his life he strove for a form of religion that was
> rational, poetic, and universal, and he worked with
> patience and precision . . . . every word was weighed
> with loving care . . . . he lived quietly, reading deeply
> and writing diaries and reflections . . . . The serenity,
> humor, and warmth . . . and his ability to quote poetry
> at length and in many languages, were both fruits of
> a single-minded spiritual and scholarly endeavour in
> which many troubles were overcome.

The grieving Kathleen Mascaró wrote to me, "If you believe in human love, you must also believe in a cosmic love." Juan had written, ". . . whatever may be the events of our outer or inner life we must ever have the peace of love."

Even this sketch at the close of a man's life reveals the possibility of and the path to peace. We hear of a life lived in so valuable a way that in the final days no adjustments are necessary; what was important then remains important now. We find adequate surroundings, with minimal attention to physical embellishments, and proximity to nature. In summer, rose bushes actually poked through their front door. We hear of open-ended study devoid of dogmas or expertise. (Juan had written, "One of the tasks of education is to reveal the joy of the Infinite . . . !") We experience personal love that opens and magnetizes seekers from across the oceans. We recognize concentrated devotion. In his first letter to me, he asked: "Can you believe that I have only seen television about two dozen times?" There is courage and acceptance of aging, illness, and death; and faith beyond content. Juan was not buoyed up by a literal, fundamentalist belief in the Bhagavad Gita or the New Testament. He resided in and purveyed their faithful atmosphere. Restraint in mood and infectious, exemplary, peaceful joy vibrate through the whole story.

In Juan's letters to me he had written, at the age of eighty-four, "I have thought very much on peace lately, as the problem of peace is the supreme problem of man: peace within us . . . the greatest definition of peace I know is in Isaiah, 'And the work of righteousness shall be peace.'" His concern was with the identity of goodness-in-action: righteousness, and internal psychic harmony: peace. Even in advanced age, he was keenly interested in the arms race; the London *Times* published his letter of moral outrage. He believed in a continuity of private spiritual life with global emotional tone. "We want an inner revolution . . . peace is an act of creation . . . a harmony, and this harmony should be found within ourselves, our family, our village, our nation, our world."

Juan's life and words were pointed toward one state of mind, which is the goal of all seekers of peace in any time or culture.

> The sun shall be no more thy light by day; neither for brightness shall the moon give light unto thee: but the Lord shall be unto thee an everlasting light.

The man or woman who has attained this depth, like the prophet Isaiah, is no longer guided by passing events such as the sun and moon. The material world is transcended. Another level of truth is known; external facts are not the final arbiter. An enduring brightness, an emotional pole star, a personal and invisible truth is now the source of vision. Inner peace is attained through discovery of the eternal within.

Before I left their house on my madcap, between-flights visit in 1986, Kathleen had given me a tiny package that wouldn't be a burden during my travels. It was a present for my son. On my return weeks later, he opened it. Her gift was magnets.

INNER PEACE IS A pole star by which individuals and groups can orient toward freedom from expansionism and divisiveness. Although population explosion, global degradation, and international aggression can devastate our earth, the most powerful counterforce is the pleasure of serenity realized.

There is a higher spiritual life, a life centered upon, resting on, an inner mood. Based upon unforgettable inner experience, cultivated in the privacy of heart and mind, the life of inner peace generates autonomy from the demands and rumors of mass man. Focused upon values that emerge from contemplation of eternal time, it liberates people from thrashing in self-protection and generates a life of equanimity, harmony, and creative expression of those values in the community. Every person who cultivates such a life is a spring where underground waters emerge into sunlight. Such people provide a source of stability and purity within the surging tides of history. They initially suffer loneliness and self-restraint, to emerge as waves on the ocean of transcendent hope and love. Across time and place, we hear their voices in chorus, expressing a unified, spontaneous, universal realization of truth: ethical sensibility and care rekindled moment by moment; concentration on purification of their own reactions; and a realistic, objective perspective.

Pursuing the life of peace, stumbling and flying, I met others going the same way, and was impelled to ask, "What strange etching in the floor of the universe has channeled me to mingle with *you*, here?" Migration by magnets and stars isn't the sole prerogative of plovers. Find peace in friendship. Seek it, fly to it across the world even at high cost. Peace embodied in memorable people imprints you to the path, creates a bond at that deep emotional level evoked only by personal encounters. Some of my best friends are yet to be born; some died a thousand years ago; and some are calling to me although we haven't yet heard of each other. I am writing this book to you.

PART II

Chapter 3

PEACE IS DYNAMIC

CULTIVATING INNER PEACE doesn't eliminate problems, but it facilitates overcoming them with a particular flavor. You can't strive for uniform bliss in the name of peace. The pursuit of inner peace is a self-regenerating way of life. As long as we live, we will be spun with demand and action, but we can design an orienting axis of stability within the swirl.

Many people who set out to find peace become disillusioned when they realize, on closing their eyes, or hiking alone in the woods, or settling into their dream houses, or attaining their career goals, that they remain granular and acetic. Their peace is situational rather than visceral. This form of disappointment derives from the error of imposing a static image of happiness over the throbbing of life. We can obtain transient surcease from comforting diversions and compelling distractions. I, too, love those moments that are free of all mucking and upwelling—pastel moments of cerulean calm. But they are only fleeting, the adolescent crush of peace, and not its repeatable consummation in marriage.

Marriage to peace is not an absence of struggle but a bond of love, a pertinacious faith in a possibility, and a determination to embody it. Peace is a persevering modulation, a direction recurrently renewed, a devotion and a discipline. Wake up with peace, sleep with peace, return at the end of your day to peace.

Peace is not an absence of problems but a set of problem-solving attitudes. Throughout this book I will expand on these, step by step. The first step is *envisioning beyond each troubling circumstance toward its resolution in the direction of peace.* Peace is interwoven with the character virtues of faith and persistence.

A twenty-year-old accounting student dropped out of Kyoto University after having had an epiphany while watching birds fly past the library window. He thought to himself, "Those birds are free, but I'm a prisoner, and have been all my life, and will be all my life, unless I fly free." He quit school, shaved his head, and joined a Zen Buddhist monastery. After a number of years, his Zen master assigned him to an affiliated monastery in the United States, and he lived here for eight years, facing language barriers and culture shock. Still, he kept up his spirits about his youthful decision by thinking to himself, "I work outdoors on our garden farm; I meditate as I have always wanted to; I'm living the free life." He struggled to improve his stilted English, and worked on translation teams with young Americans studying ancient Japanese texts, but eventually the northern climate, communication barriers, and sexual loneliness culminated in a bleeding ulcer, and he returned to Japan. From Osaka he wrote to a friend, "I'm over thirty, have no career, no wife, no job skills, no money. I'm sick, in pain every day, and back living in my parents' apartment where I was a child. I failed my teacher by being unable to last it out in America. My pain is new every day."

This might have been a wise juncture for him to reevaluate what "freedom" really means, and whether accounting isn't so bad after all. Had I been his psychiatrist, I certainly would have suggested consideration of all alternatives. But this man was set on living a life of inner peace, and he kept on meditating as well as he could. Because he spoke English adequately, a small group of American expatriates banded around him to meditate together. They were joined by a Japanese woman who had also studied in America, and, after some years, he married her with their mutual understanding that together they would keep on the path of simplicity and peace. Gradually, his integrity as a translator became increasingly widely known, and today, this man (some of whose life details vary from this politely veiled sketch) is an internationally known teacher of Zen. Whenever I get news of his recent lecture or new book, I think of that guy back in Osaka who had failed in every possible dimension . . . except one—his centering commitment to go forward according to his vision. Imagine if he had felt, "This is too hard; I must be doing something wrong; maybe there's something wrong with me! If I were really *meant* to live 'the life,' all of these failures wouldn't be happening." Incidentally, he has no more ulcers.

Like a compass needle, inner peace is a continuous returning. You will always have problems. Inner peace is cultivated when you utilize problems as inspirations to reassert the dominance of tranquil spirit over the perturbations of little matter.

RETURNING TO YOUR LOCAL FAITH throughout your lifetime is peace-giving, even though at times historical or personal events may overwhelm you, and even though you may often feel temporarily crushed. Nothing seems more enviable than concentration of the spirit in resilient determination, as exemplified by the great French Impressionist painter Claude Monet. From his life we can learn how even this one element of peace can provide us some of the calm and courage we seek. Monet's life teaches us how devotion to any one truth brings some degree of serenity. "Let everything about you breathe the calm and peace of the soul," Monet said, but he faced many difficulties in old age. His first wife had died years earlier. When the painter was seventy-one, his beloved second wife died. A few years later, his eldest son, only forty-seven, died. World War I erupted. Monet continued to paint, but at last darkness invaded even that final sanctuary. By following his struggle, we will learn about a key element in the life of peace, which is how to reorient when fate knocks you off course.

As one of the founders of Impressionism, Monet based his style on the use of diffused, soft light and a blurring of outlines and detail. Therefore it was only gradually, in his late sixties and early seventies, that the painter could no longer deny that he was seeing less clearly; Monet was going blind from cataracts, caused in part by chronic exposure to intense sunlight, with its component of ultraviolet radiation. Monet was the painter who revealed the play of light as the cardinal feature of visual reality. Part of his Impressionist revolution was to paint outdoors. He denied touching his canvases in a studio, the way Walt Whitman denied reading indoors. Monet's love of light and his lifelong self-exposure to its dazzle had blinded him and, for many years, his love of painting had blinded him to his growing blindness.

As his sight deteriorated, he continued to paint what he saw, which was increasingly diffused and abstract. His deteriorating vision, his creative urge, his denial of his visual problems, and his mastery of oil on canvas coalesced to inspire the artistic breakthroughs that led beyond Impressionism itself into the abstract art of the twentieth century. Monet's increasing abstraction was partly a refusal to be limited to any one definition of truth. Ironically, abstraction began with a determination by Monet to paint exactly what he was blindly seeing.

At last, the aging artist could no longer deny his encroaching blindness.

> I no longer perceived colors with the same intensity. I no longer painted light with the same accuracy . . . . At first I tried to be stubborn. . . freshness had disappeared from my palette! Wasted efforts . . . more and more dark.

But Monet's friend Georges Clemenceau, a former physician who had become premier of France and her leader during World War I, had talked Monet into doing a series of murals as a gift to France. In the style that led his nation to victory in war, Clemenceau railed at his failing friend, "You can still do it, so do it!"

The subsequent years of Monet's life were a saga of doubt, suffering, determination, and triumph. He underwent a series of operations on his eyes, which, in that era of medicine, was a horrible ordeal.

When a second operation seemed to fail, Monet was so demoralized he refused to leave his bed. But gradually, as he was fitted with a series of glasses which variously distorted shapes and colors, the eighty-three-year-old widower moved through despair into hope. At the age of eighty-four, the man of color and light had written, "I am terribly sad and discouraged. Life is a torture for me." By the age of eighty-five he wrote, "I am working harder than ever, am pleased with what I do . . . I would like to live to be one hundred . . . I am working with ardor." Sometimes seeing yellow color distortions, sometimes awash in a false blue tint, what was the old man doing? Until within a few months of his death, Monet worked on the paintings of his garden at Giverny, including his famous water lilies. Everyone who looks at them recognizes that Monet had not only overcome obstacles, but he had reestablished his soothing mood. Though his earlier despondency had been like the worst in any of us, his final gift helped to lift our entire civilization beyond mere sight into a visual world of calm and harmony reflected beneath rippling, vibrant surfaces. The dying artist with eye disease persevered until he unveiled invisible peace within the play of light, color, water, and green life. His water lilies are not merely beautiful—they convey Monet's determination to find peace-giving timelessness in the dissolution of his own senses, and long after his death they emit serenity to us.

It is not unusual for a person's coping style to harden in old age. As people approach death, they become trimmed down to their core. We do at the end what we have most deeply learned to do. We become what we have been focused upon throughout life. Aging purifies us. We die in our habits. There is something that whispers of heavenly possibility within life, when we consider a half-blind, weak, mortally ill old man continuing to color like a kindergartener. I can't imagine that as an act of mere willpower or artistry. Monet's last act expresses a mode of existence that is deeply practiced in self-winnowing. It is a product of decades of relentless returning to a focal point. It is not a moment of will, but a habituated recurrence that dissolves temporary agitation or confusion. Instead of clutching after the eyesight he was losing, the life he was losing, Monet kept living. His canvases express not only the aesthetic beauty of surfaces, but a cultivated fusion with the serene and formless.

Concentration is itself calming. It places our attention on life-giving order, and closes the sluice gates of background anxieties. Monet no longer worried about loss and death when he could restore his attention to painting. To concentrate on peaceful enterprises is doubly calming, from both the process and the content of focus. The more steadily, deeply, and devotedly you orient your life around peaceful activity, the more that habit will hold you within its cool, blue-green shores, through life, right up to death, and then beneath that surface.

Look at Monet's final canvases, which express more than his words, with their cobalt delight and still, inner space. From his otherwise roiled life, comfort and inspiration continue to ripple out to us from his center of concentration.

Chapter 4

SCOTT AND HELEN NEARING

IF YOU SPEND A PLEASANT HOUR or afternoon in a favorite pastime, you will be able to observe your pleasure cease as a product of one of two causes. Something outside you may change the conditions necessary to your pleasure, or an internal feeling may disrupt you. To live a life of peace, you need a way to restore the peace you've had and lost to internal or external change. Peaceful living is learning to change with the changes.

In this section of the book, I am focusing your attention on the need for a dynamic relationship to your mood and your idea of peace. Lifetimes of peace derive from flexible, problem-solving commitments that reassert peace as the core goal in the solution of your current problem, whether that problem be inner or outer, hunger or war.

One intriguing example of this dynamic process is the life of Scott and Helen Nearing, organic gardeners who inspired thousands of people to live lives honed by simplicity and peacefulness. These Green Mountain leprechauns grew powerful by following the ideal of personal and communal peace. They drew inspiration from their imagination, casting themselves as explorers for humanity. The longer they lived, the more arduous the conditions they set for themselves, like mountain climbers seeking higher peaks. Their life history reveals the role of centering focus, eternal return, tensile realignment by which lives of peace steer across the ocean of temptation, dissatisfaction, and distraction, to stay true to an internal, glowing light.

Scott Nearing started life as a professor of economics at the prestigious Wharton School of Business at the University of Pennsylvania, but was fired in 1915 for openly opposing child labor! During World War I, this premature curmudgeon was put on trial for opposing the war, but was acquitted. No university would hire such a troublesome individualist, despite his successful publications. He married a musician twenty-one years his junior, and in 1932, when Scott was already nearly fifty years old, he and Helen moved to Vermont and bought "for a song, the most isolated and rundown farm" they could find.

The Nearings moved to a high, cold region of Vermont where electricity and flush toilets were still unknown, and buying up abandoned farm property at the height of the Great Depression, they commenced a radically new life. "We thought of the venture as a personal search for a simple, satisfying life on the land, to be devoted to mutual aid and harmlessness, with an ample margin of leisure . . ." The Nearings self-consciously rejected and intended to correct the dominant world culture of 1932, which was gripped by depression and unemployment, falling prey to fascism, and on the verge of another world war. They wanted to root their life in pacifism, vegetarianism and collectivism, and demonstrate ". . . one possibility of living sanely in a troubled world." On Forest Farm in Vermont, and later in Maine, over a period of more than forty years, enduring into very old age, the Near-ings persisted in quiet, steady triumph. They wrote with deep personal satisfaction of "respect for life . . . simplicity . . . a quiet pace, with time to wonder, ponder and observe. We hoped to replace worry, fear, and hate with serenity, purpose, and at-one-ness."

The Nearings created no more than they needed, and refused to accumulate savings. Their food came from a bril-liantly informed, ceaselessly experimental, and diligently run garden farm. They cut their own fuel wood. Their economic independence not only gave them a closeness to soil and seasons, it also guaranteed freedom of thought.

Their life was a blend of agrarian idealism coupled to mastery of contemporary contingencies. After more than half a life as urban intellectuals, they built spacious, beautiful buildings that have endured after them, working with their own hands and no power tools. This ingenious output was only half their life; the other half was devoted to literary and artistic self-development and to dialogue with thousands of transient guests and admirers.

Their puritan strenuousness was only a foundation over which they built a skylight life of daring and play. They preserved and exulted in the boy in the man, the girl in the woman. When Scott was in his eighties, he dug out a farm pond by hand, counting 15,000 wheelbarrows full of mud: a sinuous old cyclone! Energetic assault on every problem marks their account of their life. In spite of the almost com-pulsive hustle in collecting stones, building houses, keeping up with the seasons in their garden, the Nearings exuded a sense of sociability and full-heartedness, becoming hosts to a generation.

Although they tried to outline a practical philosophy that guided their life and that other people could follow, they found a life that was personal and idiosyncratic—a homemade, grandparent stew. It was emblematic, but not exemplary. They progressed through a discrete series of dynamic solutions to the problem of how to attain inner peace, as the problems arose in their own particular historical moment and context. Their blend of socialistic, agrarian, New England, intellectual, literary, teetotaling hypomania is unique to them. I am not recommending an imitation of their lifestyle, nor implying that its surface features would lead everyone to peace. Their methods were pied, homespun and sweaty, but their goals and gratifications were gold thread in a wizard's tapestry. It is their essence that we need to follow: they lived with ceaseless energy, concentration, an expansive sense of the future, and a pragmatic attention to concrete details.

> We took our time, every day, every month, every year . . . we had definite goals . . . that each moment, hour, day, week, and year should be treated as an occasion— another opportunity to live as well as possible . . . we should live as decently, kindly, justly, orderly, and efficiently as possible . . . it is better to love, create, and construct than to hate, undermine, or destroy . . . as day to day training for a new way of life, our project was a real success.

The Nearings coupled a deep inspiration toward peaceful living with a dynamic sense of the process itself. They handcarried fieldstones into piles and turned the piles into walls and houses; and when retirement time came, they decided that the ski boom had made Vermont too crowded, so they moved to Maine to recommence. Even their tenacity was malleable. They built, changed, expanded, innovated barns, houses, guest rooms, and storage sheds. Every solution was temporary, but the goal was not. They sought new answers to one problem, with conviction and strength.

> The value of doing something does not lie in the ease or difficulty, the probability or improbability of its

achievement, but in the vision, the plan, the determination and the perseverance, the effort and struggle which go into the project. Life is enriched by aspiration and effort.

"We have no spare time," they told a visitor. "But what do you do for pleasure?" they were asked.

Anything and everything we do yields satisfaction . . . what we have been doing is to meet a series of challenges, each in its own time and at its own level . . . . Some of them dealt with our basic assumptions, others involved minor practical details.

True to their austere and august beliefs, the Nearings donated, rather than sold, most of Forest Farm to the town as a nature preserve, keeping merely enough money to purchase a new isolated run-down place in Maine. Their mastery of financial anxiety, which overlaps fears of illness and helplessness, was Olympian. Even Thoreau stayed at Walden only two years, and spent most of his life in his mother's home.

Deeply knowledgeable of and inspired by their antecedents—another crucial pattern of peaceful living—the Nearings quoted an ancient Chinese poem.

> *When the sun rises, I go to work,*
> *When the sun goes down, I take my rest,*
> *I dig the well from which I drink,*
> *I farm the soil that yields my food,*
> *I share creation, kings can do no more.*

The Nearings demonstrated, though they did not fully understand, that peace is not any one particular historically conditioned complex of political, social, economic, or dietary platforms. Peace is great determination in rebalancing peace. The Nearings exemplified dynamic return to peace, energy in pursuit of it, optimism in renewing it, pragmatism in fulfilling it, courage in holding true to it, and wisdom in studying the spiritual ancestry of the peace they sought. These are as essential in the city as in the hills of Vermont, and will lead you toward the Nearings' enviable peerage with kings.

THE NEARINGS' STORY REVEALS the assiduous attention that is essential to cultivating inner peace. However, absolute fixation on inner peace will not yield fulfillment. That is why I have emphasized the motile, fluid, absorbing quality of peace. If we consider religious orthodoxy, I can clarify this key point.

In all religions there are centering self-disciplines that turn attention inward, diminish engagement with mundane and secular pursuits, and lessen distraction by fixating the mind upon an object of devotion. Despite a superficial similarity of appearance, there is a vast difference between orthodoxy and peacefulness. In the former, an obsessive, repetitive ritual forms a barrier against the problems of survival. The devotee memorizes, intones, and blocks out the world and his own fears and desires, which are forcefully extruded from or denied consciousness. There is a willed repression of sex, violence, illness, and death. This determination to blot out complexity brings temporary solace, but as soon as the ritual ceases or the sealed crypt of seclusion is broken, the orthodox worshipper is flooded by realities unmastered. Avoidance triggers a subsequent anxious reaction to whatever had been left unsolved and undone. Having been driven underground, yearnings and anxieties rise up like rebellious, uncontrollable armies. As soon as the monotonic deadening of obsessively preoccupying ritual ends, the true believer must fight back, beat down, all he fears and cannot control in himself and in the world. He is unprepared to deal with his own urges and with critical, dangerous circumstances, and therefore seeks to impose upon himself and others a rigid, repeating order.

The way to peace looks similar on the surface, but is opposite to orthodoxy. A multifaceted, engaged living extends through the necessities and ways of the world, yet returns to peace continuously, like a foraging bird to its evening nest. Constantly exposed to the world, constantly aware of our own inner reaction to the welter of conditions, we faithfully seek the light in the darkness, the stillness beneath the wind. Rather than obliterate the world and the inner life it stirs, we attune awareness of them at the same time that we channel, direct, guide this awareness toward the point of peaceful living. The Nearings—ascetic as they were—had the comfort of each other's bodies. They eschewed money, but produced sugar, starch, and protein. They played music daily and flung open their doors to the world. They practiced peace that was like a garden annual, requiring continual replanting, crowned with a marigold.

Peace is the result of solution: getting things to mix and flow. It is a direction, not a station. Peace is not a possession. It is confidence, like planting tulip bulbs in autumn. Don't look for something mature and archaic; peace is the mood of continuous loss and rebirth. The re-formation of peace is outdoors, beyond walls, among the vernal and the tremulous.

THE NEARINGS' LIFE CAPTURES the middle path necessary for inner peace, utilizing their capacity for risk-taking, courageous leaps out of confinement toward peace-bearing personal freedom, but rerooting in the ordered, regularizing calm of daily toil in service of a steadying goal. They relocated, but never shifted their gaze.

The Nearings were atheists, but spiritual in their reverence for mundane tasks. The exuberant detail with which they wrote about building techniques or systematic gardening was so narrow-minded and precise that it formed a blade to cut through the minutiae in which they were absorbed. They whittled on the pragmatics of bliss. The mood of their prose and their lives was effervescent with infectious delight. After filling pages with concrete details appropriate for a gardening magazine, they penned this simple refrain: "We, at advanced ages are still questioning, investigating, searching, and aiming to build a more rewarding and more creative life."

There were two major moves in the Nearings' lives. The first was when they left urban life in 1932. The second move was when they threw off the yoke of their own beautiful, handmade, stonework farm in Jamaica, Vermont, and moved to Maine, despite the fact that Scott was already almost seventy. Of the two moves, the first was the one that plummeted them into unprecedented activity and fame. But the second move is what makes them symbols of a psychic process, the way Odysseus stands for wandering and Einstein for mathematical-scientific thought.

When Scott was ninety, he and Helen began to build by hand their new stone home. When Scott was ninety-five, he and Helen wrote: "Never for a moment did we sit back and say to ourselves: This is it . . . . we have arrived." They unconsciously echoed Martin Buber's comment: "To be old is a glorious thing when one has not unlearned what it means to begin."

Their ebullience was independent of conditions; overcoming was itself the source of their verve. They didn't retreat before the physical decline of age because they construed their task as builders, not owners; experimenters, not maintainers; flowers, not fruit. They understood their quest for peace as a continuous process that was fulfilled only in ongoing outpouring, not in storage. "To us," they wrote in old age, "life was real, vital, urgent, important." Notice how different peace is from contentment. Contentment is a temporary, static ease. For the Nearings, inner peace was a particular quality of motion, a daylong, lifelong farmer's pace, like a slow gathering of stones. They thought of peace not as anything that was done, but as immersion in just and hearty doing. They quoted approvingly Robert Louis Stevenson: "To travel hopefully is better than to arrive." Their lives epitomize the psychic fact that inner peace spoils on the shelf. Peace is not a particular social or economic solution, not pickles in a jar, but an atmosphere enveloping a lifelong series of active solutions.

The Nearings published at their own cost *Living the Good Life,* which appeared obscurely in 1954 but was reissued with fanfare in 1970. It became the bible of the back-to-the-land movement, selling hundreds of thousands of copies. In 1979, they provided a sequel, *Continuing the Good Life,* which was published when Scott was ninety-five years old and Helen seventy-four. They told their story with matter-of-fact understatement, yet like the Pied Piper, they drew a following because the facts of their existence revealed admirable accomplishment in the direction of "sane and simple living." Like Jungian archetypes, they had gained entry into thousands of people's dreams.

Scott Nearing died in 1984 at the age of one hundred. Helen continued homesteading and attracting admirers—one to two thousand a year!—until her death in 1995. The habit of peace is a form of grace that extends into the future, beyond pending death, which is only another move north to new-plowed land.

Because peace can't be grasped or held constant, faith in its possibility and resolution to actualize it are its recurrent preconditions. The dynamism of peace precludes absolutism, rigidity, finality. Peace isn't accomplished, never endures beyond a moment, and must be reborn, recreated in the next. Peace is atomic.

PART III

Chapter 5

PEACE IS SELECTIVE

INNER PEACE is cultivated by the act of choosing. If you want to live peacefully, you'll have to make a continuous series of selections that permit and confirm that need.

In Part II, I discussed the *dynamic* quality of peace, the action of returning, like a compass needle to the north. Selecting peace is different, more like writing a song. You quell the sounds of the traffic around you, and a halting tune emerges. If you let it rise and expand, but at the same time contain it, you may happen upon the invisible coherence of melody, which then flows like a stream, bounded and directional. Melody isn't merely pretty sound, but an organized, integrated channel. You have to push aside distraction—not just noise, but even tangential charm—in order to hear a melody ripple downhill within you.

To cultivate inner peace, you'll have to think like this: I'll simplify my life. Constantly returning my compass toward peace is a start, but not enough. I'll also have to trim the fat, relinquish the trivial in order to enhance the essential. Peace is also a not-doing. I may have to decide to limit my family size, or my career, or my television watching. How can I plug myself into the fibrillating, chafing, tintinnabulum of electronic stimuli all day and expect my nervous system not to be fricasseed? I'll select what I'm going to carry in my backpack, so that I'm "unencumbered by baggage," free to amble.

The life of peace is like an international flight permitting only one handbag. You'll have to leave behind some of your cherished shoes and appliances. The international traveler, the hiker, and the climber feel relieved by what they have discarded. Carrying one knapsack, they step higher, feel lighter. Not mere returning toward peace, but selecting what to abandon and what to bring along is a necessary skill in the life of peace.

Selectively trimming your life to optimize your core goal isn't comfortable, because the human mammal we all inhabit is a vigilant, expanding predator. Each of us is a survivor carefully selected by nature during eons of evolution to optimize continuity, procreation, multiplication. We are animals built to triumph in competitive adaptation, and our minds are tools for victory. Mirroring the biological imperatives of our animal aggression, our psyche is never naturally at peace. Scanning present, past, and future, we creatively anticipate, and retrospectively struggle, to master all conditions. Like hunters, we dream into the future, desiring, fearing, scheming. Like prey, we fret and remember the past to avoid reencountering ambushes. Our mental processes follow the call of our instincts to acquire, to protect.

The yearning for peace is a paradoxical struggle because it rubs against the scales and feathers of our animal vigilance. To be at peace, we must relinquish the continuous control of circumstance that our animal demands. Our self-protective environmental groomings won't go away when we solve one more situational problem. We will remain hyperalert with desire and fear unless we set up a countercurrent to prevail.

Peace is not just a more or better way to be human, the amplification of an urge. Peace is also a determination to become less human. It necessitates knowledge, choice, and effort at leaving behind our weapons and worries. It requires force: a selective pushing beyond, a rising above. Inner peace is a transformation by courage. Thoreau wrote, "Bravery deals not so much in resolute action, as in healthy and assured rest ... one moment of serene and confident life is more glorious than a whole campaign of daring."

Out of determination, peace grows like a mountain wild-flower—spontaneous, seclusive, robust, blossoming early to capture the energy of first spring sun. The hepatica seeds, scattered in secret by their antecedent generations, don't attend a gardener's permission, but punch a hole through the detritus of the wintry forest floor and open their azure petals above a sere necklace of last year's leaves. Demure and delicate as it is—nothing stops a wildflower.

Chapter 6

SELECTIVITY AND THE
AMERICAN FAMILY

AN IMPORTANT FRACTION OF the pain that brings people
to psychotherapy comes from a widespread loss of knowledge
about how to live selectively and simply. Many apparently
sophisticated American adults don't know how to generate
inner calm or interpersonal goodwill. Our contemporary
society has amplified the amount of stimuli and the pace
at which we are exposed to them on a routine basis. While
each individual unit of input may be informative or pleasant,
the sum aggregate produces an experience of flailing to keep
up, overload. This intensity derives both from obligations,
like work, and also from pleasures, so that year by year we
greet our colleagues, patients, family, or friends only to hear
a chorus of voices exclaim how busy, behind, overcommitted they've been. Phone messages pile up; friendships are
maintained by car and plane; unwanted mail spills out of the
letterbox. There's more paperwork at work, more places to
drive the kids, more worthwhile concerts and movies that
have been recommended by friends whose advice is worth
listening to. If you unplug yourself for a vacation, you are
punished on return by large cartons of printed matter waiting

like lions, and by blinking red lights that make your telephone answering machine look like a movie marquee. Every time I'm driving along a back road enjoying a September full moon, somebody drives up behind me, flicks their high beams in my rearview mirror, and honks.

Inner peace isn't just a thought; it's also a neurological tone. We can hear it humming when we learn to diminish distraction.

Restlessness, inability to be alone, ill-ease with solitude are the products of a pervasive cultural milieu in which human bodies are appendages to electronic toys, driven achievements, and consumer passion.

Our children have lost permission to dwell in their spacious reverie of newness. They no longer inhabit the structureless domes of uninterrupted afternoons. In order for us to function efficiently, we need them to be busy. We also—out of well-intended concern—want to prepare them to deal competently with our gadget-dense sphere, so that, almost from the start, children are propelled into a high rhythmic froth. This could be a sprightly animation if it were balanced by an equal but opposite emphasis on inward serenity and outward harmony, which would provide an orchestrating principle, a focus to the swirl, not precluding skillful assertion, but orienting it. The receptive neurology of a child can catch and hold real experiences in contemplative stillness and inner joy.

I would recommend, beyond any teaching at all, our sons and daughters be granted the open space and time to watch dust motes filter across shafts of light; to visit beaches in windy weather and listen to waves cleave doorways into infinity through their hypnotic, repetitive roar; to imprint in his or her heart a few mantram lines of poetry; to watch the seasons dress and undress outside his or her window; to lie in his or her room at night and hear the rustle of eternity and death that shadows make on the ceilings of children's rooms.

To feel, to think, and to understand requires free time, privacy, quiet, and solitude—even, or most essentially, in a child. Have you heard contemporary educators analogize the mind to a computer? I think a peaceful mind is more like moonlight, wind, and invisible wings: full of beautiful lights, formlessness, and suggestions.

Many children today are encouraged to live in desperate, ceaseless striving. The divorce and depression endemic in our society spring not only from neurotic quirks within individuals' personal pasts, but from the matrix of a culture that doesn't value, teach, or create people who know how to listen, receive, appreciate. We raise children who are rarely reflective and contained, who often domineer, press buttons, and keep score. Yet peace and harmony are real life skills. We anxiously, lovingly, peer into the future, wondering whether our son will be able to maintain a marriage without competing and imposing. If we only encourage and admire his success, how will he have learned to love and be able to love? With such monotonic stress on mastery and appropriation, will our daughter even have heard of deference, reverence, and awe? How will she face death and find meaning in the totality of her life that she cannot conquer? Can she really feel, or only function?

As a psychiatrist, I see what happens to these children grown up. They experience life as if an entire section of the spectrum of human emotion were deleted—as if they felt red and yellow, but never blue nor green.

SELECTIVITY IS AN EXPERIENCE of focal effort, energetic quest, self-knowledge regarding mental states of poise, and fullness in the presence of a limit. Selectivity, optimally learned in childhood, is knowledge about how to reduce inner tension by choosing foci, and by learning competence and satisfaction. Satisfaction isn't a biological state of satiety, but a learned, psychological capacity. Children who have been taught to crave the newest Nintendo game, and who argue over whose parent has the most luxurious car, are being educated in dissatisfaction. A child learning to tune in to her grandmother's life story, or to a picture book in whose illustrations tree roots blend into angels and magpies, or to the careful method of catching salamanders after spring rains, is learning focus, skill, attention, and playful kinship with the world. The child learning selectivity as a way of life isn't restrained or withheld—for obedience is the opposite of *self*-control—but she exudes a feeling of eager expectation. The capacities to choose and sustain objectives of attention, to gate out the irrelevant, and to appreciate what one has, are aspects of self-regulation that enable both action and satisfaction. Satisfaction means to feel you've done enough.

A child is climbing her first mountain. With an alternation of enthusiasm and flagging spirits, which require exhortation from her adult guides, she sweats and strains her legs until the thigh muscles shake like jelly. At rest stops she observes, or is shown, black-throated blue warblers migrating and singing among the black birch branches, or patches of painted trillium flowers sequestered behind gneiss boulders. As she approaches the summit, the child runs on magically rejuvenated legs and excitedly calls the others to come and see! She points to the expanding panorama of the world.

This child will be friends with striving, sweat, and pure water. She will eagerly guide others some day—sons or daughters of her own. In the future she will seek heights and bulldog her way out of sloughs and dare to ignore the catcalls of the gang on the corner because selectivity is a memory of the joy of the mountaintop. She knows how to choose a trail and climb to an unforgettable vista. I'm not praising a mere military hike that stalks obliviously past the vireos, violets, and visual haikus—the kind of marching that drills in conquest—nor a coaxing and begrudging upward shuffle reinforced with candy bars and the promise of terminal ice cream. Selectivity is the capacity to experience intrinsic pleasure with personal action. It breeds a trim mind that will always ascend toward the open horizon because that is where clarity and receptivity reach their maximum expanse. On mountaintops of any altitude, I have witnessed a child receiving the echo of his own harmony coming back to him from the vibration of the universe.

Ironically, scatter and dissatisfaction retain positive valuation in American life because they are assumed to be catalytic precursors to the competitive urge. When children who have been trained in dissatisfaction grow up, they may become successful, but peaceful states of mind elude them because their accomplishments simply trigger new internal demands. Their success emerges at the cost of an unshakeable irritability that is the winter imprint of a culture of acquisition and aggression, in which even human intimacy is bought and sold as a commodity. They have learned to amplify the feeling of need—which drives their striving for success—rather than having learned the art of appreciation toward near and dear people and the proximal props that share our stage. These people have never learned how to select the channel of satisfaction. They have been trained to deny the fact that peace and happiness are also forms of curtailment.

In order for children to grow up with a helpful knowledge of selectivity, precursors are best set in place in childhood: the focalization of attention and the moderation of acquisition. This will facilitate the adult love of spouse, child, friend, nearby trees, and the heavens seen through a kitchen window. I often wonder how much of our epidemic of children and adults with attention-deficit-hyperactivity disorder—allegedly a genetic disease but mysteriously sensitive to changes in culture, and as rare in England as it is proliferating in America—is induced by our sizzling and impersonal home environments. Our children can no longer hear the subtleties of the lead guitar because they've turned up the bass response to drums and guns.

Conversely, there may be societies that selectively attune their children to the simple joys of life. Camping in Alaska with his Native American guides, John Muir sat up at night and had "a long talk with the Indians about the stars; their eager . . . attention was refreshing . . . as compared with the decent, deathlike apathy of weary civilized people, in whom natural curiosity has been quenched in toil and care and poor, shallow comfort."

The selectivity that leads to peace as a life pattern is a product of example and education: the transmission of cultural wisdom. If an individual has never witnessed or experienced a sense of choice and self-responsibility, he or she will create shallow and externalized life goals. Those who grow up tasting psychological calm will seek it like bees after pollen.

Let us open the door and observe a family where selectivity is one operative valve. Their house or apartment is smaller than it might well have been because the parents have pursued their careers with energy, determination, and limits; they're the kind of people who also treasure family life. As we observe them over time, we are struck by the pool of benignity that their shared activities create. Of course, these meetings constitute a limited proportion of their daily or weekly life, which is strung out among jobs and schools, and which even at home is often merely fast and functional. But we do see them decide not to go to Boston on the weekend, and instead to listen to the audiotape of the Count of Monte Cristo together, with its dose of alerting mystery and tension. They absorb the warmth that derives from shared, silent listening to a great mood conductor. At another juncture we catch them sitting around the wood-stove, reading aloud from a book that passes around the circle among them—maybe Tolkien or Le Guin. Not that they are always nested. During the February school vacation, they are cross-country skiing on abandoned logging roads among the massive skeletons of wintry yellow birch, and traversing frozen beaver ponds. In June, they sit on their deck for a full hour or two doing nothing—no book, no talk—and listen to the copious, multiphonic concert of robins and thrushes and orioles and sparrows, whose songs have an emotional meaning that any human listener can respond to with empathic recognition. When friends visit this family, the cooking is apt to be shared; the toddlers are recognized and appreciated; problems surface and are listened to; wry political critique from Doonesbury or Dave Barry lyses the tensions of the world. We are observing a family that, when possible within the static of life, selects for harmony, mutuality, focused attention, soothing scenarios, literature, nature, friendship, and play. Their selections are recurrently interpersonal, meaningful, and compelling, and are drawn from "the simple great gifts."

Single people and childless couples have an expanded opportunity for choice and focus. At an earlier era of history, when childbearing was uncontained and labor oppressively unregulated, celibates and monastics were the only people who could control their choices for serenity. But family-less people also have fewer stabilizing buffers against dissipation and rigidification, for family life intrinsically imposes the order of nurturant routine and the captivating transformations of growth. At its best, parenting means creating a psychological eggshell for safety in which the young gradually peck holes and shatter. For parents, eggshells are nature's best reminder that growth can only follow selective containment.

Chapter 7

Selectivity in Contemporary Lives

ALTHOUGH NO CULTURE has so systematically devalued the classical virtue of selective living than twentieth-century America, with its orgiastic materialism and its frenetic work/play cycle, still I've had a few opportunities to witness this old truth working its charm.

If you would drive with me along a network of obscure dirt roads, we would at last accelerate up a steep, long driveway to the home of two middle-class Americans. Both members of this couple were raised in professional or business families and went to a small liberal arts college, where they met. Both were stirred by peaceful yearnings that initially took cover under cloudy adolescent oppositionalism: the doctor's daughter wanted to major in ornithology, while the contractor's son studied art history. Eventually, dismay about the pressures and constrictions of college education, coupled to conflict with their families, led the young couple to meld positions, drop out of college, and join the workforce early. She became a clerk in a health food store, and he, a carpenter's assistant.

This couple proceeded to do what we all do, but more consciously and concentratedly. They built a life based on a vision—in their case, one that valued selectivity. They were fans of Scott and Helen Nearing, and determined to follow those old, overalled mentors at their essence, not just their surfaces. The young couple determined to live a simple life close to nature, but custom-refitted to contemporary contingencies. Quiet and working long hours, these penniless kids who had lost their parents' support built new friendships around their interests of birding and gardening. In the summer they saved rent by tenting on a friend's land. They selected their diet to add to savings. After a few years they purchased undesirable rural acreage that had no road frontage, but a long, steep, impractical right-of-way for a driveway. Over one summer, working weekends and days off, they erected a one-room cabin, to which they commuted from work by rusty Jeep.

Lumber, insulation, and shingles are the least cost of a cabin. Labor costs more, so they did their own. Plumbing and bathroom fixtures add a bill, so the young couple dug and built an outhouse, which, they said, got them "out to look at the stars and moon every night in every weather, a real advantage." Still, they needed water. The young man explored his land and found a spring too far away, but strength, youth, folly, and the desire to prove his father wrong inspired him to hand-dig a trench, lay plastic pipe below frost line, and re-cover all three hundred feet of pipe with dirt. I've seen his back on a summer's day, and I know this story is true.

The young couple's cabin was lighted by anachronistic gas lights—no electric bill but their life was less ascetic than trim and cozy. A bathtub impertinently occupied one fifth of the floor space, bird books and art books stuffed the shelves, and the aromas of home-baked food permeated the room. The winter heating bill was paid for by biceps and deltoids in the woodlot. When friends visited in spring, they were offered home-churned ice cream spangled with wild strawberries. Their garden grew over the years as they rototilled and composted soil, the rows following the lines of strings with millinery finesse, like handsewn shirts.

This isn't just the story of a rural idyll. Let's stand back, watching as time-lapse photography reveals thirty years' unrolling, and the twenty-year-olds approach fifty. This couple carefully selected the goal of a pastoral, peaceful, nature-loving life, kept it focal, persevered to create it, and refused to be distracted, tempted, or lured away. Having met when they were twenty, they selected for twelve years of rooting lifestyle before the first of their two children was conceived. By that time they knew who they were, and could raise one, then two children in the nest of their own values, building little by little a productive and active life in a hushed and intimate setting. Their gardening, which at first appeared so quaintly obsessive, began to produce saleable herbs, initially bottled with hand-drawn, pictorial labels, and eventually more professionally packaged. It was fifteen years—both children careening around the lawn on pedaled plastic cars—before their hobby boomed large enough for them to launch as a full-time business their medicinal bottled herbs. Today, they have a three-bedroom house and, yes, a T.V. Beside the old truck with the snowplow on front sits a new Toyota that father and son use to go off to soccer practice.

In a complex society, a certain level of intricacy must be added into the life of each citizen in order to be able to functionally mesh with multiple social and economic gears. Simplicity in a farmer doesn't consist in planting a monoculture. Selectivity doesn't mean constricted, impoverished, or inviable living. Selectivity means conscious choice of what is important, necessary, and salubrious, with conscious relinquishment of what is diluting, distracting, and obfuscating. The choice is personal: live well, plant your crops, be prosperous but not festooned.

If we compare these modern herb-business people to the Nearings, we see many more points of contact with contemporary life—carefully planned marketing strategies for their products, computer and fax for handling orders, schools and cars and next-generation tuition money in the bank. Unlike their utopian mentors, this couple is economically participatory and physically stable at one location. They are modern, engaged, yet selective. Their bountiful gardens and grounds, which appear to be products of wealth, are actually the outflow of long-garnered selectivity.

As for their social impact, I see these people as more than personally successful. Who knows how far their art of selective yet lush peace may reach into the future, shaping their children's choices, inspiring me, maybe even transforming you. Selectivity forges success not just in working steadily toward a goal, but in success's flavor. Even in a confection with many ingredients, peace is a cherished bouquet. The savor of this one bowl of wild-strawberry ice cream may rotate its subtle influence through generations for untold springtimes.

THE IMPORTANT THING ABOUT THESE PEOPLE is not that they did without plumbing for years, but that they esteemed the advantages of an outhouse; not that they stalled childbearing, but that they appreciated the opportunity for prolonged foundation-building in their own lives. At the age of fifty, they have no ascetic dimension left to their life, though they remain selective. Their capacities to be patient, and to prize, made them peace-bearers to a society toxic with expectation. They form an educative contrast with many high achievers.

The ability to let go of unchosen alternatives, to experience gratification in immediacy and therefore to slough fantasies of unfulfilled possibility, these skills of selectivity often peak in early adulthood, when love and work are ordinarily channeled into marriage and career. When we choose for something, we choose against everything else. We marry only one man/woman, and, if our goal is inner peace, we have to relinquish our adolescent craving for the other five billion. Likewise with work. The manner in which channels of mature commitment are cut or blocked may in a lifetime create smooth flow or turbulence. No spiritual exercise, closing the eyes and creating one fantasy of salvation or one brain wave for twenty minutes, can smooth the eddies of misguided love and work. A life spent in alienated drudgery, cutthroat economic warfare, familial disharmony, or sexual frustration can't be palliated by a tactic. It's impossible to waste your days and save your life.

Selectivity for peace is like tree pruning. It isn't measured by the amount you remove. Your harvest is determined by the knowledge and care with which you select to cut those branches that will drain away vital energy; and by the principle with which you select limbs to receive the full thrust of spring sap and thus to optimally flower and bear fruit. Selectivity is inspiration-guided austerity.

Some of the most entrenched depressed people I have met have been stellar scholars. Those who expect to win, and who demand triumph from every circumstance, often ascend the career ladder at the price of a brittle mood. They want it all and, if talented, often appear to have succeeded during the first half of life when struggle and ascent are normative; but when life is to bear fruit, they find themselves dangling over a rapacious dragon in a pit, who must be thrown more awards, grants, applause. They don't know how to select the channel of peace. Instead, they turn again and again to victory. They come to a psychiatrist with a paradox: they are highly successful and depressed. They have overlearned the lesson about how to win, and they have avoided the extracurricular requirement of how to select their own mood independently of external accomplishments. They exclaim in dismay, "I've always been so optimistic!" The fact that peace derives from selectivity makes it an accessible goal for the limited, ordinary person. A dignified and appreciative sense of limits constitutes a greater asset than exhilarating accomplishment. For those who seek peace, insurmountable obstacles open the door of opportunity, as happened with the young couple who left college to pursue their vision.

Peace eludes those who can't pare down their goals to peace itself, and those who cannot steel themselves to resist will be drawn into the channels of banal accomplishment or irritable diffusion of purpose. Selectivity may be only a polite term for stubbornness. Peace comes most easily to the inspiredly dogged.

"Selectivity" refers to psychological differentiation and autonomy extended toward a higher principle. Many people never attain this height. Tightly pressed in mass movements, mass media, mass religion, they find security from loneliness and wonder, avoiding the vulnerability of personhood by submerging selectivity beneath the easy, the expected, the least resistant.

Of the great and good things in life—married love, parenting, friendship, communion with nature, professional help extended to others, travel, wise words, strenuous play, meditation—none arrive via dissipation or distraction. Why listen to the diffuse hum from the dense center of the hive? What can one expect to hear from all those impacted bodies? Every evening can conclude at the summit of your life.

Sometimes people who have been buffeted by fate are forced into a careful selection of lifestyle just to stay sane. Hurt souls occasionally attain deeper peace than the flamboyant and successful because selectivity and simplicity become essential and inescapable for them. Most of us have our own experience of being wounded and diminishing our concerns until we feel strong enough to reemerge from our temporary cysts, but for some people this process must be lifelong. Conviction, determination, self-responsibility, and appreciation can cure the darkest pit of the spirit. There is as much to be learned from those who recover as from those who are born graceful. Many adept achievers lack the precious wisdom attained perforce by the shaggy and the slow.

In every mature task there is a requirement of limit-setting. We surround our cherished enterprises with a protective barrier against intrusion from contrary and divisive forces. Even the most "natural" people enclose themselves in huts or yurts or tepees. Birds cup their future generations in nests. In the spring, when birds return and establish their territories by singing repetitively from limbs, we can hear the lesson of selectivity all around us, as the avian creatures design their world to protect their goals. I hope you will select for peace, and away from its antithesis, with the ecstatic truculence of piping cardinals.

I ONCE HEARD THE PRINCIPLE of selectivity described back to me spontaneously by a Maine canoe guide, who spends the six liquid months guiding campers down the Allagash, Saint John, Big Bear, Moose, and other North Woods rivers, and the six frozen months building cedar-strip canoes in the tradition of his father, who was a dairy farmer and a Yankee boat builder.

"I make canoes with the same attitude that my wife and I had toward raising our daughters. When I'm making one of these tubs, I don't build a spare. Each one gets one hundred percent.

"Every day I wake up a free man. I spend my summers among the fir trees and the animals I love. I see a bull moose raise its dripping head from the river, and I know why I'm alive. I'm outdoors every day, even in winter. I know I'm part of something bigger than myself. I'm a guide to these woods, this river, an interpreter. An old Penobscot used to do day labor on my father's farm, and he taught me what was left of his native ways. I feel I'm carrying something on. You're part of what you touch, and I'm full of sunsets.

"Boat building is a form of concentration. Each one of these canoes springs out of me, my hands, more importantly, my mind, my absence of distracting thoughts. It's not that hard manually; what it takes is unwavering attention. I don't work with a radio on. It's me and the cedar—of course there are glues and other stuff. Winters, when I do most of the building, I feel I'm bringing spirits to life with my touch. I don't feel I've given up anything, really. What other people call pleasure, to me is a dilution. The only things I gave up were all those things that kept me from living in beauty.

"A canoe has to be perfectly symmetrical, to within a sixteenth of an inch. But when it's finished, what you see isn't planes and sanders and tape measures. You see a wing, a fin, where form and function are the same. The principle is unhindered movement, lines smoothed in response to the environment it lives in and travels through. There's nothing extra on a canoe. It's trimmed and essential like a merganser after a fish, or the beak of a great blue heron. Symmetry and precision carried to a point always evoke joy, as if the mind delights in the conclusions of nature."

Selectivity is another word for "intentionality," a life in which every action points in the same direction. In the words of the canoe guide, there are fewer cross-fibers left, and he sounds more straight-grained. This delineation is not a life everyone would choose, for it's been combed free of certain spontaneous license, is muscular and energetic, and even its pleasures necessitate wool shirts in summer.

Selectivity is a scientific principle that obtains even in mechanics and optics. The barrels of binoculars encircle the light upon which prisms and lenses work their magnifying transfiguration. Without the barrels' encasement, the lenses would only distort. Selectivity is containment that leads to enhanced clarity and enlargement.

SELECTIVITY PERTAINS IN THE URBAN LIFE as well as the rural, in the mental patient's life as well as in the psychiatrist's. The selection for peaceful ways of being in all our more ordinary and incognito lives is most important, since it is we, who are immersed in society, who contribute to its elasticity or fragility, its peace or its frenzy, by our often unnoticed yet deeply reverberating choices.

I select for feelings. I listen, and I want to be heard. I participate in a family life where the light of fond and courteous attention rotates among its members. More problems are caused, more treaties struck, at my dinner table—and at yours—than in Geneva or on First Avenue in New York. In a welcoming and focused atmosphere, each person will speak the truth of his or her heart. In common parlance that is unobstructed and empathetically received, the secrets of the universe uncoil. Shut off the ricocheting distractions of the powers that want to control you, the media hype, and shut off your own anxieties, and let the family circle radiate you with its warmth. Those who share the evening, day after day, year after year, see each other around the circle of anointed opportunity. Which T.V. show called you away, just as you could have begun your initiation into this sanctuary which is the prototype for every communion?

If you haven't heard angels speaking, it's because you weren't listening. The people you live with are the messengers history has sent to your side. That seance is most remarkable when the spirit contacted is simply peace and love. Words are only the beams and lasers of feelings that originated at the origin of the world. The family circle is the lodestone of all culture and civilization. Tonight is genesis. Among all things, first I focus on this.

I select meditation, every morning, every evening. People often ask me how I find the time, but what can be more important than the most important thing? Later in this book, I will devote a whole chapter to meditation as I have learned and practiced it. I have chosen it because I love to sit still, detach myself from the narrow focus of self-preoccupation, and try to recontact the multiple perspectives that constitute reality. The immediate texture of daily problems is important, and so is the realization of the measureless expanse of unbroken and unknowable and formless time in whose cosmic geometrylessness we float and spin. Every openhearted, open-minded moment is an irruption of the *beyond*, which gives momentum to all meanings, all affections, that affirm our humanity at the moment our humanity dissolves, simultaneously washing us out, and affirming each of our moments as the best possible. Peace is a corridor beyond thought and time. All things pass, and whatever isn't damaged by the cataclysmic vertigo of that ceaseless transformation and destruction is a passageway to peace. Peace through devoted meditation is like a landscape painting that lures you in so deep that your eye passes beyond the horizon.

This focus, on the people I live with and on the perspective of meditation, forms my priority. A thousand economic, political, intellectual, social activities fan out in the wake behind it as necessary adjuncts. I can't imagine better or more powerfully positive first choices. I dwell far from uninterrupted peace, but I return to it, and I also make sure it never comes second. From a halting tune to a melody, I hear it swell in clarity and volume as I deflect distraction. I'm a child on my first hike, within reach of the mountaintop, with my head and shoulders rising into exfoliating vistas.

Chapter 8

THE SHAKERS:
THE BENEFITS AND
LIMITS OF SELECTIVITY

INTENSE SELECTIVITY IS A STOVEFUL of hardwood that can glow long enough to convect warmth into the future. But it is also a domestic hazard.

The Shakers are an example. Paragons of selectivity, they produced one of the great outpourings of spiritual peace in American history, yet their heritage is masked by an intensely ambivalent reception that speaks to the essential tension which selectivity addresses. The Shakers deserve our attention as exemplars of both the strengths and pitfalls involved in selectivity. Their example highlights how you can intensify your relationship to peace every day via rigorous selectivity, but also how selectivity can be overdone and become paradoxically un-selective. The Shakers command our attention around the question: Just how much selectivity is peace-bearing, and how much is stifling?

The Shakers were an eccentric offshoot of the Protestant Reformation in England. Their original leader, Mother Ann Lee, was an illiterate factory worker and laundress who had visions that transformed her from a downtrodden slum wife to a charismatic organizer. To her followers, she was the second coming of Christ. To the Church of England that was heresy, so fleeing persecution and imprisonment, she led her tiny band of nine to America at the time of the Revolution. In the New World, their fundamentally inspirational sect, with its fervid singing, dancing, and ecstatic shaking, gradually evolved into a principled, organized religion. Their basis was not a clear theology or dogma, but a way of life.

Shaker communities were an unusual blend of confinement and expansiveness. Based on early Christian life as they understood it from the Gospels, they were communal, abandoning personal property and possessions. They dressed alike, ate together, and followed a common timetable. Each Shaker lived in surrender to the larger order. Celibacy was absolute for everyone; they hoped to sublimate sexual energy outward into creative spiritual ebullience, transforming personal austerity into communal joy.

Yet the Shakers weren't ascetic in the manner of Christian monasticism. Unlike that of St. Francis, who made do with crusts and shivered through the winter, the Shakers' way of life was pregnant with beautiful, warm, and comfortable group homes, ample food and clothing, and inventive, competent solutions to earthly needs; and their spiritual life was lush with song, dance, and folk arts.

Possibly the Shakers' historical importance is greatest as purveyors of uncanny modernity. Their eighteenth-century guidelines sound ideal, liberating, advanced to us today. They believed in equal roles for men and women because they understood both God and Christ as male and female. They were pacifists who, by the time of the Civil War, managed to secure draft exemption on religious grounds from the inventor of the modern draft, Abraham Lincoln. The Shakers accepted African-Americans, Jews, Native Americans into their fold, and were outspoken defenders of religious and political minorities, even speaking up on behalf of communes that practiced free love. They condemned slavery and created integrated societies. Equality, justice, brotherly and sisterly love were not only their ideals, but the practical regulators of their daily life.

Shakerism has had a sweeping humanitarian influence on human history far exceeding the actual size or duration of the religion itself. Helping to create the precursor of the idea of conscientious objection to war, the Shakers not only were exempt from the Union draft, they fed fifty thousand meals to hungry soldiers of both Union and Confederate armies. They were admired by American statesmen as diverse as Henry Clay and Andrew Jackson, and by writers like Hawthorne, Melville, Emerson, Greeley, and Walt Whitman. When Mahatma Gandhi's image played over movie screens in the late-twentieth century as a symbolic representation of the peaceful individual struggling to humanize historical forces, in those moments, the "obscure" Shaker movement was subtly impacting once again upon millions of people's hope for peace as a vital, worldly force.

In 1905, at the central Shaker commune in New Lebanon, New York, the Shakers sponsored the first major international peace conference, attracting representatives of more than fifty nations, thereby foreshadowing the United Nations. When the Canterbury, New Hampshire, Shakers realized their impoverished neighbors in the Granite State were stealing their crops at night, they eschewed self-protection, legal force, or even fences and guards: they just planted more in their open fields. Their solution to crime was to increase their own efforts at generosity. The Shaker reputation for honesty made their seed businesses blossom. By the middle-nineteenth century, persecution and violence by their neighbors had given way to admiration and respect. In the words of historian Flo Morse, "People flocked to see the self-sufficient, socially advanced hamlets that had no poverty, no crime, no jails, where women as well as men governed."

To enter into the psyche of Shakerism and to appreciate their importance for understanding the role of selectivity in inner peace, we have to observe their world along two dimensions: what they selected out, and what they selected in.

They selected out sex. New members came only through converts, who might join for religious reasons, or who might enter the fold seeking food and shelter among these ultra-competent communities in a primitive and poor nation, or who might have been given succor as orphans.

Shakers selected out dirt, laziness, possessions, and personal control of time or place. They selected out individuality, college education, and urban culture, for all Shakers lived in isolated rural communes. They selected out warfare and self-defense, which meant that in the eighteenth century, many Shakers were beaten and persecuted in New York, Massachusetts, Kentucky, and Ohio.

They selected out privacy. When Shakers were interviewed about the sacrifice and ardor of their life, they attested that celibacy was less of a difficulty than the pruning of vanity and "will" that Shaker life entailed. The Shaker had to submit to others. Self-denial was the cornerstone of the structure of Shakerism. Shaker harmony rested on a watched, systematic minimization of personal preference. To the modern mind, this is anathema. Then what was its appeal?

In the 1850s, at the height of their movement, they numbered about six thousand people spread through eighteen communities in the eastern United States. From the Revolutionary War to today, there have been about seventy thousand Shakers. Despite their tiny size, they nonetheless constitute the most long-lived and influential communal movement in American history. That was because of what they selected in: universal brother- and sisterhood; community of goods, equality in labor, social security of all working for each and each for all, no rich, no poor; equality of the sexes in all departments of life; freedom of speech, toleration in thought and religion; temperance in all things; justice and kindness to all living beings; nonviolence; sanitation, health, longevity; simplicity in dress, speech, and manner; freedom from debt, worry, competition. They lived in careful, walled peace.

The key to Shakerism was its attitude toward work, which was built upon Mother Ann Lee's aphorism: "Put your hands to work and turn your hearts to God." Every action was consecrated. There was no division between daily life and worship. Every movement, every detail was done for God. There was only the sacred world, no profane—the Kingdom of Heaven was to be actualized on earth. One of the last living Shakers summarizes this core teaching: "All the Shaker does is done in the eye of eternity." Mother Ann Lee had phrased it, "Do all your work as though you had a thousand years to live, and as you would if you knew you must die tomorrow." Daily manual labor for all was a command and a sacrament that culminated in a united inheritance. "All life and activity animated by Christian love is worship."

Every day the Shaker had a prerogative and destiny to commune with and manifest the highest good. They danced with God. Hidden cupboards and closets in Shaker buildings show the same fervor for craftsmanship and excellent finish as visible exteriors because every cut of the chisel or strike of the hammer was a testament of belief. Shaker builders and woodworkers were living what scholar E. D. Andrews has called "religion in wood." The physical world was not divorced from a spiritual demand for total dedication. It appears the Shakers were living with the same attitude that animates Hasidic Jews, Muslim Sufis, or Franciscan Catholics: breaking the division between holy and mundane spheres.

The creativity that poured out of Shaker communities, consisting of mostly anonymous, poorly educated souls, was phenomenal. At the technical level, they were innovators of agricultural equipment, as well as heat and water power. They designed the energy-efficient Shaker wood stove. The first running indoor water in Kentucky was at Pleasant Hill Shaker village. They created their own breed of cattle. Artistically, Shakers have set a style for so much of American architecture and furniture, yet their preeminence was with song. According to one scholar, Shaker songs outnumber those of any other denomination, ten thousand strong. Equally striking, however, are the physical environments they created, the farms, barns, houses, chairs, tables—the material world of Shakerism. Here the psychological and political peace that lay at the heart of their communal endeavor became three dimensional.

Their abandoned villages continue to exude a Spartan lilt, like an unadorned line of song. Their ghost towns continue to convey energy, light, worldly beauty, and otherworldly tranquility. Devoid of ornamentation, Shaker barns, bedrooms, workshops all are spacious, sunny, and symmetrical, yet their linearity is often offset by a humorously twirling spiral staircase. The haunting white stillness is fascinating and attractive, and you walk as if inside of the dictum, "Let it be plain and simple, of good and substantial quality, unembellished by any superfluities which add nothing to its goodness or durability." Every museum-goer, tourist, or auction-goer in contact with Shaker relicts is drawn into spiritual communion with Mother Ann: "Heaven is a state of mind."

If Shaker life is so captivating, precious, enthusiastically embraced, Shaker society should be booming, with a three-month wait for admission tickets at Ticketron. But in the past four or five decades, there have been only three or four converts. About one dozen Shakers, mostly elderly women, inhabit the earth. All but two of their villages are abandoned and turned back to "the world" as museums, schools, and, ironically, in Sharon, Massachusetts, a prison.

The ambivalence with which humanity greets Shaker-ism is obvious. We find its outflow transporting. We want to touch it, to own it, to stay in contact with it. But almost no one wants to be a Shaker. We only dare to have vicarious reproductions of the transforming sacrificial fire of Shaker celibacy and surrender that gives birth to the simplicity, order, tranquility, and peace we crave and fear.

Most of us desire peace and desire; not pure, deep, *desireless* peace. If heaven were to be built on earth, most of us would only stand behind the cordons in our clean jeans to watch the workmen. The long experiment of human culture has provided us with the information we need to obtain a life of peace in a world of warmth, light and beauty. We have as much peace as we dare to select.

The most celebrated Shaker work of art is the eight lines of lyrics and the casual melody of "Simple Gifts," a hymn written by Elder Joseph Brackett at Alfred, Maine, in 1848. In diction and phrase, "Simple Gifts" resurrects the atmosphere of the Lord's Prayer.

For Shakers, the phrase "the gift" meant divine interces-sion. A person could be given "the gift" to pray, or to craft chairs, or to dance, or to speak for the spirit of Mother Ann. In his hymn, which he received as "a gift," Joseph Brackett described the common ground of all recipients of all gifts. He held the spirit of inner peace in view like a dove in his palm. The only analogy shaping the almost childlike concreteness of description in the song is the whirling, turning, shaking dance-worship that gave the Shakers their name.

'Tis the gift to be simple, 'tis the gift to be free,
'Tis the gift to come down where we ought to be
And when we find ourselves in the place just right,
'Twill be in the valley of love and delight.

When true simplicity is gained,
To bow and to bend we shall not be ashamed,
To turn, to turn will be our delight,
Till by turning; turning we come round right.

"Simple Gifts" is confidence in the inner compass that is free of personal will and orients by higher law. It expresses the release and grace of unresisting faith. It is sweetly social, yet solitary. Devoid of rhetoric or persuasion, it is a statement of peace. The song focuses on selectivity, simplicity, not by will of iron, but by will of light. It describes the Shaker dance in a manner that makes it transparent to our normally scattered, worldly obfuscation. Daring to surrender himself, this Shaker has lived in cloistered, chaste, possessionless remove. Descending temptations cannot interfere with the swing of his spontaneous gestures. His life of discipline has given him unerring sensitivity to a pervading rightness in the center of all motion. According to Mother Ann, every act can be filled with sanctifying love; and in the song, every place, properly arrived at, is the right place. The uncontaminated spirit is a compass needle in a magnetic field of selfless joy. A God is never mentioned. Reverence and devotion saturate and pervade everything without distraction.

For the moment of its duration, this song seems to hold all of life twirling in an unfailing solar system of love. It expresses a heart opened wide. Having selected simplicity as his guide, Elder Joseph Bracket sang with a mood of fulfillment. He was struck by "the gift" while submersing himself in the carefully culled lifestyle shared by seventy thousand Shakers.

However extreme and perverse the Shakers may seem to us, during the era of their efflorescence they were entranced by a creative communion. Their renunciations made them a transparent medium for a heaven they recreated on earth. They transmitted the light. Lantern glass, so clear and primly sinuous, doesn't endure like cinderblock, but it is luminous. Simple gifts fall only into open hands.

If you seek "the more," you will have to practice "the less." Some degree of order, simplicity, calm, and focus is necessary for inner peace to develop. I myself wouldn't give up intimacy's comfort and embrace for the promise of tranquility a few decades down a sere cul-de-sac. For different individuals at particular times and places, the location will vary, but inner peace always resides along the ascetic, renunciative, self-disciplined continuum that emphasizes careful choice and personal responsibility for the tone of one's own life. There are many kinds of cloudy skies, but only one kind of clear sky!

Selectivity is captured by the Buddha's two famous dicta: "You must walk the path yourself," and, "Be an island unto yourself."

Neighbors may find peace-seekers peculiar, but each of our careful refusals are dictated by listening, because a song, as it forms in the mind, rises from beyond our selves, from the zone of the imperturbable. If you want your life to have a point, you'll have to taper it.

PART IV

Chapter 9

PEACE IS THE VIBRATION OF LANGUAGE

IN INDIA IT IS A WELL-ACCEPTED PRINCIPLE that the vibration of language is the most powerful causative force in the universe. A similar idea opens the Gospel according to John: "In the beginning was the Word . . ." Each aspect of being derives from its own sound. Peace is not only a way of life, it is a tonal dimension. Because peace is connected to vibration, properly tuned language is an avenue into it, and an expression of it. Language can contain and express peace both in content and by resonance. Peace is what you say, and how you say it; it is both what you understand, and what you hear in your flesh and bones. From person to person, among contemporaries and across time, the electrons of language ignite the aurora borealis of peace.

Peace also travels across time and place through pictures, like art and dreams. Ultimately, the wisdom of peace is revealed in imageless silence. But guidance up to that final revelation always rests on the words of masters, whose sound and sense are uniform.

Freud healed neurotic anguish through "the talking cure."
Socrates brought his disciples to the life of self-knowledge
through dialectic. Jesus taught the Sermon on the Mount and
spoke aphorisms and parables that continue to dominate the
thoughts of billions of people. God came to Joseph Smith,
the founder of the Mormons, and to Mohammed, the prophet
of Islam, as an author of verse.

The Buddha, who embodied silent, inward Nibbāna,
gave eighty-four thousand sermons; the "three baskets" of
his words form a vast weaving of wisdom, the recitation of
which creates vibrations that convey directly the baritone
tremolo of equanimity.

Fragments of inner peace can never cohere without the
grout and bond of language. All language is a derivative of
poetry: compelling sounds that evoke revolutionizing vibration. Language is more than signative cognition; through
its buzz and beat, it transforms the minds and bodies of its
listeners until we become beings physically different from
those who came to hear the message. Bland words are only
broken poetry.

Words of peace educate us, temper us through rational
inquiry, inspire us with what has already been attained, and
transform us in the mere receptivity we have to their tremolo.
The practice of imbibing words of peace will create within
you a hum of peace. Syllabic peace sends transforming shafts
of sound shivering through its listeners. Our hearts continue
to beat in rhythmic sympathy.

Just as people exposed to traumas—child abuse, torture,
warfare—may remain crippled for years or a lifetime by one
overwhelming exposure; with the same power but reversed
direction, great teachings indelibly transform their initiates
into tuning forks resonating with received vibrations. All
prophets are poets.

Chapter 10

SPEAK YOUR PEACE

IF I COULD DO ONE THING for my society today, it would be to create community in which everyone was encouraged to speak from the heart, and to listen to the messages of others. I have spent most of my life listening to varieties of justified complaints that no one listens to or understands. Unfortunately, we live in a non-listening, mass-market, person-inattentive society. The emphasis on efficiency, productivity, pleasure, and hurry that pervade society leave little room for building personal relationships around resonant communication of feelings. We live in a society uniquely devoid of conversation about the backdrop of infinite reality, through which every shaft of light that falls on us has passed. We see the tint of this passage everywhere, but we suffer from derealization when we try to speak about its presence in our lives. Yet this cultural repression is changeable, every time we ourselves dare to refer in our talk to the reality always present around us.

Autumn in New England is an example—a season in which leaves color a kaleidoscope of mountain ranges and regions. How can we pursue our business in silence when the world is turning in death and revelry? Not just the panorama, but each tree, every limb, goes pointillist. A creation usually hidden within summer's green is suddenly unveiled, and dances in *deshabillé* across the landscape.

If you collect a batch of autumn leaves, as you are apt to do with your four-year-old child, who babbles to you that each one is a jewel, you can see that one leaf alone mirrors the wild russet and umber pigments of the whole hillside. Across its segments, down its veins, the one leaf is as flagrant and glorious as the Shenandoah. Each parish of the spectacle shivers with the unrestraint of the whole. Every maple leaf is its own Canada, intricate provinces and territories to explore. Every cell is alive. Not billions, not trillions, no numerical concept can capture what our dazzled eyes reveal: we are members in an infinite host of presences. Not all life is human, or even visible. Each cell is as alive as is our mind. The complexity, beauty, and importance of autumn derives from the hosts of contributors within its colors.

Within cells also, no doubt, there are patchwork hillsides, because the world is mottled by components within components, and they turn color and change ceaselessly. Autumn colors reveal ineluctable change at every level, at last made visible. Beauty derives from the egoless mortality of parts, tiding out at their own pace. Autumn leaf magic reveals the mosaic microcosm beneath all surfaces.

Each one of us is also a cell, a leaf, ablaze and dying in an oceanic infinitude of change upon change. Yet we spend much of our brief passage here unable to speak about the reality we feel. We all yearn for that moment in which we could express to each other the feelings generated by the disruptive, majestic, ego-shattering realities of nature around us.

A sense of expansive belonging is available to us. We are born into membership in a panorama of presences.

Exemplars of peace, like Walt Whitman and Mahatma Gandhi, spoke freely about their expanded belonging—Whitman to a poetic cosmos, Gandhi to millions of people, dozens of social political and religious reforms. We can be elevated by speaking with each other about what we deeply know. We love the leaves not only for their color, but for the whispering sound of their fall, which we intuitively understand as a language we once shared with all beings.

ALL WORDS ARE IN RHYTHM, all thoughts are in rhythm. The written word, the spoken word, is like a hand feeling its way into a dark room, looking for a switch. Its search is noiseless, unpoliceable.

Words of peace enable solitude in elevating company. Reading, at its best, is friendship at its rarest. If you are seeking peace, visit the lands of the forefathers of peace, who have suspended entire invisible kingdoms in the deep Alps of their words. Behind every Whitman is a Krishna and an Isaiah; behind every Gandhi is a Thoreau and a Socrates. The Buddha himself knew the poetic forms of his time. It is the struggle to understand and communicate that kindles peace. Buddha said: "By seeking truth I have discovered peace of mind." Our passage into the recess of reverie, analysis, and dialogue in silence is permitted by the serenity and unfinality contained in words of peace.

The Shakers were wordsmiths via their song lyrics. Shakers corresponded with Count Leo Tolstoy. Tolstoy's book was one that transformed Gandhi, and Shaker and Gandhian ideas re-molded Count Tolstoy into Christian peasant Tolstoy. Whitman and Thoreau met and influenced each other, and Thoreau's "Civil Disobedience" became the manifesto for Gandhi's social action. Scott and Helen Nearing read Whitman and Thoreau, as did Rabindranath Tagore. Tagore and Gandhi had a long relationship. John Muir's favorite author was Thoreau. Thoreau "carried *Leaves of Grass* around Concord like a red flag." Seekers of peace read each other, write to each other, influence each other. The quiet life of inner peace isn't a vacuum. The silence of peace is only possible after peace has spoken.

GREAT WORDS GO BEYOND their informative, evocative, transformative properties, to seminal ambiguity. They point to a specific cone of darkness; they delineate an essential unknowable. Ultimately, words are important on the path of peace because they point beyond whatever they say. They call on, evoking in the reader or listener an urge to direct personal experience. The role of words in the life of peace is paradoxical: they are essential, and they must be abandoned and transcended. Socrates exemplified this two-sided process, and he set the stage for Thoreau and Gandhi, using words of peace for social betterment yet pointing to a peace deeper than words.

For Socrates, philosophy was a way of life, built around the cultivation of emotional calm. He understood philosophy to be the generation of liberating dialectic—conversations whose goal was to free the mind from rigidity. The true test of the rightness of philosophy, according to Socrates, was that it brought so much serenity that the philosopher could face the vicissitudes of life—ostracism, persecution, murder—with equanimity. Philosophy was the art of dying well, which was the litmus test of living well. Words vibrating in face-to-face dialogue were the tools through which intellect could dilate to a mood, an atmosphere of virtue and limitless unknowing. Socrates passed his own exam, dying under persecution with aplomb and, of course, conversation.

When we read the Socratic dialogues recorded by his student, Plato, we come away with a sober delirium, as if we had inhaled a mind-altering vapor. We feel immersed in dynamic single-mindedness of purpose and austere selectivity, and we ascend into a realm of unrelenting good will, deep conviction, and uncertainty. Conviction and uncertainty sound like opposites, but in Socrates' Olympian thought, the conviction is of uncertainty. Even imminent death is a curious topic of unknown import. He inspires his listeners to continue to ascend into the unknown, even at the last moment. Underlying his unflappable ease is his confidence that all of our fears are only superstitions. We have nothing to fear but unexamined thoughts.

Words, with their precision at expelling false knowledge, yet their inability to ever define a final truth, are the medium of an unending playful search. Socrates calls us on to live through fate like a boy exploring a mud-hole for frogs. The dirt hides leaping wonders. His words are the verbal instillation of courage, faith, and peace.

The exactness of words enables them to shatter illusion; their abstraction prevents them from ever pinpointing an absolute finality. Socrates used them to continuously go beyond.

Words of peace, to be effective, must resonate with our experience, and be free of parochial attitude or reference. They rise out of an aquifer of possibility underlying all cultures and places that can't be divided or owned by one group.

THE BUDDHA SPOKE WORDS of Dhamma, truth that liberates. The Dhamma is both content and tone of voice. The Buddha used words both educatively—to counsel the importance of moral precepts, for example—and suggestively, to inspire his listeners to transcend words and ideas in direct experience of Nibbāna.

Not only did the Buddha spout a fountain of sermons, he placed great weight on right speech. The *way* a person converses will be a critical determinant of his fate. Our spiritual progress will be hindered or facilitated by the flavor of our talk.With our words, we can sow discord, suspicion, fear, and hate; or love, peace, harmony, cooperation. The Buddha carefully defined right speech by both content and tone.

> He speaks the truth, is devoted to truth, reliable, worthy of confidence . . . he unites those who are divided . . . concord gladdens him . . . he speaks words that are gentle, soothing, loving, such words as go to the heart, and are courteous, friendly, and agreeable.

Avoiding vanity, trivia, and the parade of ephemeral distractions, "talk of kings and robbers and empires," he instead "speaks at the right time, in accordance with the facts . . . like a treasure, uttered at the right moment, moderate and full of sense."

Right speech outlines an entire continent of life. I have often thought that if a person were to adopt only one aspect of the peaceful life, this would be it because all morality, relatedness, and self-knowledge are merely provinces within the conglomerate empire of right speech. If I want to live by right speech, I have to know what I think and feel, in order to be able to actually parlay the truth that my posture and tone may already be conveying. But to blurt out abrupt, hurtful words, even if they are accurate, isn't acceptable to Buddha's ideal, and so I not only have to search for my sense of the truth in the moment of interaction, but I have to simultaneously find a channel that is "gentle, soothing . . . . courteous." Finally, right speech demands loving words that are honest—this is its apex. To live by right speech, I not only have to be a self-psychologist and a linguist, but I have to learn how to find love in the ordinary gray-day facts. Right speech is predicated on disregard for calculation, on cohesion of word and act, and on honest affection, sentence after sentence.

Gandhi attempted to live by right speech. Louis Fischer, Gandhi's biographer, visited him at Sevagram Ashram and wrote:

> . . . nothing remarkable about him . . . I felt no awe in Gandhi's presence . . . a very sweet, gentle, informal, relaxed, happy, wise, highly civilized man. I felt the miracle of personality . . . he radiated his influence . . . . One has to go back centuries to find men who appealed as strongly as Gandhi did to the conscience . . . . He was a good man in a world where few resist the corroding influence of power, wealth and vanity. There he sat, four-fifths naked, on the earth in a mud hut in a tiny Indian village without electricity, radio, running water or telephone . . . . He encouraged banter . . . joked with all . . . . He himself was sometimes surprised by the things he said. His thinking was fluid. He thought out loud; he revealed each step in his thinking . . . he talked like a friend.

Gandhi spoke from the heart to the heart. In ordinary interaction, Gandhi followed the codification of right speech as taught by the Buddha, not because he was a Buddhist—he wasn't—but because he understood that to live a life of inner peace, each of his apparently inconsequential conversations had to flow out of and into peace.

An intimate, unguarded, spontaneous conversation with the inspired dead and the circle of the living places us in the ebb and flow of words beyond pretense. There is a particular pool of sound that bathes us in friendship and peace. Words of peace contained in the collective human treasury, or murmured anew in obscure corners of the world, manifest in sound the seamlessness of the universe. All boundaries are temporary. Listening to unifying words, speaking them, repeating them, acting in accord with them, we tune up our nervous systems to the voices of time and timelessness. Like geese, we travel in formation behind trailblazers. We migrate by listening to the beckoning call of those who have already pierced the clouds and are flying higher.

Chapter 11

WALT WHITMAN'S POETIC PEACE

ONE OF THE WONDERFUL INSTANCES of language in service of inner peace can be found in the biography of Walt Whitman. He placed himself inside an oscillating language field of peace to ease his own heart, then created a field in which we, too, can stand for similar benefit.

A hundred years after his death, Whitman's life transpires the atmosphere of outdoor freedom. He is known as America's pagan poet, who set the style of bohemian bard, beckoning to listeners today from old photographs that capture him in his rustic livery, cocked Stetson, open collar, and spirit of dusty rambles on timeless summer days.

The story of Whitman's relationship with his literary ancestors is not only instructive but intriguing, since he intentionally distorted fact to sculpt a poetic truth. Both what he initially intended to hide, and what his writing and later confessions reveal, highlight the role of the vibration of language in his journey toward poise, since Whitman's life, for all its breadth and creativity, was an increasingly dynamic, selectively honed pilgrimage into peace.

Whitman came from a large, poor, semiliterate family devoid of accomplishment. He had minimal schooling and, as an adolescent, began various jobs, living alone in Manhattan rooming houses until he became the editor of a series of short-lived one-man newspapers. We have spare information about his young manhood, but out of his nondescript, unpromising background, at the age of thirty-five, Whitman erupted with one of the masterpieces of world literature, *Leaves of Grass,* which he continued to rewrite and expand until his death almost four decades later.

When Whitman's poetic breakthrough occurred, he was aware of both the historical significance and the apparently mysterious personal transformation that underlay it. An important feature of the original edition of *Leaves of Grass* was his emphasis on the unaccountable emergence of his poems without forelearning or art. He underscored for his readers that an unemployed carpenter's son, who had never completed high school, had seemingly erupted with volcanic originality. He reinforced the impression that the poems sprang out of common soil like wildflowers, or a rose dripping like a god from the sea. The poetry claimed to be the voice of the universe, or of a spokesperson for the universe.

> *My tongue, every atom of my blood, form'd from this soil, this air . . .*
> *I harbor for good or bad, I permit to speak at every hazard,*
> *Nature without check with original energy . . . .*
>
> *I and this mystery here we stand . . .*
>
> *These are really the thoughts of all men in all ages and lands, they are not original with me . . .*

His verse surged like a geyser, steeped in the secrets of molecules, soil, rock, and sky. He tried to expound a trans-human perspective, to create an independent frame of reference, as if his words flowed from a rootless universal sage. In his real life, as in his poetry, Whitman followed his own dictum: to dive down into his soul, to disobey all else, and to pursue his own way. If continents and grass blades could write, they would do so without going to the library, but Walt Whitman's literary voice was an intentional artistic effect that belied the origins and methods behind *Leaves of Grass*. In fact, Whitman's personal transformation was a slow and careful process based on years of focal quest for vibrating words that could heal, soothe, and bring peace to himself, and to his contemporaries.

Whitman spent a decade or more in intense effort of self-transformation and ardent private tutorial. His was not an apprenticeship nor disciplehood, since it was autonomous, but it was not, as he wanted his readers to believe, a *de novo* cosmic cloudburst. He immersed himself. Part of the mystery of Whitman's genius lay in his uncanny absorptive power:

> *There was a child went forth every day;*
> *And the first object he looked upon and received*
> *with wonder, pity, love, or dread, that object*
>   *he became;*
> *And that object became part of him for the day, or*
> *a certain part of the day, or for many years,*
>   *or stretching cycles of years.*

The depth of his literary genius is a blessing that nature bestowed on Whitman, but his method of cultivating it follows a common method of the peaceful life. Whitman educated himself, quaffing the peaceful wisdom of all antecedent teachers. He absorbed the peaceful vibrations of Bibles and birds. He suspended himself in currents of art and music— and his poetry is remarkable for both its visual and rhythmic power. He was an eager audience for science, and among all writers of his age, he went furthest to pursue and incorporate into his poetic vision the expanding scientific knowledge of the nineteenth century. He bathed himself in influences that led him toward harmony, never self-satisfied with what he contained, eager to receive. And of all influences, the vibration of language was foremost.

Although in his notes to himself he advised: "Make no quotations and no reference," and though he attempted to create a style that, in the words of one of his biographers, read "as if literature had never existed," his original outpouring tapped the roots of world literature. Literary caterpillar Whitman spent his larval years wrapped in the pages of tomes.

He took on a purely naïve written voice partly to produce a literary effect, but mostly because he wanted to cleave an opening for himself between models of education that were classist, authoritarian, and divisive. Whitman's homemade education enabled him to tumble together in one vision ideas, images, experiences, and insights that were generative of peace that was deeper and truer than anything in his environment. He read and studied with an agenda: to make whole, unify, integrate—himself and his contemporaries. He was transforming Western civilization at the same time that his literary efforts had a psychological urgency beneath them: to escape the misery of his own background and personal conflicts. To do so, he had to harness his unique array of protopeaceful talents. He learned to write on war, politics, sex, or history, but he became preeminently the bard of synthesis, overview, embrace, ecstasies, and peace.

IF WE TAKE OUR OWN Whitmanesque amble through the poet's literary voyaging, his exemplars, and his temperamental style, it will become clear how he became not merely a poet, but the poet of liberation, the prophet of the open road, even as he stayed home and read.

Whitman's chief literary ancestor was the King James Bible. He rejected its doctrines, but he absorbed through continuous study two of its essences. The attitude of revelation and the rhythms of free verse are the containing seashores of Whitman's otherwise poetic formlessness. Throughout the "New Bible" he felt he was creating, whose content varied from personal love poems to patriotic chorales, a recurrent ambience pervades all of *Leaves of Grass*—an overarching, incorporative relinquishment, acceptance, restoration, calm. Whitman's lifework is an insistent reconstitution of relief within the hurricane of suffering. The quality and style of address in *Leaves of Grass* is unique; no poet before or since has shared in the idiosyncratic vantage point from which Whitman looked at life and spoke to his readers, with its gush of exuberance, omnivorous incorporations, grandiose proclamations, and intimate innuendos. Yet through all the fanfare and whispers there is a consistent derivation from the prophets. His poetry shines with primeval daring, unfiltered witness, and expansive, organic harmony like the desert Hebrews who founded Western religious verse.

Whitman described his literary foreground more candidly than he had originally in the poetry itself, explicitly referencing himself to the Old and New Testaments, Shakespeare, Homer, Sophocles, Dante, the Bhagavad Gita, and many other classics of East and West—all of which he claimed to have read on beaches or in the woods. Whitman's insistence that he read outdoors—known to be a liberty with observed fact—is reminiscent of Monet's insistence that all his paintings were done spontaneously outdoors—also known to be a lovely lie, the intent of which was to link art with pastoral tranquillity.

Late in Whitman's life, long after his years of questing study and self-transformation were complete, his devotion to antecedent literature continued. The aging poet perused books that littered his tables, chairs, and floor, books of every kind from every field of endeavor, with Whitman moving from topic to topic in a sequence dictated more by his curiosity and intuition than by logic or by table of contents.

The distracted, idiosyncratic style of Whitman should not be mistaken as casual or haphazard. The kind of studying Whitman exemplifies is an existential studenthood that differs from the obedient, narrow incorporation of information and technology promulgated in school, and differs also from the prudent, objective completeness of a scholar. It is the passion for truth channeled by a focal quest. Whitman wasn't chaotically feasting on words. His studies revolved around a hub, a unifying theme and a dominant mood, that he sought both in his personal life and which he wanted his poetry to express foremost: inner peace. His unifying core is what enabled him to wander so far, to be so multichromatic and panoramic, without becoming tangential or irrelevant.

Walt Whitman crafted a psychic world of words of peace as a balm for his inner torment of childhood deprivation, fears of paternal rage, conflict over his homosexual feelings, dismay over social injustice, and heightened awareness of death. Emerging from a degenerating family and living in a tumultuous era, he sought excitement, freedom, membership, and health, but predominantly, peace of mind preserved in poetic beauty. His writing is relevant to us because it was so personally motivated. The priority of inner peace organized him and gave his fragmented self a coherent personality. He recreated reality with pain-diminishing intent, wrapping himself in the poultice of peace.

WHITMAN'S STYLE OF STUDENTHOOD illustrates one feature of the life of inner peace, but his literary and personal pursuit of ameliorating harmony did not rest on that alone.

The poet of peace had more than one dimension. Whitman's immersion in words of peace became numinous because he integrated it with his absorptive temperament, his scientific-historical gnosis, and his courageous spelunking in death's cavern. No portrait of him can shortchange those other healing powers and developments. Let me focus now on the way he rose out of turmoil to transpire peaceful poetry, because it is both so inspiring and instructive.

Whitman's capacious drinking-in of literature, the hidden, indoor side of the author of "The Song of the Open Road," was one aspect of a pervasive capacity he had to receive. The same gleaning characterized his relationship to nature. He was a continuous, outdoors walker, wanderer, observer. Even in his late years, partially paralyzed, he would immerse himself in the solitary woods of Timber Creek and study the minute perturbations of bees and leaves. Psychiatrist R.M. Bucke wrote:

> His favorite occupation seemed to be strolling or sauntering about outdoors by himself, looking at the grass, the trees, the flowers, the vistas of light, the varying aspects of the sky and listening to the birds, the crickets, the tree-frogs, the wind in the trees, and all the hundreds of natural sounds. It was evident that these things gave him a feeling of pleasure far beyond what they give to ordinary people. Until I knew the man it had not occurred to me that anyone could derive so much absolute happiness and ample fulfillment from these things as he evidently did.

Whitman practiced a mode of being that forms the basis for many of his great poetic passages.

> *Going where I list, my own master total and*
> *absolute . . .*
> *Pausing, searching, receiving, contemplating,*
> *Gently, but with undeniable will, divesting myself*
> *of the holds that would hold me.*

This peaceful, embracing, permitting, nonjudgmental freedom is the psychological center of Walt Whitman, poet and person; it is the way he interacted with the world, and the way he read. To find and express peace was his goal; his method was to stand back, unattached, to ". . . witness and wait." Whitman described himself: "The poet judges not as a judge judges but as the sun falling around a helpless thing . . . both in and out of the game, watching and wondering . . . ."

Whitman related to words in a particular way, and then he used those words to recreate the world in a vision that derived from the same mental operation: the cultivation of states of self-detached absorption. The content of his poetry expressed a neuromental mode of being, making himself an unresisting conduit of reality. He absorbed vibrations of peace, then re-combined and emitted them.

> *My ties and ballasts leave me, my elbows rest in*
> *   sea-gaps,*
> *I skirt sierras, my palms cover continents . . .*
> *Speeding through space, speeding through heaven*
> *and the stars . . .*
> *Speeding with tail'd meteors, throwing fire-balls*
> *   like the rest*

From this psychological altitude, Whitman could expand his understanding of time and space. So laid-back, so high above, he could envision human history consistently with the scientific literature he read so assiduously.

Whitman's words of peace are cradled in cosmic time that neutralizes personal pain and guarantees continuity and meaning to private acts in the interstices of the universe. An important part of Whitman's breakthrough as a poet was to bring scientific cosmology into poetic language.

> *A few quadrillions of eras, a few octillions of*
> *   cubic leagues . . .*
> *They are but parts, any thing is but a part.*

Nowhere in world literature, outside of the Sanskrit religious classics of India, have time and space been treated so realistically, objectively, and psychologically as in *Leaves of Grass,* and this floating in timelessness underlies the atmosphere of accepting peace. Whitman diluted his individual suffering in the ocean of eternity. His literary work was poetic, scientific, and personally reconstructive and therapeutic. He envisioned his individual creativity to be part of an eternal liberating evolution. He forged a new theater of meaning, based on empirical astronomy, that made his pain inconsequential, and his existence miraculous and opportune. Listen to Walt Whitman transcend identification with his own body and with his historical moment, sweep open a vision of the future exceeding any limiting imagery, and launch himself, and us, into a cosmic optimism that affirms his potential as it obliterates his small self—all through his command of peace-evoking language.

> *And as to you Life I reckon you are the leavings of*
> *   many deaths,*
> *(No doubt I have died myself ten thousand times*
> *   before) . . .*
>
> *To conceive no time, however distant, but what*
> *you may reach it and pass it . . .*
>
>
> *I launch all men and women forward with me into*
> *   the Unknown . . .*
> *We have thus far exhausted trillions of winters and*
> *   summers,*
> *There are trillions ahead, and trillions ahead*
> *   of them . . .*
> *I am an acme of things accomplish'd, and I am*
> *   encloser of things to be.*

. . . and still I mount and mount . . .
Immense have been the preparations for me . . .
Cycles ferried my cradle, rowing and rowing like
*   cheerful boatmen,*
For room to me stars kept aside in their own
*   rings . . .*
All forces have been steadily employ'd to complete
*   and delight me,*
Now on this spot I stand with my robust soul.

The world mirrored in *Leaves of Grass* reveals a stagger-ing complexity of time and material, organized into human-ity: the culmination of the universe's potential for joy, love, peace, and freedom from suffering. Whitman's poetic vision explodes the narcissistic time-scale of mere decades and cen-turies, but paradoxically affirms each individual as the apex of an evolutionary ascent towards compassion, sympathetic joy, loving kindness, and equanimity. He said of himself in the third person, "As he sees the farthest he has the most faith. His thoughts are the hymns of the praise of things."

It is one thing to declaim expansive astronomical poetry, and another thing to turn toward personal, individual death with equal embrace. Yet any time scale so vast immediately presses the individual toward confrontation with mortality. According to Whitman, the key to and the source of his po-etry was death.

Whitman reconstrued death not as an interruption, an end, but as a source, a principle, the fundamental nature of the universe out of which life was a scent from the flower. Fertile, enclosing, creative, restful death is the matrix from which life arises like a song from the throat of a bird. Whitman's confrontation with suffering and death wasn't a philosophical or literary pose. His ability to dwell in proximity to suffering and death and to rise strengthened and affirmed was what enabled his years-long, heroic, sacrificial watch over hundreds of thousands of Civil War soldiers, wounded and dead. This real-life vigil derived from a rare faith in the integrity of the human drama and in the restoration of the cosmic tides.

An important source of Whitman's sense of peace was his depth of conviction that life is only the fluttering emblem of something invisible, eternal, and tranquil. Historic cataclysms and personal anguish were diluted to ripples in a galactic ocean whose depths remained dark, pregnant with infinite life, and painlessly serene.

The poet's serenity was a conscious victory; it does not tell the whole story of the man's life. Whitman struggled frequently with personal loneliness. The man who could embrace the universe lived alone. He did make personal friends, and late in life was surrounded by admirers, but his writing, with its revolutionary style, challenging realignments, and bold sexuality, brought vilification, rejection, and frustration. Yet, surrounded as well by his sick, deteriorating family, Whitman overrode despair or bitterness.

> *. . . from any fruition of success, no matter what,*
> *shall come forth something*
> *to make a greater struggle necessary.*

Part of Whitman's poetic power was the compression of what is wise, serene, and complete with what is troubled, unfinished, rough, and real. He was a poet not of complacent aplomb, but of ignorance revising itself. His poetry was a gift, his abilities titanic; his peace was a slow and careful construction with common hand tools.

Whitman's relative victory over suffering, though partial and filled with troughs, was not peculiar nor a product of his unique literary genius. He followed a well-worn, reproducible, psychological method, one salient element of which was his literary studenthood to words of peace. Not a pure example of anything other than himself, he did place his boots upon many other common stepping-stones of inner peace: dynamic devotion to that focal concern, love of the outdoors, and his particular style of absorptive meandering; passionate compassion exemplified by his service as a volunteer nurse-savior during the Civil War; and courageous confrontation with suffering in wartime hospitals. Above all, he used language to think, feel, and convey an expanded reality. He heard the *sound* of the moment stretching back like an accordion to the birth of the universe and out toward an expanding future, then compressed again to the note of the now. This oceanic immediacy, and the task of verbalizing it, create the mood of Whitman's poetry. He saw infinite multitudes of the future, poised within today like unseen buds in a continuous cosmic spring. His envisioning was caused by, and was an effect of, his continuous effort to speak peace, to sound the libretto of the seashore in human tongue, to evoke in uniquely American diction the mood of ebb tide, hermit thrush, and starry night. His discipleship was to all books, all songs, all sounds that carry us beyond ourselves to sibilant rest.

Chapter 12

MAHATMA GANDHI'S
MANTRIC COLLAGE

INDIA'S GREAT POLITICAL AND RELIGIOUS LEADER, Mahatma Gandhi, intended his monumental public life to be merely an extension of his inner cultivation of peace. Foremost among Gandhi's peaceful qualities were his reverence for world spiritual literature, his awareness that words transmit feelings as well as ideas, his steady immersion in peaceful language, and his use of linguistic vibrations to transform his followers.

Gandhi was different from Whitman in almost every dimension. Whitman had little formal schooling, whereas Gandhi had trained as a barrister in London. Whitman's language was limited to colloquial American, whereas Gandhi was an educated master of English, Gujarati, Hindi, and other Indian languages. Whitman was primarily solitary and economically marginal. Gandhi made a fortune in South Africa before he took his personal vows of poverty; he was married, fathered four sons, lived in collective households and ashrams, was a beloved, celebrated leader of a nation, a household word around the world in his own lifetime. Whitman was fired from being a clerk in a government office; Gandhi

conferenced with prime ministers and kings. Yet the way
Whitman and Gandhi studied, read, tuned up to the sacred
rhythms around them, then conveyed peace to others, reveals
a kinship in their methods of living and self-elevation. Both
developed their proto-peaceful inklings through immersion
in illuminated language.

Gandhi's life became a series of charismatic self-trans-
formations that swept up millions of people in his idealistic
reforms. Until late middle age, he lived in South Africa, where
he struggled for justice against racial laws and forged his eccentric personal path of vegetarianism, sexual asceticism, and
political activism in the service of pacifism. When he returned
to live in India, he was already a world figure, and he gradually
assumed the mantle of leadership in India's fight for freedom
from British rule, and also in his own comprehensive social
reform program for India. A description of his enormous
power and accomplishments, and his hand-carved personal
lifestyle, doesn't account for the effulgent love and awe that
he evoked in his followers and that has made him symbolic
of a new hope for peace as a pragmatic force in the world.
That was the product of his spiritual ascension.

Mahatma, as he was called by Tagore and came to be
known (Mahatma means "Great Soul"), broke out of his
narrow British professional education and became a self-
educating seeker. He shucked his formal schooling and set
off alone on an odyssey through world literature, seeking
words that would enclose, mirror, explain, and animate the
inner truth he intuited but had yet no way of expressing.

Throughout his long leadership, Gandhi stressed his debt
to his literary ancestors. Like Whitman's, Gandhi's idiosyncratic studenthood did not inform his mind; it transformed
his personality. For him, reading was yoga, a sustained discipline directed at liberation from ignorance and suffering.
His quixotic and creative leadership of Indian national rebirth

was constantly and explicitly referenced to the passages of literature that had inspired him. He didn't invent in a vacuum. He called forth from the collective library of possibility its most treasured catalogue numbers of tranquil strength. Like Whitman's extensive reading, Gandhi's was a deep inhaling that reconfigured his molecules. He soaked in words of peace to dye himself with new hues of being.

Most famous of Gandhi's self-proclaimed literary ancestors was Thoreau, whose essay "On Civil Disobedience" became the kernel of the Gandhian revolution. Gandhi first read it, appropriately enough, in a South African jail. Gandhi had begun to disobey laws he felt were unjust before he ever encountered Thoreau's writing, but he found the essay to be a "masterly treatise"; "it left a deep impression on me." Gandhi biographer Louis Fischer concluded, "There is a Thoreau imprint on much that Gandhi did." What Fischer meant is that from Thoreau, Gandhi captured more than a tactic. He absorbed a mood of indomitable determination to actualize peaceful idealism in daily life.

Gandhi's literary pilgrimage wandered backwards to Thoreau's roots in Socrates. Gandhi dissolved himself into the Socratic dialogues, into the world of a faith so deep that tyrannically imposed death was too trivial an incident to interrupt the quest for higher life. Gandhi made the first translations of the Socratic dialogues into his native Gujarati.

Gandhi has also recorded in reverential detail how his reading of art critic John Ruskin's book *Unto This Last* and Leo Tolstoy's *The Kingdom of Heaven is Within You* provided the inspiration that reorganized his life from bourgeois barrister to prophet and saint. He explicitly stated that he became the man he was as a product of an inner revolution created by passages in Ruskin and Tolstoy.

Among other deviations from accepted Indian traditions, Gandhi the holy man never accepted any guru, although that transformational teacher-student relationship is usually considered the essence of Hindu spiritual life. In place of a guru, Gandhi accepted three people as "having left a deep impress on my life and captivated me." One was a real friend of young adulthood, Raychandbhai, but the other two were his literary heroes only: Tolstoy and Ruskin. Tolstoy's Shaker-influenced "independent thinking, profound morality, and truthfulness . . . overwhelmed me" and Gandhi went on to make "an intensive study of Tolstoy's books," from which "I began to realize more and more the infinite possibilities of universal love." Don't you find it intriguing, and even a revealing dissection of the pathways of peace that are woven beneath the visible world, that a bunch of semi-literate, rustic American herb farmers, like the Shakers, after their demise reached out and reformed a twentieth century, literary-intellectual lawyer and politician, like Gandhi, thereby putting their peaceful imprint onto modern Asian nation-building?

But of Ruskin's *Unto This Last,* Gandhi wrote:

> The book was impossible to lay aside . . . it gripped me . . . I could not get any sleep that night . . . I determined to change my life in accordance with the ideals of the book . . . an instantaneous and practical transformation in my life.

The Mahatma's guru was books. Of all books, the Bhagavad Gita ultimately became most important to Gandhi, functioning as his bible. The Gita is a poem in rhythmic couplets; not just its philosophy, but its pulse influenced him. Gandhi himself was a prolific writer, but his full feeling for words of peace emerged not in his private reading nor in his public writing, but in another medium altogether: the prayer service he invented to anchor the life of his ashram. Here he stirred up words of peace from the human collectivity to whirl in rhythmic catalysis and inspirational transformation.

The prayer service at his ashram was the psychic center of a man, of a collective of men and women, and of a political, social, and spiritual revolution. Here was the divine communication intended to inspire and inform fasts, poverty, beatings, prison sentences, service to and love of all living things.

Prayers at the ashram began at 4 a.m. with Gandhi sitting cross-legged under a tree, while his followers seated themselves in a semicircle in front of him. Prayers from many religions were recited and always in their original languages, to keep their vibrations true, while Gandhi, like a schoolmaster, would stop the whole service to correct an individual's mispronunciations! Buddhist chants in Japanese, Hindi prayers to Vishnu, Arabic verses from the Koran would follow each other. Then came the affirmation of dedication to Gandhi's principles.

> We will be nonviolent; we will be truthful; we will not steal; we will be continent; we will not hoard; we will all wear *khadi* [homespun, not store-bought] clothes; we will work with our hands; we will eat simple foods; we will be fearless; we will treat people of all religions equally; and we will work for the eradication of untouchability.

This was followed by verses and chants from many Indian religions and languages, mixing Hindu, Islamic, and Zoroastrian scriptures among Christian hymns, with the participants all singing, clapping hands, or keeping time with small cymbals, finally culminating in the *dhuns*, invocations of God under his numerous, mellifluous Hindu appellations, recited faster and faster, louder and louder, in thrilling, surging climax. Gandhi was in ecstasy as the names of God rolled over his lips and rocked among his disciples.

To close the meeting, someone read in Sanskrit from the most important book in Gandhi's life, the Bhagavad Gita, which could be heard aloud, repeatedly over the years, at the ashram. At 5 a.m., Gandhi returned to his hut and sat down cross-legged on his bed, alone.

Gandhi's prayer service was like a church service, except that it embraced all religions rather than one: "I am a Christian, and a Hindu, a Moslem, and a Jew." Also, the service didn't sanctify the collective routine, but inspired ascetics toward sacrificial rebellion. In that sense, it was more like a tribal war dance. It was intended to focus his followers on the exalted and dangerous life and social-political movement to which they had dedicated themselves without reservation: peace in action, peace at all costs. The service lit a bonfire of intention. Unlike a war dance, Gandhi's prayer service unified means and ends: it had to inspire risks for peace by inducing not mere courage or fanaticism, but inner peace. In that sense, the prayer service was a dawn lullaby. It tuned the earth around them like a vast harp. Even the echo of this ceremony, recorded on the page and long after its originator's death, makes me feel as if I had just awakened from a dream-irruption from another dimension. It is both excitation and soothing, a fusion, a mantric collage of humankind's songs, prayers, and rhythms of peace.

With its participants seated in a mandala centering on Gandhi himself, and with the beat accelerating, rolling outward from them, among them, and beyond them into the sympathetically vibrating membrane of the atmosphere, the process became, in the eyes of its creators, the navel of peaceful, unifying, conscious and preconscious communication on earth, among the worlds. They were not merely praying, singing, reciting: they were pulsing the heartbeat of peace into their own arteries, and into the waiting environment. Peace is a product of both insight and physics.

Every fast, strike, and day for Gandhi commenced and ended with scriptural poetry from diverse sources. His use of words was rhythmic, musical, and vibratory. They helped him to retune the strings of himself and his followers daily, like a concert-master violinist. He avoided reducing words to intellectual sectarian dogma, but he became an extension, a manifestation of them, carrying their notes in his atoms while he attempted to spend the rest of his day in "right speech."

PEACE MILITANTS WILL SEEK and use words differently than hermetic poets. But Gandhi and Whitman rose to their fullness on wings of rhythm, recitation, and resonance. Their lives reveal a common pattern that would also be found—if we were to pursue more biographies—in the lives of most people who attain some degree of peacefulness.

Many people spontaneously use literature in this living way, as the path of peace dictates, looking for suggestions and provocations that push you back on the U-turn toward possible reconstructions of your own life the rectifying and illuminating perceptions of the elders. Yet there are dangers in mere book-learning.

Thoreau cautioned, "we are in danger of forgetting the language which all things and events speak without metaphor.... No method or discipline can supersede the necessity of being forever on the alert.... Will you be a reader, a student merely, or a seer?"

On your own path, peace means listening and speaking as if your words and actions were playing one instrument in the orchestra of the universe. What you say, read, listen to, will influence how your molecules and nervous system dance, and what messages you will conduct and broadcast. Whitman's poetry may spring you free of foreshortened time; and Gandhi's *dhuns* might, if you could reconstruct them, prepare you for noble social action. The words that you absorb will be important contributors to the peace that you will transmit, intentionally or not.

Peace is partly a product of dipping yourself down into a strata of sound. If you were to learn Vipassana meditation, a teacher's chanting might facilitate receptivity in your tissues and fibers to the Dhamma as the Buddha revealed it, because the Dhamma is not only a way of life, but also a vibration.

As you orient toward peace and select out distraction, stay tuned.

PART V

Chapter 13

PEACE IN NATURE

A CONTINUOUS, DEVOTED, LIFELONG relationship to nature is one aspect of a life of peace. This may be due to a fundamental evolutionary law. Possibly we can't feel at ease without contacting the environments in which our minds and hearts evolved. The rush of wind in trees, rain pattering on earth, falcon wings scything the sky may be more than esthetically pleasing; they may be biological necessities for our psyches, as food is for our bodies. Children are born with a kinship for animals. No one grows up hugging a plush, stuffed traffic light.

But mere proximity to nature alone doesn't induce peacefulness; murderers too can grow up on farms. The Khmer Rouge, who created the killing fields of Cambodia, where millions of their countrymen were killed for no clear reason, were mostly rural young men who had grown up in rice paddies and jungles. The wisdom and calm found in nature isn't automatic. It doesn't reach everyone; it doesn't occur with every exposure. Yet without exception, across time and culture, people of peace have always lived in kin-ship with the world of natural things. What, exactly, is this natural power; when does it "take" and participate in peace; why does it often fail to do so? The following story will help us tease apart critical elements of this question.

An engineer resigned his industrial position, packed up his young family, and moved to the country. He bought a dilapidated farm and, inspired by Thoreau and Scott and Helen Nearing, set about living a disciplined, simple, natural farm life. The family worked as a unit, repairing the old build-ings, repopulating the pastures with goats, digging, turning, enriching, and harvesting an organic garden. The engineer reminded his wife and kids as often as he could how beauti-ful the dawn mist was, how aromatic the earth smelled, how free and happy they were now to hear doves cooing in the nearby pines.

But they weren't happy. The children felt displaced; the wife felt trapped, bored, confined. The engineer himself felt harried, frantic—equipment broke, cash was depleted.

The adolescent daughter became pregnant. The son be-came brooding and lonely, resigned to outsider status in his class. The youngest girl, still new enough to life to have few habits, made the only successful adjustment.

In less than a year, the engineer resold the old farm at a significant loss and returned to the suburbs where he sought psychiatric help for incapacitating depression. Long ago, so-cial psychiatric research dispelled the myth that rural people are happier than urban people. The peace that is to be found in nature is a form of communion requiring two parties, an exchange. It is not something that nature creates and hands over, nor something that nature can impose or enforce. It is a cultivated receptivity, a learned appreciation. The student of peace in nature is, ironically, a product of civilization and culture. Jumping into a new environment doesn't concoct a new man. The engineer had romantic notions that were squashed rather than confirmed in nature. In a sense, his brief excursion worked, for it brought him up squarely face to face with the depression his move to the country had been intended to deny. His contact with nature revealed pains, not inspiration, in his inner life. It forced him to enter a less romantic but more honest and helpful psychotherapy, where he could know himself as he was, not as he yearned to be.

Nature is a stern guru. Those who are not simultaneously knowing themselves as they study nature will be shaken into rude awareness of the great dark truths of the natural world and of their own psyches. Just as nature is the realm of light and beaches and bluebirds, it is the realm of the shadow winter, storms, cold, and death. Immersion in the natural world doesn't provide a sanctuary from human suffering; it augments and clarifies the deepest origins of distress. When that augmentation is a step toward confrontation and resolution, it is also a step toward inner peace.

To run your hand over ancient granite domes or to poke through the woods in search of spring beauties is to open yourself to both peace and disruption. We imagine we can hide from our neighbors, but our deepest secrets are known and shared by newts and rabbits. When you let yourself identify with other fragile lives, you unzip your own vulnerability. For many of us, a hike in a national park, snorkeling on a reef, or watching an endangered neotropical songbird through binoculars has brought us face-to-face with the unnameable. Soothing and shattering innuendos of eternity pulse from mountains, oceans, and orioles.

An outdoor life is a hallmark of a peaceful life, but it must assimilate combat with the Great Adversary, with the helplessness of all life. Everything that lives and grows dies. Human activity is now the source of the greatest extinction in animal life on the planet since the demise of the dinosaurs. No ocean or tundra is free of some sign of human incursion and desecration. If you take a simple walk outdoors, or maintain a back yard garden, you are on the path of peace, because of the organic sympathy that connects us in prehistoric kinship to all our brothers and sisters in life, and death. The greatest benefits of contact with nature are the flowering of sorrow and perspective. "I do not value any view of the universe," Thoreau wrote, "into which man and his institutions enter at once . . . and absorb a great share of the attention." John Muir wrote: "Why should man value himself as more than a small part of the great creation?" This humbling, diminishing, implosion of realistic perspective can be peace-inspiring, but it can backfire.

I know a small town boy who grew up in a society that stressed male aggressive prowess, but he felt afraid in the woods. Sensing something vast and obliterating in the forest solitudes surrounding his home, he took to carrying a gun. Decades later, he remained mentally entrenched behind his self-image as the great hunter. He buttressed his security by reiterating how much and with what skill he had killed grouse and geese and deer. Millions of men arm themselves with rifle and scope to shoot down the immensity that would reveal their moist, ephemeral palpitations. Nature drives some men towards peace, and others toward defensive self-aggrandizing murder. A man in the act of murder feels momentarily immortal.

Not all the wisdom of the universe is in humanity. The ability to understand the language of birds and animals has always been considered a stigmata of higher life. John Muir heard the trees and birds speaking clearly to him. "It is still the morning of creation," Muir wrote, "the morning stars are singing together." The robins in their rotunda chorale, the bobwhite in their ventriloquistic soliloquy, the wood thrushes in their shadowy allurement, are not just mechanical toys with instincts run by gears—as mass-man science promulgates regarding birds. They sing to us with recognizable emotion. Whenever a person listens open heartedly, streams and hemlock thickets echo distinct feelings, for locales are alive. Every ravine is an unfolding thought. The earth itself is a work in progress, being continuously revised before its ultimate publication.

Humans are one family in the neighborhood, and the general loss of our attentiveness to cloud, brook, and gull accounts for the restless, thirsty loneliness among us. We need to be upbraided by the incongruous boldness of wrens. The taste of wild black raspberries is not only a flavor—it is also a communication to us about how bacchic and languid it feels to be roots and leaves in July. The blueberries of August in the Traveller Mountains of Maine translate ice storms, spring mountain-winds, and summer heat into rhymes of sugar that eight-year-old boys consider sonnets. I find that wild fruit often *tastes* the way the Bhagavad Gita and Ecclesiastes sound. The wild tiers of berry flavors string out in all directions like unruly harmonies of great free verse. The language of plants is as clear and no less wise than ours. When they wave their leaves at each other and rustle, they may be saying more and better than I have mumbled in the bank or at breakfast all week.

Chapter 14

John Muir

THE ENVIRONMENTS IN WHICH we human mammals evolved into our current form calm us like a womb. How many people have recovered from depression, renewed a dilapidated marriage, or soothed their self-esteem with walks in the woods! This is a ubiquitous discovery, requiring no doctor's suggestion, a spontaneous return home to health and the outdoors. To live a peaceful life, you have to regularly expose yourself to weather, wildlife, and the roll of topography. If you think back through the preceding chapters, you'll easily recognize closeness to nature as a recurrent theme, without exception, in every story I've told.

To fully clarify the connection between nature and inner peace, I'm going to start with the story of a great man whose life captures the effect of this free radiation treatment.

John Muir, America's greatest conservationist, almost disappeared into a compulsive indoor existence until a dramatic accident forced him to rediscover the transforming power of the outdoors in service of a life of peace.

Young Muir was a budding genius. Working alone late one night by candlelight, the industrious and ambitious young man, who was "busy almost to craziness . . . inventing machines twenty-four hours a day," leaned closely over his tasks. The awl in his hand slipped and the point stabbed into his eye. Muir felt his vision dripping out into his hand. Due to the trauma in one eye and the sympathetic spasm of the other eye, his promising life seemed to close. John Muir was totally blind: "Closed forever on all God's beauty."

Fortunately, the injury wasn't critical, and had only punctured the aqueous. He lay in bed blind for a week, and arose resurrected. His new goal was to learn the secret of the universe "from a weed's plain heart." "I might have become a millionaire, but I chose to become a tramp." He wrote on his journal his new name and address: "John Muir, Earth-planet, Universe," and he started to walk. Muir lived the rest of his life with the passionate appreciation of a man seeing the creation for the last time, all the time.

Muir began the lifelong rambling, wandering, botanizing, geologizing, and writing that were to become the central activities of his adult life as "Nature's own prophet." Initially, he walked from Wisconsin to the Gulf of Mexico, wandering fearlessly through the anarchy of the post-Civil War South, and got as far as Florida on his way to the Amazon before he was halted by malaria. He then went to California, to rest and recuperate in solitude as a shepherd. Here he encountered Yosemite Valley and the Sierra Nevada mountains, and fell into one of the greatest love affairs of all times, writing prose that has been analogized to that of the Christian mystics, doing solitary scientific research that made him one of the most significant geologists of his century, and becoming champion and spokesperson for conservation throughout the world, the guiding spirit in the creation of Yosemite National Park, as well as founder of the Sierra Club and author of many books.

Few people have poured out such sustained ecstasy in prose, or have lived as appreciatively. Along with his rare mechanical, literary, poetic, and scientific intellect, Muir was an athlete of supreme, almost eerie proportions. He climbed and conquered the entire Sierra Nevadas, hugging its rocks and seams to his scrambling bosom, studying mountain glaciation more thoroughly than any person before him, squeezing through obscure canyons looking for subtle traces of moraines, and standing on top of all major peaks and divides throughout the range. Almost all of his mountaineering was done alone and without technical equipment—two things that would mark him today as far over the lunatic fringe. His mountaineering in Alaska was to be equally risk-taking and ground-breaking.

From the early journals of his walk to the Gulf, to the books of his late old age, Muir was a careful, popular, and successful writer. He exemplifies these aspects of the peaceful life: an unbounded sense of time and history; a sense of harmony with and community among other life forms; a modest deference to objective truth; attunement to his own body as part of "nature" and as a source of wisdom; a sense of love for and service to all living beings.

The first striking feature of his writing is its scale. For example, the opening pages to *The Mountains of California* take the reader flying north and south along the entire "range of light," as if riding on the back of a grand raptor. The prose leads us to see hundreds of miles of snow-capped peaks as one living backbone. At the same time, Muir portrays the shaping of the Sierras through eons of geologic history with such clarity and conviction that the reader may be induced into believing that the author had been there for the whole process. He makes you feel he watched—not deduced—the whole thing. Like Walt Whitman, Muir hovered over the earth with the attitude of cosmic accomplice. He didn't surmise nature's scope and method; he seemed to participate, hand in hand.

Another feature of his writing is its tone. Muir's prose is laced with extremity, like an alpinist poised to fall off the edge of the English language. In one passage he writes of rejoicing, abundance, stupendous, spirituality, miracles, glorying, eternity, ineffability, and enchantment. This would seem forced and ingenuine if he were not able to sweep us up and waft us along in thrilling transport, enabling us to see trees as "condensed sunbeams," to feel "the very rocks tingling with life," and to see the sky as "a vivid sunfire . . . irradiating . . . luminous . . . like very angels of light." He helps us feel "God brooding over everything," and the whole world responding in reverence, as "the mountains seemed to kindle to a rapt, religious consciousness." In Alaska he viewed an entire mountain range at dawn ". . . transfigured, hushed, and thoughtful, as if awaiting the coming of the Lord." At the heart of John Muir's passion about nature is one word, one insight, one mood: "All chanting and blending in glorious harmony." The subtle, continuous repetition of the word "harmony" is Muir's signatory state of mind. "I quietly wandered away . . . free as a bird . . . independent of roads . . . harmonious . . . a bee in a garden . . . plain simple relationship to Cosmos."

Muir made harmony his orienting point and built a lifestyle around it. He refused teaching positions at Harvard and the Boston Academy of Science, and instead cleaved to the environment he wrote about.

> I drifted from rock to rock, from stream to stream, from grove to grove. Where night found me, there I camped. When I discovered a new plant, I sat down beside it for a minute or a day, to make its acquaintance and hear what it had to tell.

Struggling free of even well-meant social bonds, Muir, in a manner similar to Whitman's receptive mode, stepped outside the weave of mundane entanglements. His rambles, his books, and his eco-activism all hung, like objects on a mobile, around a central thread.

> We all travel the milky way together, trees and men. . . . Everything is so inseparably united. As soon as we begin to describe a flower or a tree or a storm or an Indian or a chipmunk, up jumps the whole heaven and earth and God Himself in one inseparable glory.

He experienced even the inorganic as melodically alive and communicative. Commenting first on larksong, he added, "Music is one of the attributes of matter, into whatever forms it may be organized." He went on to describe the songs of water, air, and flowers. He heard the world singing to itself. "Every atom in creation may be said to be acquainted with and married to every other."

John Muir's intimacy with nature deepened to mental states of fusion, during which he lost his sense of individual identity to blend with the whole. "You bathe in these spirit-beams, turning round and round, as if warming at a campfire. Presently, you lose consciousness of your own separate existence; you blend with the landscape, and become part and parcel of nature." By "nature," Muir always meant one mood: harmony in every thing, harmony over and over.

Muir's intuitions of the interpenetration of all lives in a synthesizing cosmic order never arrested the precision of his discriminating, probing, scientific mind. The poetic, shaggy goat-man, who had memorized the entire New Testament Gospels as a ten-year-old child, was both an altered-states-of-consciousness mystic and a painstaking scientist. The rhapsodist who saw "everything hitched to everything else" was also an empiricist of detailed precision and observation. In both aspects of his personality, he subsumed himself as obedient student to overarching truths.

It is easy to misread John Muir as a romantic landscapist, when, in fact, his harmonious receipt from nature sprang from somatic self-observation. His realizations were based upon austere self-discipline. John's father was a former Scotch soldier who became a Protestant fundamentalist fanatic, and these two influences made him stern and tyrannical; thrashings, deprivation of food and heat, and severe physical labor were the daily bread of John's childhood and adolescence. Although his siblings grew up normal—doctors and businessmen, teachers and homemakers—the forced asceticism of his youth was probably one influence that tempered holy-wanderer Muir to tolerate so much daily hardship in adult expeditions. John Muir didn't merely endure; he thrived. His ". . . inexpressible delight in nature's secret chambers . . . and grateful sequestration in the deep hushed calm and peace" was the fruition of living for days on a crust of bread, camping without tent and often without blankets, accepting prolonged exposure to cold, wet and wind, not for a night, but recurrently over decades. At times only ninety pounds of sinew were stretched on his Herculean frame. But he was not—as you might suspect based on his history of child abuse—festering in anesthetized denial of his body.

Muir's unmatchable mountaineering was accomplished by the dual discipline of highly attuned awareness to the subtlest proprioceptive messages, with detachment from pleasure and pain. Spontaneously, he was practicing a self-discipline similar to the Vipassana meditation I will discuss in Part IX. He didn't deny his body; he knew it, utilized and mastered it—through sensitivity, not through force. He turned his body into a vehicle of awareness. He serves as an example of attunement and discipline rather than mere machismo or asceticism.

I'd like to linger for a moment on one of his most compellingly told climbing exploits, in order to emphasize and convey his mixture of toughness and receptivity. Muir was the first person to ascend Mount Ritter in the Sierra Nevadas (as well as many other "firsts"). He climbed above the tree line, alone, in his shirtsleeves, without any equipment, no rope or ice axe, no coat or blankets, a hard crust of bread on his belt. For an ordinary mortal, this would simply be nuts. His account of the ascent is an extraordinary literary gem by a psalmist-athlete possessing demons of courage and strength. Feeling the rocks beneath him "rejoicing like living creatures," he draws his readers into his own concentrated worship and hypnotic intensity.

Reaching a point on the unknown rock face halfway to the top, "I was suddenly brought to a dead stop, with arms outspread, clinging close to the face of the rock, unable to move hand or foot either up or down." Realizing his death was certain, "I became nerve shaken for the first time since setting foot on the mountains." But in a moment "life blazed forth again with preternatural clearness." He felt possessed of a new sense.

> . . . every rift and flaw in the rock was seen as through a microscope, and my limbs moved with a positiveness and precision with which I seemed to have nothing at all to do. Had I been born aloft upon wings, my deliverance could not have been more complete.

Muir ascended himself as he scaled mountains. He used his body like someone skillfully pulling taut the strings of a living guitar for it to be optimally expressive. He made his body the instrument of his spirit. For someone with a history of traumatic blindness, his expanded senses on Mount Ritter was the ultimate undoing of the past, a corrective healing. In this anecdote we encounter not only the mountaineer and the storyteller in Muir, but also the student of self-as-nature.

Though his example is extreme, the general point is universal and applicable: detached observation of one's own body through all its vicissitudes leads to breakthroughs of healing clarity. This forms the basis of meditation.

Exquisitely attuned to his magnificent body, yet determined to overcome pain and fear, Muir cultivated his own human nature as he absorbed the lessons of the wild outdoors. This yogic path led him, like Buddha, to see in creation "incessant motion and change . . . eternal flux."

An East Indian poet visiting the United States, on hearing about John Muir for the first time, exclaimed, "Why, he was a Rishi!"—recognizing in Muir one of the legendary hermit-sages of yore who wrote India's sublime scriptural literature in prehistorical eras on Himalayan forest slopes. John Muir was not all holy man. He married, ran an orchard in California, was an actively involved father and a doting grandfather, was politically engaged, a lecturer, and a counselor to presidents Teddy Roosevelt and William Taft. Like any peace-seeker, he himself sought out fellow peace-seekers, and he listed his few days in the company of Ralph Waldo Emerson as one of the high points of his life.

The trace John Muir left behind him is marked by a prophetic obeisance to the natural world and its creatures. He referred to animals as people, and related to flowers and squirrels as fellow mortals. The peace he found in nature was animating, not sedating. It elevated his personal agony into a historical force, which gave new, worldwide momentum to conservation movements. He sublimated the compassion he felt for the beaten child he was into compassion for all; and he fought his cruel father by battling "progress and civilization."

However, his feisty, optimistic suffusions of joy seem short of repose. A slightly rigid, repetitive, didactic insistence on "exhilarated thrill" and "majestic sublime" imply his ill-ease in confronting the sorrow he was constantly hurtling over. He overcame his sorrow at the devastation of pristine nature through energetic ecstasies and practical politics. One does not find in this madcap crag-conqueror mellowness, even equanimity. The harmony he sought and found in nature was a mood he cultivated to overcome psychological pain, a process we have also seen in Walt Whitman.

Away from wilderness, Muir fell sick. He needed to immerse himself in wilderness to counteract an internal ill-ease. His prose seems to spring from irrepressible emanations of temperamental ebullience, like the trail of a comet of the psychosphere. But his high spirits in adulthood couldn't be taken for granted. He had dark moods, he had ill health. Removed from nature, Muir paled. When he went exploring, he wasn't camping out; he was restoring himself through worship. His divine fire required constant stoking with mountains and skies. Muir claimed he was "always happy at the center," and while this was probably an extension of the truth, he could always find optimism and energy by recontacting nature. "Religion," he said, "is on all the rocks."

Despite his garrulous and wide-ranging affability, a painful split separated Muir from humankind. His writing pits pristine, divine wilderness against destructive, ignorant humans. He fails to search for the womb where the human monster itself emerged from his goddess, Nature. He couldn't assimilate the fact that the dark forces he fought were not outside of nature, but part of the world-evolving, just like his beloved, creative-destructive glaciers. In glaciation, but not in civilization, he could see "that what we in our faithless ignorance and fear call destruction is creation." For all his cosmic imagery, Muir remains one of the supreme scientist-poets of the surface of the world. His pagan worship of storm and pine made him the earth's high priest, but he wasn't anchored in the inner light. He couldn't find harmony apart from rambunctious muscularity. The "essential love, overlying, underlying, pervading all things" that he found in wilderness he couldn't find in the trammeled twentieth century world.

We feel in Muir not quite a patriarch, but the most magnificent boy of all. He inspires us all to dare, to strive, to ascend, to temper our edges, and to nuzzle with camaraderie, "warmed and quickened into sympathy with everything."

Several aspects of John Muir's biography deserve emphasis. Young Muir, having grown up in a world of seemingly endless Wisconsin wilderness, could follow the call of an indoor fortune because he fantasized that he and nature had some unimpeachable future tryst. The dramatic blindness was like a divine herald, a reminder of life's transiency, a call to activate his real purpose. The rest of his life was counter-inspired by a sense of nature's fragility. The sight of every tree and rock he now understood as an ephemeral gift. His experience reveals that emphasis on the transciency of our good fortune isn't depressing, but heightens our continuity of appreciation.

Muir's love of living was boundless. Woodrats were innocent, fine companions. Lizards were: "Small fellow mortals, gentle and guileless, they are easily tamed and have beautiful eyes expressing the clearest innocence . . . and they will teach you that scales may cover as fine a nature as hair or feathers or anything tailored."

John Muir made himself "a flake of transparent glass" through which humankind would be brought to new truths: "I care to live only to entice people to look at nature's loveliness." The peaceful person is always a conduit rather than a vault.

Muir built no walls between science and literature, science and religion, religion and politics, prose and poetry. He lived in a complex whole. The thread connecting this diversity of inspiration and talent was a freshet of harmony that flowed through him from his contact with nature. The depth of his inspiration enabled him to infuse many aspects of a whole vision without feeling fragmented. John Muir's story echoes aspects of the peaceful life that are not limited to his harmony-oriented, self-reflective, time-opening, care-taking love of nature. He returned from distress to peace in dynamic self-reminding, and he practiced selectivity—to an extreme! He was fundamentally not a writer, scientist, or conservationist, but an ebullient emissary between humans and the whole he communed with in nature. Like a Scotch druid reborn for a cause, he was carried to the New World by his father, then swept on to California to speak for the trees.

Getting rained on is part of the way we are born to be. Muir heard with trumpet and tympani what the rest of us also hear, but in whispers—the self-diminishing, self-confirming beauty and love that radiates from unadorned nature. On every walk, in our own neighborhoods, there is a Mount Ritter moment when our blindness is lifted.

Chapter 15

HENRY DAVID THOREAU

LOVE OF AND CLOSENESS TO NATURE is a hallmark of the peaceful life, and Muir's bounteous genius is a prototype of a universal phenomenon. Moses, Jesus, and Mohammed also were seekers in natural solitude. The authors of the Vedas, the focal texts of Indian religion and mysticism, were inspired nature poets. St. Francis, recently redubbed "the patron saint of ecology," is the Western world's legendary nature lover and man of peace. For three thousand years and more, Chinese literature and the Far Eastern literatures it influenced—such as Japan's—have equated harmonious natural imagery in poetry with spiritual attainment. Chinese philosophical traditions became embodied in Sung dynasty landscape painting, in which softly blending scenery of the natural world revealed the painters' own communion with peaceful inner realizations. Retreat to the forests has been the enduring trademark of Indian holy men, from legendary gods like Krishna and Rama, to historical figures like Buddha and his close followers. The poetry of the elders who succeeded Buddha—the *Theragāthā*—overflows with love of the forest life.

We have already seen how Juan and Kathleen Mascaró lived under thatch in the twentieth century and wrote to me of roses and sparrows; how Scott and Helen Nearing created an entire way of life around their back-to-the-land philosophy; how Whitman submerged himself in ocean and woods and pastoral scenery to emerge as one of the great nature poets of all time. For two-thirds of his productive life, Claude Monet painted scenes he encountered walking or boating within two miles of his home at Giverny. His inspired concentration was not just on painting, but on painting a natural world that he studied in all seasons and weather.

Henry David Thoreau stands at the pinnacle of this worldwide tradition of keeping nature in focus as a method of tuning the heart to peaceful vibrations. Of all the people I have written about so far, Thoreau probably attained the most abiding equanimity. His story will perfume your mind with peace.

Thoreau lived in the first half of the nineteenth century and died when Muir was still a child. Although he has been posthumously canonized as the greatest nature writer of all time, he didn't directly catalyze a conservation movement, nor create a national park, nor found an organization, nor make a major scientific discovery. Despite a core similarity to Muir's, his life evokes a more contemplative atmosphere of local walks, old books, magnifying lenses, and sagacity. Thoreau was an appearance. As you will see, his inner peace was luminescent and unforgettable.

Thoreau was born, lived, and died in Concord, Massachusetts—its unofficial Dalai Lama. The son of a lower-middle-class family, he attracted the attention of Ralph Waldo Emerson, who promoted the younger man's literary career to little avail. Thoreau disappointed his mentor—as Muir was later to disappoint his—by becoming what Emerson disdainfully called "the captain of a huckleberrying party rather than a captain of men." Thoreau selected the private, contemplative life, never married, raised a family, or held a job for any significant period of time.

Thoreau's initial attempt at work was as schoolmaster of Concord, a post he obtained by dint of his Harvard degree and a recommendation from Emerson, and he taught by the principles that guided his life, leading field trips and turning the schoolroom into a hubbub of spontaneous activity. He eventually founded his own school with his brother, John, and their three years of teaching has been hailed as a major advance in American education for its emphasis on experiential learning and informal atmosphere. But John Thoreau was ill and was destined to die young, and Henry Thoreau couldn't bear the school alone.

He held multiple shifting positions, as Emerson's houseboy, as carpenter, as assistant in his father's pencil factory, as tutor, but he eventually settled down to earning his living as part-time surveyor, a job that had him tramping outdoors, free to be a full-time . . . Thoreau! An apparent idler, he was busy within. Although his writing expresses a normal range of emotion, including annoyance, sarcasm, and anger, his emotional life, as recorded by both him and his contemporaries, was remarkable for the recurrence and depth of his vibrancy, joy, and creative, passionate ecstasy. He often analogized his time and place to heaven. He seemed to feel that all goodness and well-being rained down upon him from the Concord clouds. He felt predominantly the emotions of dawn.

Thoreau was a student and acolyte of language; he translated Greek and Latin. He was a serious scholar of early English poetry, a devotee of Chaucer, and knowledgeable in such esoteric literary corners as Scandinavian mythology. His knowledge of Northeast Indian lore was derived from an exhaustive and original labor of love, as was his knowledge of botany and zoology. He made minor scientific contributions throughout the fields of natural history, particularly in ecology, where he was the first person to understand the succession of forest trees. He played the flute and wrote poetry. In general, he exemplified the kind of existential studenthood that Whitman and Gandhi also followed: broad-ranging, personally selected, lifelong pursuit of knowledge in the service of personal development. His commonplace books, into which he copied chosen quotations, filled five or six thousand pages, onto which he had copied close to one million words.

Thoreau was foremost a spiritual seeker, a Transcendentalist, a student of the inner light. Keeping himself free of social institutions like governments, churches, and jobs, he studied, thought, and wrote out his innermost thoughts, and sauntered through nature, observing every detail as a communication from a higher sphere. He lived a "Brahminical, Artesian, Inner Temple life."

For the bulk of his adult years, Thoreau worked at most half a day, and spent the rest of his time outdoors and journal-writing. His main self-appointed task was to ceaselessly study nature, in every hour, season, and condition. In *Walden*, his most famous book, there is an extended rhapsodic description of the beauty, shapes, and varieties of sand. Nothing escaped his eye. Nothing was trivial in nature. Just as importantly, nothing was unworthy of a note in his journal. Walking and journal-writing were his lifework. "Nature never loses a day . . . I have the habit of attention."

His trim, clipper-ship philosopher's life contrasts with the libertine poses of Walt Whitman. His journal of fourteen posthumous volumes exceeds *Walden* like the Milky Way does a star. It is one of the most important spiritual-psychological documents of all time. In it, we have the record of a life of peace as it unfolded day by day, and sometimes even from hour to hour. In one year alone, 1852, his journal covered seven hundred pages; the following year he added another six hundred pages. It is probably the most eminent, extended, personal, spiritual statement in history.

Usually, we have from a great writer selected, codified, ordered thoughts: books. A journal is less groomed and preselected. There have been other lifelong journals: Ralph Waldo Emerson, Thoreau's mentor, inspired Thoreau's journal with his own. But Thoreau's journal is unique in several ways. It is extensive, covering the bulk of a mature lifetime with regular entries. It is intensely focused on a main goal: to capture in words the elevated feeling for life that Thoreau felt while perpetually instilling and drenching in nature. The journal contains forays into many other topics literary, poetic, scientific, social, and political—-but day after day, year after year, Thoreau refocused himself on a singular point. Through verbal artistry, he transmuted into prose his recurrent, ecstatic harmony with a purposeful, benign universe that he found in fish scales and fox tracks and flower stems and rain storms. "What in other men is religion is in me love of nature."

One of his greatest gifts to us is the systematic, enduring intensity of his reverence for the commonplace and his determination to record it. Zen poems and St. Francis's aphorisms read like postcards compared to the encyclopedic, tinkling galaxy of exquisite observation in his journals. Muir was the prophet of great mountains and unique valleys; Thoreau was the Isaiah of muskrats and phoebes. He ceaselessly received from communion with nature a sense of peace and splendid import. There is no record in the human condition of a person who—despite irascibility, petulance, even temper—transcribed more hours during more days and years of transporting, elevating realization.

Thoreau was not merely or even primarily a naturalist. His dynamic return to his exploratory, literary, daily outdoor ramble was his central concern. Some of Thoreau's most renowned rhetoric was spent regaling the principle of selectivity.

> Most of the luxuries, and many of the so-called com-
> forts of life, are not only indispensable, but positive
> hindrances to the elevation of mankind. . . . To be a
> philosopher is not merely to have subtle thoughts,
> nor even to found a school, but so to love wisdom
> as to live according to its dictates, a life of simplicity,
> independence, magnanimity and trust. It is to solve
> some of the problems of life, not only theoretically,
> but practically. . . . A man is rich in proportion to the
> number of things which he can afford to let alone.

Gandhi echoed and summarized Thoreau, whose writing he had first read while in jail, with a book he later wrote
in another jail: "Civilization, in the real sense of the term,
consists not in the multiplication, but in the deliberate and
voluntary reduction of wants."

Thoreau avoided possessions or activities that required
material or social debt. After a saunter through his holy land
of Concord, at which he typically spent more than four hours
a day, he would return to his desk to spend the evening rewrit-
ing his notes and studying literary sources for his ideas. He
pursued the Latin etymology of words, botanical textbooks,
and travelogues. He was one of the earliest and profoundest
students of Hindu and Buddhist texts in America.

The ordering principle of his life was a mood.

> Every morning was a cheerful invitation to make my
> life of equal simplicity . . . with nature Herself . . . to
> affect the quality of the day, that is the highest of arts.

> If the day and night are such that you greet them
> with joy, and life emits a fragrance like flowers and
> sweet-scented herbs, is more elastic, more starry, more
> immortal-that is your success.

I think I cannot preserve my health and spirits unless I spend four hours a day at least—and it is commonly more than that—sauntering through the woods and over hills and fields, absolutely free from all worldly engagements . . . so we saunter toward the Holy Land, till one day the sun shall shine more brightly than ever he has done . . . and light up our whole lives with a great awakening light.

In the midst of a gentle rain . . . I was suddenly sensible of such sweet and beneficent society in Nature, in the very pattering of the drops, and in every sound and sight around my house, an infinite and unaccountable friendliness. . . . Every little pine needle expanded and swelled with sympathy and befriended me. . . . Why should I feel lonely? Is not our planet in the Milky Way?

Knowledge does not come to us by details, but in flashes of light from heaven.

Thoreau's journal is flooded with passages of such serene high spirits. As a reviewer once wrote more than a century ago, "On closing the book we find ourselves in love with the author, satisfied with ourselves, and at peace with the world."

Like John Muir, Thoreau cultivated nature within as well as through observation. His manual dexterity and physical fitness were legendary within his lifetime. A student of diet and inveterate foot-traveler, he turned his body into a perfect tool for exalted purposes. According to Emerson, Thoreau (despite smoldering tuberculosis) could "outwalk, outswim, outrun, and outskate" anyone.

More than a writer, naturalist, Transcendentalist, Thoreau was a yogi, a practitioner of a state of mind. He confided in his journal flatly:

> I am a mystic . . . the woodpath and the boat are my
> studio, where I maintain a sacred solitude. . . . Ask me
> for a certain number of dollars if you will, but do not
> ask me for my afternoons.

Thoreau scholar Walter Harding wrote that *Walden* can be read on many levels but is, above all, "a guide book to the higher life." Thoreau's existence was the successful cultivation of optimistic ebullience and inner peace.

Thoreau intuited that his existence was one in a chain of rebirths. He felt that the thread connecting past, present, and future was a simple experiential immediacy. He did not believe in a fairy-tale series of self-referential legendary transmigrations, but he surmised a continuity in his most exquisite promptings, a uniform source to his self-discovery. "The oldest Egyptian or Hindoo [sic] philosopher raised a corner of the veil from the statue of the divinity; and still the trembling robe remains raised, and I gaze upon as fresh a glory as he did, since it was I in him that was then so bold, and it is he in me that now renews the vision." This sense of coexistence with the Undying made Thoreau feel that every moment was genesis. This was the inspiration behind his delight in detailing the minute anatomy of each snowflake in his journal.

Thoreau had to face the normal allotment of woe. Despite periods of robust well-being, he suffered from crippling recurrent tuberculosis throughout his entire adult life; he was continuously rejected as a teacher and as a writer; his few books were largely ignored and most of his writing was unpublished; he suffered snubs and ostracism for his eccentricity, and was attacked for his unabashed free-thinking "heresies"; his beloved brother died young; and he was rejected by the only woman to whom he proposed marriage. In the face of suffering, Thoreau struggled to rise higher.

In his early forties, the intermittent weakness from which he had suffered in a life of overall vigor became continuous. Gradually, he lost every function that characterized him. His staunch rambles to Maine or Cape Cod became impossible; his daily walks shortened, then ceased. It was obvious that he was slowly dying of tuberculosis. Finally, he became too weak to write. Still, he lingered for six months more, through a bitter New England winter. What would Thoreau be, how could he anchor himself in sanity, without walking in nature and journal keeping?

The vast body of his life's work, an attempt to substantiate the Transcendentalist atmosphere of *Walden* with precise natural history, a literary unification of faith, science, and poetic love of nature's details, the culmination of all his journal-keeping and the distillation of his life, lay unpublished. Only half his life lived, Thoreau faced closure.

And yet, Thoreau's premature death at forty-four was exemplary, a confirmation of the depth of equanimity he had established in life. He remained focused on the present, interested in books and men, unconcerned with the future. He averred it was just as good to be sick as to be well, and said he was enjoying existence as much as ever.

If a person has really found deep inner peace, it won't be shattered by life, or death. This is the ultimate goal of cultivating inner peace, a light that shines from within when the outer light fades. Thoreau found through his love of nature, an inner nature, an inner peace. Listen to the beautiful echos of his death, like cellos, the voices of his contemporaries who observed him, as collated by his devotee, Walter Harding.

His friend Bronson Alcott wrote:

> I know of nothing more creditable to his greatness than the thoughtful regard, approaching to reverence, by which he was held for many years by some of the best persons of his time, living at a distance, and wont to

make their pilgrimage, usually on foot, to the master—a devotion very rare in these times.

Among those who came to witness the dying of the master of peaceful living was Sam Staples, the constable who years before had clapped Thoreau in jail. Staples commented: "Never saw a man dying with so much pleasure and peace."

Fading Thoreau maintained a remarkable balance. He was rational, worldly, objective; refusing to pander to cozy delusions and religious claptrap. Yet he was oak-rooted with unshakeable faith in spiritual immortality. When he could no longer sit up, he requested that the little cane bed he had used at Walden be brought down and placed in the front parlor of his mother's house. His mother remembered: ". . . he was always so cheerful . . ." When the long winter of his demise was ending, a friend told him of seeing a spring robin, and Thoreau replied: "Yes, this is a beautiful world; but I shall see a fairer." Yet, when another friend asked, "You seem so near the brink of the dark river, that I almost wonder how the opposite shore may appear to you," Thoreau answered from the present moment, "One world at a time!" When his religious Aunt Louisa asked him if he had made his peace with God, he quipped, "I did not know we had ever quarreled."

His devotion to sober objectivity was as strong as his absence of fear or regret. He refused pain killers because he ". . . preferred to endure with a clear mind the worst penalties of suffering, rather than be plunged in a turbid dream . . ." His sister said:

> Henry was never affected, never reached by his illness. I never before saw such a manifestation of power of spirit over matter . . . his perfect contentment was truly wonderful . . . he accepts this dispensation with such childlike trust and is so happy that I feel as if he were being translated rather than dying in the ordinary way.

No man lived and recorded in halcyon prose a longer string of luminous mentations and occasions. His journal reads as if all the small and secret wonders that compose the universe had found their spokesman. The motto of his journal and days could well have been the phrase he penned in 1855, seven years before his death: "The age of miracles is each moment." Thoreau's graceful and transcendent dying was the outcome of a series of incandescent confirmations of the omnipresent inner light. The peace he exuded at death expressed the mastery of a well-practiced skill, as if he had died confidently many times before. The solar system is unperturbed by a transient eclipse.

Chapter 16

CELEBRATING WITH EVERYONE

WHAT WE CALL "NATURE" is the community of lives with whom we share our time. Our attitudes toward our fellow travelers on Earth-ark will influence our mood. Domineering and destroying will not bring us peace of heart. Identification with our fellow mortals will open us to sympathetic joy shared with redwoods meditating for a thousand years on California hills, or with chickadees flying back to their holes in apple trees with delicious samples of sunflower seeds, or with loons, wild and boisterous, calling across lonely Canadian lakes.

A peaceful heart celebrates with everyone. "Nature" is a construct, the imposition of a category over the living, vibrating, collections of atoms and molecules, shaped into hearts and minds that are swaying, flying, and yodeling around us today. When even the concept of "nature" is removed, rivers and bears are seen to be as consanguineous as spouses and store clerks.

The sparrows that winter in the ivy on old buildings in urban ghettos and the ailanthus trees that sprout up in neglected city lots may well be paratroopers of a companionable army that is invading our darkest corners to liberate us from ourselves. Mountains grow and die; vast spruce forests of the North quiet down to watch boreal sunsets. "Nature" is everyone with a different kind of face and a similar fate.

The process of impermanence and change unites the world. Nature and people have no clear demarcation. We are all tumbling on together. What we subsume under the rubric "nature" is the screen onto which we project our own love and compassion—or lack of them—and when we say "love of nature," we refer to our capacity to pour out nurturant and fond delight toward all or any "others." "Nature" is inner peace flashed back and forth between a human being and any other kind of cloud.

"Nature" is everywhere, not just in the Serengeti or the Brooks Range, but wherever we awaken to the commonality of our own life with all life. It is as grand as the Sierras, as minute as the ant wars over which Thoreau peered. It is in our bodies, and in snow. It is urban as well as rural. Sweet-smelling riverine winds sweep through Manhattan on clear November days. Unique species of oak cling to their prairie ancestry in cramped backyards behind Chicago tenements.

"Nature" teaches about cosmic time and personal transience. The natural world can be an inspiration for a self-discipline of cultivating increased awareness of and detachment from one's own body. For John Muir, Henry Thoreau, and throngs of bikers, walkers, runners-in-the-rain, and gardeners, nature is the setting that facilitates spontaneous development of the beginnings of the Vipassana meditation that led to the Buddha's Nibbāna.

"Cherish the forest depths," emphasized the Buddha, who retained his appreciation for quiet woods as nurseries of rebirth. He taught that attachment to body sensations creates a false, myopic perspective, and that awareness of and detachment from them leads to liberating compassion for all.

Muir's ascent of Mount Ritter and Thoreau's Concord deathbed describe men schooled in laws of nature within: this life is a temporary aggregate, but it is not in vain. That is why Thoreau and Muir were more than athletes, naturalists, or poets. They found peace by using nature as a teacher that led to cultivation of their own bodies as loci of dissolution with harmony. Nature for them was not just a floral garden, but an experience of perpetual transformation, a pathway beyond physical life. Your body changes, changes, passes away. Will you be able to dissolve, pass on, with no regrets, like a melting Sierran glacier; like Thoreau; like a ripe blueberry being burst by the tooth of the cosmic eight-year-old boy? "I laugh at what you call dissolution," proclaimed Whitman, who revealed to us the source of his insouciance:

> *Now I see the secret of the making of the best*
> *persons,*
> *It is to grow in the open air and to eat and sleep*
> *with the earth.*

PART VI

Chapter 17

PEACE IS FACING SORROW

IF A READER WERE using this book as a practical guide to cultivating inner peace, he or she might now be thinking: I know that mere situational adjustments won't essentially improve my life, which gains its trajectory only from my own actions and feelings. I want to sail toward peace, easy in the currents of myself, harmoniously related to people and circumstances, and to achieve this I have to consciously steer with peace as my polestar. When life storms and batters me, my goal is to return to course, and the will to do so creates the dynamic resilience I need. I'll limit myself to sail light and trim. I'll absorb the wise directions of those who've already negotiated these straits, soaked in the soothing sounds of peace, and my own words will add to this score. I'll befriend all I meet on wing and wave, an unwalled, welcoming life.

But you might feel confused to find, having taken these steps, that you are oppressed by a cloud of sorrow. Yet this would be a good sign, because impersonal and surprising grief is the harbinger beyond the known world of yourself to the horizonless peace you seek, as the story of the Buddha will show.

Siddhartha Gotama was said to have been born a prince in the lap of luxury, handsome, intelligent, athletic, beloved by his parents and wife. This opening mythic image entices us because of our yearning for restoration of the complete security and love of childhood. In spite of that, the prince remained unhappy. Lush physical gratification simply isn't fulfilling. Against the demands of his beloved father, the king, who was guarantor of his son's worldly delights, against the plan of the castle and kingdom, which represent the practical, established order, the prince sneaked out of the palace of comfort, aided by his loyal charioteer, to find something more, beyond, deeper.

Still cushioned within his royal chariot, the prince made forays around the capital city. The prince's castle of enfoldment was breached, and his sense of safety punctured, as he saw first an old man, then a sick man, then a corpse. His charioteer, the voice of fact, assured him that everyone will age, sicken, and die. The prince, at the sunset of his childhood under the protective parental roof, became distraught. He would suffer! He would die! There was no escape! His restless premonition had been objectified. Even if he were to remain a prince bathed in boundless gratification from day to day, his life and pleasures would be ephemeral, and he would tumble on blindly toward pain, helplessness, and darkness.

But on his fourth secret excursion into the city of the world, listening to his charioteer narrate the stark outline of existence, the prince, now primed to shed his childhood delusions, saw a spiritual seeker, a man of peace, calmly traversing the rutted, crowded lanes of worldly affairs. The image of the holy man is a symbol of the prince's own aspirations, maturation, and incipient wisdom. This vision of a transcendent possibility catapulted the prince into a personal revolution.

Like every young adult, he must and did flee the castle of false security and pleasurable distraction. Siddhartha Gotama abandoned comfort, his parents, even his beloved wife and infant son, because each person is essentially alone. No one can hide from fate behind others. The prince closed the door forever on his palace of ignorance.

Siddhartha Gotama, no longer a prince, spent years in search, years of determined, heroic hardship, as a student of others, as a solitary hermit, as a fellow traveler of the hopeful and austere, in the wilderness of his inner world. When he emerged after six years as the Buddha, the fully enlightened one who is free from suffering, it was because he had plumbed suffering so consciously, staring into the cobra's eye.

The core of the Buddha's enlightenment was his confrontation with the suffering intrinsic to existence. Everything born dies. Along with the birth of consciousness is the birth of suffering, because life is built over loss. Prince Siddhartha, like all of us, wanted to remain young and strong, sexual and safe, loved and happy forever. Every known form of happiness was guaranteed to evaporate at his death, yet he was unwilling to accept a merely pragmatic hedonism. He sought and found a way of life that connected his transient life to an ultimate truth within this one, mortal lifetime. The bridge Buddha walked over suffering was the fourfold noble truth, the mastery of suffering, a psychological practice leading to liberation.

All eighty-four thousand sermons of the Buddha are built on the four noble truths. He said that the essence of Buddhahood—the absolute transcendence of suffering—is full mastery of just these four.

The first truth is the realization that life is suffering. Not that suffering might happen, or can occur if one is unlucky, but that life by nature is transitory, filled with loss, and always terminated. The cause of suffering—which is the second truth—is that intrinsic to ignorant life is the craving for pleasure and the fear of pain that are built into our animal organism. Since no life can consist of pure pleasure—even the mythic prince in his pleasure palace would eventually age, sicken, and die—craving and fear will always culminate in unwanted suffering. The third truth is radical optimism: the cycle can be *reversed*. A human being isn't a mere pleasure machine. Insight can prevail; transformation can occur; the craving for pleasure and the fear of pain can be overthrown in favor of enduring values, timeless, selfless peace flowing past the universe. The fourth truth outlines the path by which the third truth can be actualized: the eightfold noble path of virtuous living, insightful meditation, and liberating perspective that points beyond oneself toward Nibbāna, pure peace.

In the legend of the Buddha, he is born destined for liberation, but he still sought and suffered for seven years. That time frame reminds us that we need to grow on the path with patience and work. When we read or hear claims of peacefulness based on a mechanical training of the brain or on a facile philosophy or practice, we know these claims are inauthentic because we haven't heard about struggle. *Conscious depth* of suffering, your own problems and despair, are the Rosetta stone messages by which you can decipher peace. Your personal truth comes to you as a wrestler. Peace is dynamic because it must answer the deepest human questions that you have, stirred by suffering and death as they manifest themselves around and within you.

A person may be busy, engaged, successful, even happy, but inner peace is a product not of what you accomplish, but of how you are. Inner peace is a skill in how to be. The spiritual dimension of life manifests itself as urgent questions, and peace must plumb as deeply as our dismay is rooted. Inner peace can be found only through confrontation with the potential bottomlessness that yawns when our life is seen in the perspective of cosmic time and certain death. Peace is discovered in a realm that is independent of conditions, an "everlasting light." The more thoughtful and intelligent the person, the deeper their scrutiny of life, and their despair. Despair is the lash that turns our ill-ease into full-fledged knowledge of our plight, and into resolute quest for a solution.

The path of peace must lead through a cataclysmic realization of our future because our forethought and cunning, which makes our species skillful predators, also precipitates abstract questioning, insight into death, and dismay about mundane time. Every hope is merely a fantasy of more life. No political platform or social action can ultimately solve our problem: What will happen to me when I die? Where will I be, how can I endure being nothing forever? I feel trapped, how can I get out of this horrible, total erasure? I have accomplished so little, the remainder is so brief. Historical memory endures only a handful of generations. My children, my family, my religion, my culture, are themselves insubstantial, temporary. Our planet floats in a milky way of worlds. What is the point of my life?

As people approach death through age, illness, or danger, the fairy tales that were formerly employed to bind anxiety into the background of daily life lose their persuasiveness. The comforting proximity of loved ones presages only separation and loss. Directly or fleetingly, as foreground or background, everyone knows what the Buddha found: Life is suffering. All children, all adults, hear a whisper of terror in the night. How can any intelligent person be at peace?

I know despair. I perceive the world as dead, empty, a machine. Bodies emerge from bodies; they consume bodies as food to grow themselves. Without observable origin or goal, the parade of flesh and form flows across time, and every form is temporary, a ghost that dies, disappears, loses everything.

We ride a planetary rock in a repetitious orbit through an endless clockwork void. I think of ancient Egypt: for thousands of years, generation upon generation grew food, procreated, worshipped hawk-headed illusions, each one believing in a life after death, each one fantasizing some significance to this or that tiny twist of their personal fate; and thousands of years have passed; hundreds of generations, millions of lives, each imagining their daily concerns as overwhelmingly real, yet not a footprint in the sand is left of each of those lives.

I think of the Nazi death camps: millions of bodies packed into heaps of ashes, year after year an entire continent operating factories of death running full steam, vast stadia, cities, nations of peoples choked and burned, and each one, in their personal agony, totally unknown, gone, pointlessly feeling and suffering before the final anoxic agony of oblivion. Of those who died in comfort nursed by a daydream, and those who died in horror, equally nothing is left. Those who claim to never forget will also die, pass on, be long forgotten. Time swallows all life down a gullet of darkness. My death leads to nothing. I have no purpose. I'm trapped in a narrowing tunnel that ends in total black. Logically, life is hopeless.

Beyond logic, I feel faith. It dwells in me separate from reason. Regardless of my despair, my heart doesn't stop, and faith beats with my ventricles. Before I ever thought about meaning, before I knew about science and religion, life parted in front of me in virginal flirtation. Pregnant import pervades every turn. Poems, gray-bearded men remembering ospreys, the upturned hand of a chanting singer, grasp me, redirect me with unaccountable fervor. The events in my days are syllables in a great aphorism, pieces in a puzzle I feel destined to complete. I feel a loft to my work that defies mere assessment of its measurable impact. Evanescent intuitions burst inside me like spices, and I taste thoughts that I never chose, which were born inside me along with my brain. Particular patches of earth have drawn me around the planet to make my shoe-prints in their dust. Words I heard one August dusk, spoken from a perspective beyond historical time, flashed into my neurons and linger for years in an alpenglow of thought. My mind, Odyssean since boyhood, my heart, intractably rehoping, were born to search beyond the known. Messages from lives past whisper goals, purposes, directions to me. Every obstacle is a semaphore. There are words I must write, meditations that must be followed, in spite of any finality or absurdity. My deepest inner promptings infiltrate the impenetrable black and keep on traveling through it on wavelengths unknowable even to me who rides the beam.

Faith is inner experience, not ideation, belief, attestation. Faith is a felt experience of significance that is independent of time, life, death, and that shapes all future behavior. Faith isn't salvation or liberation, but the deeply felt, indelibly imprinted precondition for work on the path. It provides the hope and energy that enable spiritual life. It is not the prerogative of prophets and poets. On the contrary, it is commoner among unknown, ordinary people whose self-esteem is not dependent upon achievement or recognition. Faith is an animated knowing that affirms felt salvation alongside the logic of meaninglessness. Faith doesn't cancel despair; it is lit by that subterranean pressure. As dark as is the inner night, that much phosphorescence must be pressed into existence within. The more you care, the deeper your despair, the brighter the light of your faith will be.

I STARTED THIS CHAPTER by pointing out that if you had followed this book chapter by chapter so far, you would by this time have found not a soda fountain of joy, but the claret of sorrow, and I told the myth of the Buddha to clarify the role that direct immersion in sorrow has on the path to peace. The path from suffering to peace is a psychological truism independent of religious ideology or of "Buddhism." Anyone can experience growth in this direction. A modern Catholic-American autobiography illustrates this point, providing us with a vivid example of someone initially trapped in a static ideology that prevented deeply felt despair *or* faith. The author's spiritual rebirth toward peace depended upon his discarding his old belief, and experiencing enough doubt to kindle a truly kinetic faith.

Jesuit Dan Berrigan has recounted in his autobiography, *To Dwell in Peace*, how he grew up with a religious ideation that was all he had to cling to in his childhood, because the other pillars of life seemed rotten. He experienced his father as mercurial, threatening, mean. Their poverty was more than material penury, but a fearful, bitter state of mind. As a boy, Berrigan felt ethnically and religiously alienated from dominant American culture by his Irish Catholic roots. He experienced schooling as humiliation rather than education.

Young Dan's adherence to traditional Catholic dogmas at least gave him a route to higher education, and by becoming an obedient Jesuit acolyte, he could study history, literature, and language. In spite of this vigorous and extensive education, however, Berrigan felt constricted. Life seemed burdensome. He felt imitative, regimented behind closed doors "both horrific and final . . . I was a wooden Indian Jesuit."

Eventually, doubts and questions erupted in him. His festering dismay was exploded by the deceit, hypocrisy, and anti-Christian spirit he perceived in the support that the Catholic establishment gave to the American government during the war in Vietnam. This shattered an elaborate realm of ritual and concrete belief, nourished in childhood and amplified in decades of priestly education. Berrigan began to doubt his church, his elders, his beliefs. He slid down through serial depths of despair: "The imperial Christ looming above, blazing there, ordering all things strongly and sweetly—He is shaken . . . . What remains is impoverished, diminished, a mere breath on glass . . . beyond all images."

It was this elusive, pulsatile hint that turned his dreary cardboard life into a dynamo. Free of dogma, liberated from wrongful images he had "coveted and concocted," yet in his own view remaining faithful to Christian spirit, he catapulted into leadership of the anti-Vietnam war movement. He became a daring, clowning, imprisoned priest of conscience and morality. His literary output mirrored his political somersaulting: he has written more than thirty-five books on politics, religion, social commentary, and poetry.

The living, wavering, nameless breath of his faith was more generative and peaceful than his previously imposed certitude. His faith persisted not in the content of church dogma, but in an intangible softness too elusive to fracture. He could feel the living breath of faith only when deep, honest doubt and historical forces coupled to explode institutionalized belief.

Although Dan Berrigan witnessed other antiwar activist priests back off in fear of church or state, or leave the priesthood, as did his firebrand brother, Philip, he didn't feel disloyal, he didn't resign. He gave his undefinable faith back to society as his urgent antiwar outcry.

Dan Berrigan's story reminds us that a life of peace is opposite from a life of compliant membership. Because peace rests on answers to unanswerable questions, it must dip down into felt faith that is invisible and impalpable. The reader of his biography wonders what about caustic gadfly Dan Berrigan is, after all, Catholic. His verbal excoriation of the church is unparalleled by any other continuously participating member. Somewhere in the mist of his breath on glass, he finds droplets of a continuously rejuvenating formless faith and personal peace.

Berrigan's experience also reminds us to beware of those who can account for their faith too exactly, like the robotic Jesuit that Berrigan claims he was as a young man. Those who have arrived at the breath of living faith cease to be imitators, repeaters of memorized formulas. They express themselves through right speech and authenticity of action. Father Berrigan added: "It gives me joy to report that I still seek out the Mystery." His passage through sorrow and despair enabled him to emerge into the infectious delight that has characterized his public years.

Gandhi said that God couldn't be seen, but came to him through action. Seeking inner peace brings you to the stage where your own inner life is like watching a solar eclipse. Direct looking will burn your eyes. You must follow the movement of a shadow.

Inner peace isn't established upon the denial of despair, which would give despair the power of the underground enemy; nor in the attestations of faith, which would weaken faith with affectation. Faith isn't an answer but a breath, a pulse, a shadow cast somewhere by an unbearably brilliant light. If you've seen it . . . that's not it. Your own thoughts, fantasies, conclusions, can never guide you beyond your own thoughts, fantasies, and conclusions, which are all toys in the box of your brain.

Inner peace speaks in two languages. Despair and faith are the language of the Christian and existentialist West; they describe the loss of individual-centered time and meaning, to enable the discovery of peace-giving, felt truth. The four noble truths are the language of the East; they describe a pathway beyond the personal ego, because the ego is encased in the transitory history of one personality and is preoccupied with its own pleasure and pain. The four noble truths activate a holistic enterprise of ego-transcendence, enabling the realization of Nibbāna, pure peace.

These languages of East and West may differ only semantically. Even if they capture different experiences, they certainly contain homologous insight, sympathetic overlap. Both Buddha and Berrigan had to crack open the platitudes of their backgrounds and face the darkness. Sorrow is a canyon, and downriver from it are the expanded capacities of a more encompassing peace, deep pools of turquoise equanimity.

Chapter 18

Sorrow Is A Skill

SOME PEOPLE CAN successfully avoid the depths of life, but if you try to deepen your feelings of peace, you'll unearth within yourself and the world profound unpleasantness. We saw this to be true in the lives of ecstatic visionaries like Walt Whitman, and in the lives of great nature lovers like Thoreau and Muir. Logically, the world is unknowable to us, who are brief visitors. In spite of that, because of that, to find peace, we have to confront our despairs, ignite our faith, and learn to feel sorrow. Hold on, Reader! We're headed toward a magnificent campsite, but first we have to be roped for safety across an icy traverse.

What I want to describe, using the word "sorrow," is an integrated association of human capacities that dwells inside the developing person and that is essential for peace to gain ground in our harried lives. Sorrow, in the sense I am using it, is not a reaction, like tears or retreat to bed, but a response that actively evokes personality traits to operate upon the torn soul and cushion it, until it can heal and reemerge. In this sense of the word, sorrow is not a passive result of life events, but is a learned skill, an achievement. When life weighs heavy, sorrow is an emotional response that must be attained as one step toward a life of inner peace.

To describe what I mean by sorrow more fully, I would like to portray an agonized person who is *unable* to experience sorrow. By pinpointing its absence, I will be able to describe sorrow's constructive function, and to differentiate active healing available through sorrow from passive or reflexive misery.

This father's story is grim. He has just heard his daughter is addicted to heroin and is exchanging her body for drugs. Picturing this in his mind, his daughter naked, degraded, trammeled, he is overwhelmed by an onslaught of horrible reactions within himself. Sick and fearful of his own impulses, he seeks a psychiatrist.

This is not the first misery of his life. His childhood had its own set of prison bars. After his parents divorced, his father withdrew, behaving deceitfully, such as leaving a telephone message that he couldn't visit on the weekend because he had to be out of town, only to be spotted on Saturday night, in town, with a new girlfriend. His divorced mother buried herself beneath two more unfaithful husbands. He grew up a psychological orphan, determined to make a home for himself.

He met and exceeded his goals. Real estate sales came easily to him; he married, had a daughter and a son, and over time imagined himself buttressed from the abandonment and humiliation of his childhood by middle-class, middle-aged success. But a scar persisted from his childhood, an inability to feel emotions of normal amplitude. He had overlearned how to ignore the voluminous hurts to which he had been subjected, and therefore, as an adult, he was oblivious to the fermentation of anguish in his nuclear family.

His wife was passive, anxious, many years younger than he. She clung to his determined optimism, but was tantrumy and blaming as a mother, slapping her children when they disturbed her, and projecting her own sense of badness onto them. Home life was turbulent and childish, without a guiding adult voice.

The father was busy supporting his family in comfort without the college degrees or the family backing that his neighbors could count on. He worked hard to provide what he had once lacked. He had no role model as a father. He had no skills to sail the storms that his wife and children stirred in their kitchen. Sometimes to placate his children, he bought them stereos and ski vacations; sometimes he tried to create a united front with his wife by yelling at them about what brats they were; sometimes he pleaded with them to be good, asking them to do it for him. His son found a channel upward through football, peer gangs, and the air force. His daughter responded to the arguments, blame, negative projections, materialism, and helpless pleading with a contempt that helped her feel superior to a world that seemed tawdry and chaotic. She quit high school to seek her fortune as an actress in Greenwich Village. About a year after she left, a cousin brought word of what she was doing.

The father reacted to the news about his daughter's descent with rage. He wanted to kill her. The urge was compelling; he knew it was insane; that's why he sought out a psychiatrist. He imagined her on her back beneath men of color, then sticking a needle in her arm. "I just want to kill her." But, skillful self-made man that he was, he instead persuaded his son to get emergency leave from the air force, and with his wife, they three went to confront and rescue his daughter. To his surprise, she eagerly, willingly followed them home and entered a substance abuse program.

For several weeks his fury turned from his daughter to drug dealers. Clearly this demure, help-seeking girl was the victim of nefarious seduction. He wanted revenge. Racial slurs alien to his naturally democratic heart poured over his lips. This attitude changed when his daughter signed out from the hospital against medical advice and disappeared.

That his daughter was not merely the victim of others, re-evoked the father's murderous rage, but only briefly. He slowly slid into depression. His daughter might be dead, drug addicted, a prostitute again; it was too horrible to fantasize, and ultimately didn't matter. His life felt destroyed, like a barren house. The trajectory of his lifelong leap over neglect and rejection into career, home-ownership, and family, was exploded. What had been the point of it? To bring into the world an unhappy fool who was wretched herself and destroying him as well? The optimistic surface of his aspirations and accomplishments peeled off to reveal a hollow. He became sleepless, suicidal.

As he wondered about the meaning and value of his own shattered life, he began to focus on his hatred for his wife: all those years of yelling and accusing and slapping! Surges of fury and blame welled up in him. Clearly, he now felt that their daughter's plight was his wife's fault. How could he have let his life come to this; why had he ever married such a shallow, selfish bitch; why had he not divorced her, as he had often fantasized? He threw down the gauntlet, told his wife he wanted a divorce. She readily agreed.

He panicked. How would he live, what would he live for, without wife, children, home? His murderous rage was gone; his yearning for revenge was gone; his hopelessness was gone; his blame was gone. He rattled in terror like a house with broken windows.

The father of this story was incapable of sorrow. He reacted to the darkness of life with rage, revenge, depression, blame, and panic. These reactions not only followed upon misfortune; they may have been lifelong undercurrents of primitive reactivity that were partially the cause of the destructive home atmosphere that they subsequently also followed, in an ongoing downward spiral. No one had ever held him, made him feel safe enough to learn sorrow.

SORROW IS AN INTEGRATED STATE in which multiple emotions are synthesized, like the blending of primary colors into pastels. It prevents the dominance of individual reactive fragments of the type that the father extruded. Sorrow facilitates mature function in the presence of the assault of the world upon personal existence. As humiliating and lacerating as the father's situation may seem to us, still we can feel in his reactions a deficiency of depth. We want to teach him about weeping, empathic reaching out, pondering. We want to facilitate an interior quest to solve, to understand, to cope, to master, to help; but we hear instead of impulsive action fragments exploding in thoughtless angst. The father could not think and feel because he was unable to hold together his plight with sorrow. Instead, he fractured into irresolute discharges. While the capacity for sorrow might have brought him salve, perspective, plan, he sorrowlessly exploded into emotional shrapnel.

The sorrow this father needed to learn descends into darkness and holds the sufferer in its buffering modulations. It is a surrender of expectation. This father's overwhelming loss and vulnerability could have created an incorporative receptivity, opposite to rigid conviction. Those who can bow do not break. When tears flow over the top, fresh growth rises beneath them.

The paucity of parenting in the father's own childhood deprived him of the opportunity to learn how to sorrow, and the culture in which he lived gave him no encouragement. Sorrow has almost vanished as a culturally transmitted wisdom. The rage of rap music has displaced Joan Baez's grief and Beethoven's melancholy. Contemporary people have forgotten how to approach the placeless temple of peace with the wish to deepen their capacities to feel a full range of feelings. Cleansing, sustaining sorrow is blocked not only by personality fragments like rage and despair, but by the demand for a unilayer of happiness, in denial of the depth of our entanglement with life and death.

It should be clear that I am using the word "sorrow" to stand for a learned, developmental attainment of character. I do not use it to imply overwhelming misery of those broken by tragic calamity, nor lugubrious wallowing in negativity and self-pity. I do not want to be misunderstood as romanticizing or prescribing indigestible horror, or rationalizing injustice. I am using sorrow with a specific denotation: a higher adaptation in the human animal, which facilitates a broader engagement of reality and which we observe in those who persevere against reason, thereby catalyzing hope beyond prediction.

Sorrow is the capacity to jettison delusion, to grieve the demise of innocence, to inhale and absorb the brevity and loss that accompany all life, to empathize with this identical plight in every being, and to cleanse the wound with faith's sustained direction. The absence of sorrow, according to this definition, isn't happiness, but fantasy. Based on acknowledgment of inescapable aspects of reality, sorrow is a component of well-being unrelated to sullenness, truculence, or panic. Sorrow is suffering transmuted through meaningful and masterable aliquots of insight into the positive, provocative value of loss.

The father was distraught not about events, but about his own fantasies. Based on hearsay, he painted pictures in his mind that enraged him but which were his own creations in delusional color, not real events. Not only his reactions but even what he reacted to represented a fragmentary, sorrowless, impulsive character. His crisis occurred in reaction to the cousin's rumor and his own obscene imagery. He forgot to pursue the facts of the case, as he didn't seek constructive solutions.

While his daughter was depressed and drug abusing, she was not as deteriorated as his fantasies. As he learned sorrow, rather than trying to domineer or excoriate her, he gained the capacities to understand and reach out to her. Would you believe the irony that, as the years of his psychotherapy unraveled, and he became less brittle and volatile, he, and I, had the pleasure of hearing about his daughter's enrollment in law school? The deeper and richer our capacity to face reality and stand firm, the more we can positively and peacefully help ourselves and influence others.

Chapter 19

THE GATEWAY TO SYMPATHETIC JOY

A PERSON WHO HAS LEARNED the skill of sorrow paradoxically will be lightened by kinship and communion with all beings, and will spontaneously speak in phrases of empathy and saliency. Words and sorrow are a couple with a long, strong marriage. An ancient myth from India provides a metaphor for this relationship.

Once there was a ruthless dacoit who had no pity for anyone. He created such havoc that God himself was alerted to the plight of the robber's victims, and determined to intervene, though in his own instructive style.

God came down for a little stroll in India. He gave the impression of having forgotten the multifacetedness of his own creation, however, because as he sauntered along in his peaceful tourist mien, he let himself be accosted by this mugger, who demanded money or traveler's checks and who threatened his life. But our metaphorical murderer quickly discovered that his gruff demands were being parried by the cunning victim into a skillful repartee. By the time their wordy philosophical exchange was ended, the highwayman had been verbally disarmed by the tourist's sagacious charm, and had become convinced that he ought to do what all ancient India myths convince all their protagonists to do, which is to seek the divine wisdom and liberation within his own heart.

The robber adopted the life of a religious hermit, pinnacle of Indian cultural values. He gave away his ill-gotten jewels, and possessionless, clad only in loincloth, in forest solitude he lived the yogi's life. He turned his previous avaricious tenacity with equal fervor toward spiritual quests, and meditated with such unrelenting concentration that ants built their hives and hills on him while he endured motionlessly. In this way, he became known as Valmiki, which means "the guy who wears anthills for clothes."

After years of arduous *tapas,* spiritual self-sacrifice, Valmiki decided he was at last liberated, a sage free from suffering. Nothing could distract him, nothing could trouble him, and there was nothing more to be gained through meditation by someone with no problems, so Valmiki arose, scattering anthills like a water buffalo shaking rain from his hairy hide, and walked down to the river to bathe. Dreaming that "freedom from suffering" meant isolationistic imperturbability, he imagined he had attained the supreme goal of yoga, which is unshakeable joy. Now, he felt, it was time for him to become an avatar, a missionary of inner peace, bringing his self-absorbed tranquility to others.

While Valmiki at last indulged himself in a long-overdue bath, he watched two white herons courting on the springtime riverbank. His self-satisfied and crusty old heart picked up speed as he vicariously delighted in these beautiful forms of the Creation dancing in the rapture of love. But someone else was also observing the white plumed birds.

As Valmiki watched, one of the birds dropped, killed by a hunter's arrow. In spite of his years of unwavering meditation and his yogic joy, Valmiki was pierced. Hardly a few moments had passed from his reentry into the world outside of anthills, but Valmiki, the most indomitable religious hermit of all, was stricken with love, compassion, and sorrow for his beautiful birds.

The arrow of sorrow burst his theistic satisfaction. Valmiki's anguish, called *soka* in Sanskrit, swept out of him in a cry of sympathetic kinship with all lovers and losers, and *sloka*, which means poetry, was born.

Actually, his meditation had worked perfectly. He had only assessed it one stage too soon. Rather than mighty in remove, he had made himself so vulnerable to sorrow that it could flow through him unimpeded. He had not become an unemotional narcissist, but a witness against cruelty and a spokesman of love. The name "Valmiki" today remains the only name we have for the great and unknown poets through whom poured the thousands of *slokas* that form the Ramayana, the epic in which animals and people share their heroism, grief, and fealty.

Every bird must leave its nest, and every person must relinquish the hope for a simply safe and pleasant life. Like fledgling birds, peace must tremble at the edge, and fall; only then it can fly.

THE MOMENTUM GIVEN TO INNER PEACE by passage through sorrow is missing when peace is sought through avoidance. A flat life of calibrated retreat may appear placid and ordered to the neighbors, but those who live minimally and timidly tread water, enduring a life of chronic anxiety-depression. Here is a typical psychiatric case to illustrate that.

A mathematics professor felt sick in his being, but couldn't name why. He was so troubled, he secretly sought out a psychiatrist; though he didn't believe in that subjective, emotional realm, he didn't know where else to turn. His life was nearly perfect.

Long since tenured, economically and professionally secure, he was stably married, and his two brilliant children were launched on their own careers. He had achieved every reasonable life goal; besides family, finances, and career, he was a stalwart churchgoer. But every day for years his step had gotten heavier, his work more tedious, his feelings for his wife dimmer, his sleep thinner. Thoughts of suicide or death wafted through his waking moments in the middle of the night like breezes over the windowsill. As his inability to sleep worsened, nameless dread crawled upward from his palpitating heart. He was sick and he couldn't figure out why.

In psychotherapy, reflection on his life led him to the realization that he lived in a basement of caution and calculation. He had no tolerance for disarray, ambiguity, and uncertainty. He sought precision, predictability. He created and cleaved to routines. Heir to an irritable and recoiling temperament and blessed with high intelligence, he had mustered adequate power to climb over the top of success as a scholar, teacher, parent, and citizen. But his life had no point.

Unlike a soldier of a captive people struggling for freedom, unlike a scientist on the scent of nature's secrets, unlike a Buddha going forth to find Nibbāna, he had only the absence of irritation as his goal, and having achieved that, he had nothing at all to live for. A man of moderation, prudence, and routine, he sought peace in individualistic remove from perturbation. He was hidden under anthills. He saw causes as immature, passions as degrading, goals as unsettling. Having so competently held the reins of daily life, he had forgotten only his human nature, which cannot find peace in the empty crust of a single self.

Anxiety-depression in late middle life is a very common syndrome. To a psychiatrist, it is like the common cold. An exploration through the inner world of these patients invariably exposes a value system, a belief, a way of life, that reveals the human paradox. A librarian home alone surrounded by her cats, a dentist with his large home and well-hoed field of investments, the mathematician with his formulas for safety, have failed to answer the call of life that even the prince in his palace of perfection must heed. Those who do not drive out toward suffering, despair, and sorrow will be attacked within their own castles. The security available in American life has created a plague of successful avoiders who can sidestep mortality well enough and long enough to be at last imploded by it from within.

Inner peace is not entrenchment. Those who have not heard of war, anarchy, and time's ocean, and wept, contributing their tears to the salt sea of pan-human identity, pay interest on their life of savings. Peace and its antithesis are known most truly at night.

Ironically, the mathematician's illness was hopeful, an outcry from within to escape his own house arrest. He was properly troubled. The best in him was stirring and about to crack his shell. He met the Buddha as a neurosis.

Don't worry, there are two white herons everywhere. Each one of us is Valmiki. All of our restless nighttime awakenings are poems waiting to be born with a cry. Inner peace comes near when we join in the grief of the hunted. Our work will never be done because there are many, many hunters.

Regardless of what we believe the meaning of our life to be, we *feel* peaceful when our sense of concern is directed outside ourselves toward others, not as a substitute for self-care, but as an extension of it. Sorrow is what enables pity, dread, or condescension to become compassion. This is one of the deepest ironies of human nature, that our sorrow also contains a leavening celebration. Gandhis, Whitmans, Berrigans, and Buddhas remind us of an alleviating energy and joy that sweeps over us when we can convert dumb anguish into sorrow, compassion, and then participation. Human nature didn't evolve in an anthill. We were born to cry out, to join in with the white herons, who save us as we save them on our common ineluctable riverbank. Sorrow is the only gateway to the meadows of sympathetic joy.

PART VII

Chapter 20

Peace Is Humility
or Egolessness

I WANT TO START this chapter on egolessness by re-evoking the word "humility" in its classical meaning, which is related to "humus," soil, and signifies "near the earth." The humility I want to talk about is neither fawning self-deprecation nor social modesty, but means awareness that at the biggest, we stand seven feet small, and if the whole earth were populated with basketball heroes poking their heads outward toward the stratosphere, our earth would still be a smooth, not a quill ball. We are all near the earth, its own true cells.

Generally, we experience the details of our week as earth-shattering. To live a life of inner peace, we need to cultivate detachment from those gripping ups and downs on which our well-being *appears* to depend, because it is the delusion of importance that blinds us to the real panorama. The humility that will help you cultivate inner peace is a continuous falling back down to earth, like the leaves of birch trees spilling down in golden autumn showers.

An infinite tide has flicked us up onto the visible shore. Beyond a few little details that we can rearrange, we are recipients, products of an unknowable ocean. We are born-of.

In our birth, we fall down to this earth. Humility, closeness to the earth, is looking upward, outward, while a freshet of other-awareness pours over us in tides. This is the attitude that is devoted and pious, but also skeptical of convictions and claims, a reverential and irreverent attitude of someone who senses the scope of things. No sand flea debates the reality of the Atlantic, nor listens to her fellow flea declaim on its dimensions. She gulps and swims in its nutrient-rich breakers. Humility is a primeval swallowing and bathing in the oceanic depth of reality.

Humility is ultimately washed into us by the ebb and flow of life, so that, often enough, people find more humility and peace as they age. But the opposite can also happen, the pathos of the aged clinging to their self-serving dogmas that become increasingly brittle, and increasingly grasped, as the realities of life challenge them. In this case, the accumulating years, which ought to be the great teacher, seething in and out with the alluvium of detachment, become glutted instead with polluted deposits, old plastic bags of arrogance, bitterness, or fear.

The growth of humility, downward, creates an upward expansion of starry sky to contemplate. Traditionally, this attitude of greeting toward the world has been called "egolessness" in the East and "humility" in the West. I want to remove humility from its churchly old lace and make this realization helpful and regular as denim.

"Egolessness" is defined by an absence, rather than by a presence. It means "absence of the fantasy of self-importance," and it implies the growth of social rather than selfish motivation. It is unrealistic to expect that we can all become totally egoless, like a Buddha, but we can all gradually emerge from local to open perspective, from personal to participatory concerns, from historical time to eternal immediacies. We can come to experience ourselves as a cosmologist might see us, a drop in the ocean of time, but also a tiny force field bending the rays of the world ever-so-slightly into universal, peaceful directions. Instead of a personal ego struggling to solidify itself against the tides of time, we can become channels through which the stream of peace flows.

HERE IS A BALANCING POINT in the cultivation of inner peace: We want to dig in and treasure the simple, glistening immediacies of our existence, the parade of opportunities and gifts of moments, like Scott and Helen Nearing among their pea vines, like Thoreau, the Homer of mosquitoes. But we want to see the big picture, take ourselves out of the operatic, fantastic egocentricity that makes us think that every acne blemish of our routine is Mount Vesuvius; understand ourselves as we really are—a hot dog vendor in the bleachers in the last of the ninth inning, the stands emptying, and no consequences resting on how much mustard we've got left.

If our humility is mere cosmic unctuousness, we won't find this balance. But even minute water molecules freezing and thawing in the right spot can crack granite. Strength and size aren't proportional. Perspective and purpose aren't at odds. Delight and diminution go hand in hand. The point I am emphasizing is that egolessness, the shrinking of the sense of self, is what creates panoramic perspective. The smaller we are, the more awestruck we become, and the more precious our days. It's possible to balance between the apparent opposites of engagement in the precious, transient moments that constitute our life, and detached, impersonal, objective perspective.

When I think of the sturdy joy of insignificance, I think of Nyogen Senzaki. He kept a low profile in a small corner, lived and died with remarkable calm, yet held an iron lever against the boulder of history. Almost totally unknown in his time or after, he had a profound influence on the history of culture and civilization. His life story is a metaphor for the mixture of creative, constructive, freedom with humility.

His beginning was vulnerable and inauspicious. A traveling Japanese Buddhist monk found a baby beside the frozen body of its mother in Siberia, and brought the infant back to Japan. His first name, Nyogen, means "like a phantasm, a fantasy." He was attracted to Buddhism early in life, anchored himself in scholarly study, and became a monk, training under the famous Zen master Soyen Shaku, who became the epitome of religious fame in Japan and had been chosen to represent Zen at the World Parliament of Religions in Chicago in 1893.

When Soyen Shaku returned to America in 1905 to give more lectures, he brought two disciples with him. One was D. T. Suzuki, who was to become the most prominent writer on Zen in the English language. But the other disciple of Soyen Shaku, a former monastic-training roommate of D. T. Suzuki, Nyogen Senzaki, arrived as personal helper to the abbot.

Before he left America, Zen master Soyen Shaku took a walk with Nyogen Senzaki through Golden Gate Park in San Francisco and, setting down his disciple's suitcase which, in role reversal, he had been carrying, he said: "This may be better for you instead of being hampered as my attendant monk. Just face the great city and see whether it conquers you or you conquer it." Soyen Shaku left and Senzaki never saw his spiritual father again.

In a breathtaking act of devotion to the master, Nyogen Senzaki remained in America the rest of his life, initially working odd jobs such as houseboy, porter, and cook. He lived like a mushroom, "without a very deep root, no branches, no flowers, and probably no seeds." After seventeen years had passed, and he had nourished his own life in austere and lonely obscurity, he began to teach Zen. Unlike Soyen Shaku or D. T. Suzuki, Senzaki taught actual Zen practice, and was the first person to transmit Zen *as a way of life* to the Western world. He ordained the first Americans to become Zen monks.

Rather than founding a temple, he inspired only a "floating zendo," a transient room to practice Zen that moved from place to place in Los Angeles and San Francisco in the 1920s and 1930s. He wrote his credo for himself in the third person: "A Buddhist monk is celibate and he leads the simplest life possible. He never charges . . . he accepts used clothes or old shoes and wears them. Any excess food or money he gives away. He sleeps quietly without worries, having none in his possession." He didn't even consider himself a Buddhist, but aspired to be the Buddha's friend, seeking to place himself in "the same responsive relationship to the universe." He inspired Robert Aitken, who was later to become the first American Zen master, and Paul Reps, with whom he successfully coauthored books in English.

Senzaki was serious about extending his way of life as an option to others. He was modest, but not devaluing. He deemphasized his name, but not his mission. He taught and wrote with commitment. He wrote both prose and poetry, and when he coauthored books, he left out his own name, giving full credit to his coauthor.

During World War II, Senzaki was imprisoned with ten thousand other Japanese-Americans at Heart Mountain, a desert camp in Wyoming. He continued to meditate and to inspire others. He corresponded with a score of American students, telling them that the handful of Japanese who meditated with him were "the happiest and most contented evacuees in this center." The poetry he wrote during the internment reflects unruffled constancy and his determination to maintain goodwill toward everyone, including the

American government, and to turn hardship into opportunity. With characteristic humor, he referred to ten thousand Japanese "guests" of the American government, and wrote:

> *Evacuees who follow Buddha, learning*
> *contentment,*
> *Should attain peace of mind*
> *Even in this frozen desert of internment. . . .*
> *They can admire only the gorgeous sunrise*
> *Beyond the barbed wire fence. . .*

He wrote of his three-year internment as an opportunity to practice compassion, and to "face the world with equanimity" in a "snowstorm of abuse."

When he died, after fifty years of life in America, he left these instructions, read posthumously to a packed hall of Japanese and American students.

> Friends in Dhamma [truth], be satisfied with your own heads. Do not put any fake heads above your own. Then minute after minute watch your steps closely. These are my last words to you. . . . Keep your head cool but your feet warm. Do not let sentiments sweep your feet. . . . Remember me as a monk, nothing else. I do not belong to any sect or cathedral. None of them should send me a promoted priest's rank or anything of the sort. I like to be free from such trash and die happily.

His only personal effects worthy of mention were three cardboard boxes of manuscripts, which were to become his posthumous literary legacy.

Nyogen Senzaki fulfilled the teaching his master had given him almost sixty years earlier when the young disciple, ill with tuberculosis, had asked, "What if I should die?" and Soyen had replied, "If you die, just die."

Nyogen Senzaki's life manifests the way of inner peace. In the wry California lingo that his fifty years in America enabled him to master, he gave his piquant definition of selectivity: "minute after minute watch your steps closely." He lived with exceptional personal selectivity: "insistence on self-discipline and simplicity." He internalized the understanding that peace is a victory over the stray yearnings of the infantile self; he endured the solitary, seventeen-year test his teacher had given him, and faced persecution with humor, poetry, community, and impish goodwill, constant to the goal of equanimity. Continuously aware of nature around him, in every poem he referred to sunsets, flowers, stars, and seasons to symbolize his own sense of integration with the processes of life, time, and death; yet he was a city dweller, and, for all his solitude, a social man, immersed in a circle of multicultural friends. Raised in a culture that he experienced as inflated with self-importance and stultified by competitive hierarchies, he maintained his autonomy and his attunement to transiency through raffish iconoclasm. Nyogen the fantasy, the self-proclaimed mushroom, was an orphan who passed through grasping at nothing. How intriguing that such a self-effacing fellow became an historical and cultural linchpin. His story reminds us of the realistic possibility of humorous, dedicated, fuss-free living and dying.

Nyogen Senzaki's life story also portrays a balance that is essential to peaceful humility. On the one hand, Senzaki bowed. He expressed awe and obedience for his teacher. Hearing about the casual exchange that led to his seventeen-year internal exile, we can understand why Japanese Zen teachers are called Zen *masters*. Soyen Shaku's casual suggestion to his student was internalized into a rod of command. Senzaki wrote about his relationship to his teacher as a person might revere a deity. On the other hand, Senzaki's attitude is far from that of a man with an "authoritarian personality"—an insecure follower who fawns on overlords to complete his own persona. His humility was not even that of a loyal member of a religious order. He understood his relationship to Soyen Shaku in spiritual not material terms. His obeisance was not to a man, but to a universal reality for which the man was an envoy.

> *. . . he passed from the world, and his body was*
> *cremated.*
> *What is the use to poke the remaining ashes?*
> *Look! The moon depicts . . . the autumn tree.*
> *A naked branch stretches itself and casts a slanting*
> *   shadow . . .*
> *Let us pay homage to the real being of Soyen Shaku*

The Soyen Shaku that Senzaki revered was an essence visible through the fleeting revelations in nature, including man. Senzaki bowed not to a personality, but to a realization of a truth that liberated him to seek on his own. While interned in Wyoming, he wrote:

> *I saw the stars strewn in the heavens,*
> *Each twinkling its eternal loneliness . . .*
> *Nothing could I do without my teacher . . .*
>
> *. . . I have carried his Zen in my empty fist*

Bowing was balanced by separation, individuation, and self-directed living. Obedience was only a step in his development; it was not a point of permanent arrest. Humility is not obsequiousness. A star shatters our pretensions; there is no need or possibility to cringe and grin in front of it. Senzaki lived as if both he and his teacher were puddles of fresh rain in which glittered reflected stars and moonlight.

HUMILITY IS RELATED TO COURAGE. In the increasingly egoless life, as a person diminishes cocksure, self-proclamatory conviction in favor of seeking, open-endedness becomes a traveling companion. To travel without ideology and with curiosity is an act of courage. True humility is not-knowing. At its best, egolessness simply means constant willingness to learn.

Journeying skillfully between the rocks of belief or cynicism, we find the spirit of egolessness on deck, questioning and sincerely open to the unknown. Every individual who can stand free of the security operation of dogmatic closure is involved both in intellectual humility and in a secret, undistinguished act by which, in repetition, the human collectivity can steer toward harmonious relations. Authentic egolessness is intrinsically edgeless, like clouds, and softly peaceful.

Sometimes, as a person progresses in this direction, there may be moments of panic, as old safe harbors of self-importance disappear beyond the horizon. Then the path to egolessness can backfire. Pretension of knowledge is one way people can react against this loss of previous landmarks.

The imagination in reaction against the voyage of peaceful humility may concoct a fantasy world ordered for one's own personal protection and happiness. Our childish wishes are essentially egocentric; they imply the world is revolving around us. Though they may bring comfort, such wishes don't bring peace, since they must be buttressed against the inevitable vicissitudes of fate. The attempt to bolster this desperately comforting delusion often leads to the strident self-importance with which churches, tribes, and nations proclaim their centrality to the cosmic scheme. Peace lies in the opposite direction from this proclamatory bombast with its assault on everything that contradicts it. Peace emerges when there is no position to protect.

Another reaction against egolessness may be the adoption of a guru or charismatic leader who claims to teach humility, but who exudes power and authority on which followers can anchor themselves like barnacles. This dangerous and ironic outflow of the search for humility is sadly recurrent.

Flattered by his followers' adoration, the teacher of egoless-ness feasts on his coterie and claims that his commandments are really benign lessons in accepting egolessness, so that he conflates humility with willingness to be humiliated, and he becomes grandiose as he purports to model egolessness. But humility doesn't mean cowering in compliance before a psychopath; nor does it mean a covertly ambitious alliance with a tyrant whose power is vicariously participated in by those over whom it cracks. Many cults teaching Christian humility or Buddhist egolessness have wallowed in this miasma of aggrandizement and fawning.

Soyen Shaku, Senzaki's teacher, taught humility and obedience, but manipulation for gratification never entered his relationships, and his disciples blossomed into healthy, self-directed people. He conveyed authority but not power. He generated reverence and awe, not desire and complicity. Soyen Shaku's famous lay disciple, D. T. Suzuki, wrote that Zen meant absolute passivity, absolute obedience and humility. But no saltier sojourner ever extolled and spanked the civilized world.

Peace within is an encapsulation of a peace that is already possible in the universe. We can only decipher it, obey it, and exemplify it. We have to accept it, drink it in, but no benefit is conveyed to us if we become inebriated by proximity to a drill sergeant's epaulet.

Inner peace is as strong and pure as the flow of the Other around us. Facts are empty shells from which the truth has scuttled forth. What we think we know is only the glow of a flashlight held up to an ongoing flood.

To understand ourselves in light of peace, we must die to fantasies of individual attainment, and soberly experience continuity beyond personal death. Our bodies and minds have sprung out of past causes; our knowledge and intuitions are products of interaction with culture and nature; our entire being is saturated in receipt and gift. Breathing itself is a borrowing and returning. Reality is intrinsically humbling and needs no petty officers.

When all the leaves on all the trees, bushes, herbs, and grasses explode into green each spring, how many trillions or quadrillions are there? Nyogen Senzaki lived as if he were a grass in the field. Spiritual humility, or egolessness, is the realization that the processes we call spring and autumn are omnipresent, instantaneous, and identical.

Every day is inconsequential, and every moment, a whole summer.

Chapter 21

Individual Identity
Within Egolessness

PEACEFUL LIVING DERIVES from balance in a world of torque. The world shakes, but our gyroscope must remain upright. The student of peace envelops deep habits about how to live intentionally, selectively, naturally, knowledge-ably, and harmoniously amidst losses, defeats, and gradual decline. Like an acrobat with eyes fixed on the horizon, peace focuses beyond self. Peaceful people inhabit landscapes where perspective derives from an infinitely distant vanishing point. Peace is transcendence of flux. Mountains erode, continents and oceans slide into one another, stars burn out. Still, men and women find within themselves an unshakeable something-else. Regardless of language, culture, religion, or its absence, inner peace means detachment from anxious narcissistic immediacy and entry into the impersonal. Peace is the simultaneous expansion and contraction of the world beyond measurement.

Sometimes students of peace confuse egolessness or humility with identitylessness. Egolessness means realistic perspective about your own or any individual life. But every life, no matter how relatively egoless, also has an identity that occurs in a cultural and historical context. On the one hand, peaceful living rests on the ability to see through your own and your neighbors' self-importance; on the other hand, you eat the food your neighbors grow, and you interpenetrate with them as their doctor, teacher, or friend. The Buddha lived universal truths, but he spoke Pāli, not Greek, and he ate rice, not manioc. Egolessness does not mean extracting yourself from the everyday texture around you. To find inner peace, you have to accept yourself.

This is a difficult but critical balance: how to diminish your ego while you remain your plain old self, blue jeans and sneakers, wool suits or dresses. In our world of libraries, jet travel, and polyculturalism, many peace seekers become lost by donning new costumes. Humility isn't about self-defeating poses, but about how to be who you really are, which is yourself in passing. To have a full perspective, we need to mingle egoless perspective of our own transience with identity-confirming appreciation and service to our moment-after-moment life. In the following story, you'll be able to observe this apparent tension between humility and self-confident self-expression, and watch it work its way down toward a peaceful resolution. This story captures the possibility of firm, meaningful personal identity within an impersonal perspective.

THE CHILD WHO WAS TO BECOME the wildlife biologist was born into a casserole of mediocre problems and options. His father was sales manager of a hardware firm, and he grew up in a blue-collar neighborhood of a small industrial city. His mother was anxious and preoccupied. Her parents had survived the genocide of Armenians in Turkey and had managed to escape to America, where she grew up, hidden from the facts of the past yet suffocating in its atmosphere. Constant suggestions of hatred and fear had withered something in her. She palpitated like a rabbit, persecuted by a past. At nineteen, she married her bona-fide midwestern American boyfriend and started having a family. Two others came first, so that when the future wildlife biologist was born, the home was lively, crowded, busy, inattentive. He remembered little of his early years, his father hardworking, reliable, and mostly absent, his mother's harried warmth and dark side-gazes, and her affection for their cocker spaniel, with whom she shared something different from what she did with her children. The first clarity in his memory were summer weekends at his father's brother's farm. It was not a real farm, but a hobby, a vestibule of avuncular hope in an otherwise drained life. His uncle, like his father, had joined the workforce early, was uneducated, but became a plumber and had managed to buy an abandoned poultry farm in what was then still a rural abutment to the city. These few acres were the home of a handful of sheep, a half-dozen black angus steers, and a swirl of dogs, cats, and chickens on the loose. The unmowed rims of the farm supported a large ash tree in which scarlet tanagers stowed their secretive nest, a creek hidden in willows and guarded by mosquitos, pastures full of dandelions and swallows, and backwoods that ran into shadows and imagination.

Here the future wildlife biologist first felt a happiness that he associated with summer and nature, and escape from the arid world of pavement and stickball. I think that one of life's secrets emerges in those people who are early and deeply drawn into an inspiration, one arena that calls to them and holds them, and wakes them up at night with wishes and urgings, as if an unfinished past were inescapably creating the future. This boy's brother and sister found the farm boring: they missed the tribe of children who quickly gather on a city street in summer around a baseball game or lawn sprinkler. But he felt the world opening on the farm, as if walls did not exist and the future were a sky. He helped his uncle mow. When robins flew into a tree repetitively, likely there was a nest.

Truly inspired people progress toward unpredictable futures where the sources of human creativity lie waiting in front of them. Nevertheless, all choices are also pressured from behind by past events. The future wildlife biologist felt his family home to be dreary; there was neither nurturance nor stimulation for his incipient character. His mother's anxiety suffused the atmosphere. Her respite was her own childlike attachment to her dog. Animals brought peace. On his uncle's farm, the future wildlife biologist found an intriguing, complex environment, an escape from his dreary urban confines, and lots of animals. He synthesized these two influences into a symbolic and realistic rebirth for himself by aspiring to become an outdoorsman and friend of animals. Through his career aspiration, he could rebel against his mother's fragility and his father's sterility, at the same time that he remained loyal to his mother's ability to love and to his father's family.

By the time high school graduation was approaching, he had managed to acquire a scholarship to the state university. He majored in wildlife biology, excited to find himself out of his factory neighborhood and among professors and intellectuals. But slowly, over his four highly successful academic years, he felt himself choking in unexpressed tears. One by one, his hopes and ideals were being ridiculed and dismembered by an invisible Joker. He had imagined himself befriending wild animals, visiting them in their homes, learning their language and their songs. Instead, he learned how to memorize textbooks, pass multiple choice exams, kill and dissect life and model the activity of its carcass on the principles of a machine. In advanced courses, he learned how to apply for grants, read government documents, and develop tactical career cunning. Majoring in wildlife biology did not mean becoming a Native American scout; it meant learning to compete for economic survival as a research scientist. For a wildlife biologist specializing in the white-tail deer, he learned, the only employment would be managing hunting research of state departments of wildlife. The job of a deer biologist was to augment the state herd to maximize hunting kill. The goal of his degree program was to prepare him to facilitate the mass killing of the fleet creatures who had called to him of a new life.

The discipline he had chosen to study in college was in fact only marginally connected to, and in many ways antithetical to, his personal agenda. The shadowy anxiety that had haunted his mother's life, and atomized into his own, was the cross-generational residue of mass murder. The career he had naïvely selected to heal and correct that past instead descended into a realm that was unbearably similar: human delight in killing. He wanted to study and befriend wildlife to rectify his fear of a violent world, but he found his career opportunities as a deer biologist to be catering to an element of the very cruelty he felt impelled to transform. The life riddle he thought he had solved once again deteriorated into a conundrum.

After graduation from college, this career-focused idealist and scholarship student, who had superseded his social background and excelled in school, began several years of disconsolate odd jobs. He worked on farms, drove tractors and combines and helped to coat fields with pesticides and fill livestock with antibiotics. He was a substitute high school teacher, a carpenter's assistant, and repaired chain saws. A small savings, and pressure from his draft board to induct him into the Vietnam war, squeezed him out of America. He hitchhiked across Europe and into Asia with a vague goal of working on a sheep farm in New Zealand, on his way joining the stream of hippies traversing Iran and Afghanistan in the early 1970s on their way to India. He was shiftless and cynical, but not lost. An unformulated hope set his directions.

From other Western travelers in India, he heard about ashrams, Gandhi, reverence for life. Among the dust and filth and crowds of India, where there was no visible evidence of anything other than the struggle for survival, he heard about ideas that concretized his intuitions: a kinship with animals, vegetarianism, nonviolence, and a search for the divine within. As his uncle's farm had come to him like a beckoning spirit, so did the mystique of India. He put his knapsack down in an ashram on the banks of the Ganges in northern India.

There he studied meditation. He heard that world religions, despite their diversity, have a common theme, and that the creative spark within the universe resides within the individual and can be known by every person. The method of this knowledge is self-restraint, scriptural study, and inward meditation. He was taught that all living forms evolve; life is a kinship.

A practiced student and self-transformer, the wildlife biologist progressed through increasingly intense and lengthening meditation retreats. In solitude, with a minimum of food, clothing, and comforts, under the guidance of ascetic religious celibates, he faced the fear and hatred within himself, the quivering flutter of his mother's tenuous hold on life as it trembled within him, his bitterness and dismay about his mechanistic, opportunistic college training and the war in Vietnam. As these rose up in front of him and passed, he found an untouched pool of faith. Initially, it seemed localized to memories of his uncle's farm. After weeks of isolation in a meditation cell, thin from gradual weight loss on the restricted diet, trapped behind the bars of his own mind— instead he began to remember barn swallows careening over pastures in the August dusk.

Meditating alone in his cell in a Hindu ashram on the banks of the Ganges in the Himalayan Foothills, the biologist reenvisioned his first encounter with wildlife. This was the moment that had inspired his initial profession. Of course, he had seen deer before, fleeing tail-flags bounding off in fear of him. But this memory was of his first pungent meeting. It was August; the mosquitos and deerflies had abated, and he could wander in the woods on unmarked land stretching around his uncle's place. About eight o'clock in the evening, as the light began to fade, he rambled down an old logging road and emerged at a swamp. Across fifty yards of open water he saw a doe feeding. The wind was blowing from her direction and she couldn't smell him; the light was fading, he was in a thicket of alders, and his profile was obscured. He watched the doe move and feed. Flanking her, in thicker brush, were two fawns. The adult deer wasn't at ease. She fed in an atmosphere of vigilance, ripping off vegetation and chewing, then halting, watching, listening, wide eyes and taut ears. She stepped precisely with a snap; her whole body seemed like a poised arrow. Here was a wild being of the woods, nonaggressive, yet unrestrained and unbeholden, born free in the forest from a mother born the same, back generation upon generation into the Pleistocene when ice covered most of the northern hemisphere, back into the Pliocene, the Miocene and before, for fifteen million years this genus *Odocoileus* had sprung forth, a lineage of wild watchers. Her tawny dignity emerged from an unbroken series of cunning, attention, and autonomy that had passed from body to body across hundreds of thousands of generations. The young man brushed away a mosquito from his forehead—the doe turned, eyes and ears burned into him, and she shot off in parabolic leaps of power and ease, other noises crashing in the brush beyond her as the fawns fled. It seemed to him her departure was due less to fear than secrecy. She vanished into unknown spaces in the forest, where the spirits that run and listen survive, outlasting ice ages and hunting seasons, to observe earth's history from a coiled, sublime remove. The planet is inhabited.

The Indian meditation teachers of the wildlife biologist were middle-aged monks who had surrendered their sexuality to follow their guru. Long black beards descended from their detached faces. They encouraged their unusually austere American student to search for something beyond his memories. Unpleasant thoughts of mass murder or cynical bureaucracies, or pleasant memories of woods and wildlife, were personal, transient. What could he find that lay beyond, within; not ephemeral, evolving forms, but something immutable, eternal, true?

For the wildlife biologist, time in India was anchored only to the ritual of visa expiration and renewal. After emerging from an extended meditation retreat, he was informed that his visa would not be extended. He had to leave India. He had a departing interview with the guru of the ashram, a slender, elderly, retired physician who had left secular life to follow his own guru some forty years earlier. The guru retained a knowledge of worldly mechanics at the same time that he followed his own celibate, restrained, ashram life, guiding others on the quest for *moksha,* spiritual liberation. His sincerity, integrity, and depth were unimpeachable. He was impressed with the wildlife biologist's modesty and perseverance. The guru told him he had bright karma from a long chain of previous lives filled with austere spiritual practice. In this incarnation, he was intended to bring true meditation to America. Would he return home, found a small, quiet center, and begin to teach what he had practiced here in India? There was no need for pretension, no need to claim spiritual insight or power, but the divine light would be with him to guide him.

The wildlife biologist thought about this dream come true. He could represent, speak for, and spread the culture of self-restraint, inner search, humility, and fellowship of living beings in America. He took a long last look at the rushing Ganges, speeding out of the Himalayas onto the Gangetic plain at Rishekesh, a fulminant torrent in a dry land. Clearly, he would never be the same person who had arrived on this riverbank. He had entered an inviting, open, yet secret society, had suffered and received unspeakable gifts. He thought of the incense, the Sanskrit chanting at dawn, the unsewn white cotton clothing fluttering in the riverbank wind. Could he teach the way of obeisance to Shiva, the one principle and force inside the life of the universe and all things, the unnameable, worshipable, symbol of the unformed All?

It took the wildlife biologist three years to earn a master's degree in outdoor education in Australia, because he had to earn his tuition on outback sheep ranches. The Vietnam war and the military draft had ended, and he returned to America, where he became a trip leader, climbing instructor, and survival skills teacher in Colorado. It was not until his midforties that he joined a group of professionals who had a meditation study group, and told his life story.

By this time, the wildlife biologist was married to an outdoor education instructor from Colorado; they had a daughter and had moved to Maine, where he did population research on mammals and taught wildlife biology and outdoor education at a state college. His main intellectual concern now was human population growth. He felt that restraining the surge of billions of people on earth was the fundamental key to the environmental crisis. His animal research was intended not to "manage the herds" of Maine moose and deer, but to explore models of population control and balance in large mammals. He was an active volunteer representative for Zero Population Growth. He and his wife planned to limit their family to two children.

The wildlife biologist as a middle-aged man was a muscular, bearded, prototypic rural "Maine-iac" in his characteristic flannel shirt, jeans, and boots, a sales manager's son who might be pumping gas in Bangor or Patten. His life revealed an outpouring of productive energy: research, teaching, volunteer organizational work. In addition, he was writing a guidebook to "environmentally conscious recreation": how to live in the wilderness without leaving a trace on it—no fires, no footprints, no noise, no meat.

He felt that his social productivity came from the fact that he was unable to differentiate work and play. He didn't have a job, and then free time with recreation. His work was play; his play was work. He was called, focused, alert like a wild animal to his love of wilderness, his desire to preserve it and teach what he saw in it.

Despite his creative, externalized energy, his life also had a laconic flavoring. He lived in a small house that had taken on the style of rural Maine: a chaotic mixture of neglect, repair, tight budget, and defeat by weather. Newly replaced, unpainted clapboards mingled with older ones, painted, but peeling. Right around the house, grass was mowed, but in the field behind, tall stems choked the view and mingled with orange hawkweed and black-eyed Susans. Cleanliness and order played second fiddle to tramps for moose-watching, reading wildlife bulletins from Alaska and Manitoba, and meditating.

He continued to meditate, rising at 4:30 a.m. as he had done in India so many years before. One evening, after a slide show about a canoe trip in northern Maine, he told an inquiring friend:

> My fate is to love the world as it is being destroyed. Why did I take birth in an era when human hordes are penetrating every last stronghold of rain forest and tundra to chop down or hunt the last wild things? The peace I have, comes from the conviction that I am incarnate here, now, to witness this wave of destruction with compassion and love. I spend my life outdoors,

doing what I love, showing others how to find what I've found. The history of the earth is very long; no matter how much destruction or creation we humans perpetrate, it's just a transient up-swell in a population of locusts. Dinosaurs lasted one hundred and fifty million years; we've been here one million or so. One avaricious monoculture is dominating the earth, stamping out whales and elephants and caribou and salmon, but I listen to the cries of anguish and death with a wide perspective. I can also hear the voices of millions of years. Chain saws in the Amazon and oil rigs in the Arctic Ocean can't touch that. Every life is in a series. When I wake up in the pre-dawn—and at 4:30 A.M. in winter in Maine you've got a long way to sit until dawn—I am in the company of spirits that embody themselves in mountains, lakes, and wild animals—before or after they are embodied. Do you think this visible, tangible world is the only dimension of reality? Do you think the creative outpouring of beings on earth will stop tumbling out of that greater dream? Do you think this one planet is the only stage? Next week my wife and I will be leading a trip to observe loons—they are becoming endangered because acid rain on northern lakes is killing the fish on which they feed. My ability to love in the face of mass death, mass murder, comes from inner peace. I'm not caught in one moment as if it were the totality. I'm a witness for the wild and beautiful. This planet is inhabited.

The wife of the wildlife biologist described him more succinctly, "He's the most focused person I know. He's always alert and interested, but he just doesn't attend to the chaff. People catch his enthusiasm. He's really as quiet as he seems, but I always imagine he's humming."

A friend commented, "He seems to be half in another world—and I know it sounds like a paradox, but that makes him more alive in this one."

He had no further contact with the ashram in India. His guru had died and been replaced. He had no further interest in religion per se. He had not adopted an exotic religion or lifestyle. He did not feel cut off from that world, but evolved.

> I find the guidance I need in my own meditation, and in contemplation of the natural world. The truth is the same everywhere. Every life is a creative and loving message. There could be nothing; instead, we emerge. Death isn't the tragedy we conventionally take it for, but a breather, a stopping place, like a period at the end of a sentence, that enables a fresh start. Each salmon has a desperate fight to get upriver; they all arrive depleted and exhausted; but if you can stand back and absorb the phenomena of millions of years of salmon migrations as a reliable, recurring, presence on the earth, then each spring run is just like one inhalation, and the spawn is actually effortless breathing in and out.

The wildlife biologist's story commences with a constellation of problems and tools, but his adolescent visions, born in solitude, were disjunctive with social reality. They shattered. Carrying only fragments of hope with him, he launched into a deeper, guided quest, and emerged with a sense of things that was not rigidly pinned to either an ideology or an image. His functioning adult identity was anchored in a mood of delight, reverence, sorrow, and faith. Like his meditations, his life came to express energetic penetration of nature's secret places, fond awe for the wisdom embodied in other lives, and sorrow for the ceaseless death that accompanies the vast transformation of the planet. He felt blessed with the same time-transcending purpose that he espied in the lives of the deer that inspired him with their enduring, watchful consciousness. He had accepted his guru's request at its essence, though rejected its Asian dress. He had recreated the core elements of the life of inner peace: dynamic acceptance, self-discipline, selectivity, studenthood, closeness to nature, conscious suffering, self-effacement, and loving action, and he felt and radiated a playful, animated, energetic equipoise. Peace is found anywhere that you cease measuring the world by your own casing.

His story exemplifies egolessness, not to the degree of being absolutely free of personal needs and preferences, but in the development of life-transforming and life-directing calling as a servant of higher peace. His perspective is both epochal and immediate. He experiences himself as both insignificant as an individual, and vitally important as a participant. Rather than banging on the doors of time to proclaim his power, he lives as if life and death were a seamless flow, imperturbability were the soil, and he were rain. He has a clear identity and historical context that embrace his work, play, home, and style, but he listens to and follows something far beyond himself, a deep, silent gong.

An individual peaceful presence transforms its environment. In the instance of an ordinary person, like the wildlife biologist, he influenced family, friends, and students. He felt purpose in a world whose goals he couldn't know. His egolessness wasn't located in fidelity to gurudom or in affected modesty, but in breadth of conception and concern. There are many men and women like him, anonymous, doing a small good job well, carrying forward a great and mysterious agenda, like fawns.

PART VIII

Chapter 22

PEACE IS AN AMBIANCE:
RABINDRANATH TAGORE

THERE IS A CHARMED QUALITY to Rabindranath Tagore's biography that enables us to inhale the fragrance of a life of peace-in-action. Not only the facts, but his atmosphere inspires peace, like the smell of transpiring grass on a summer evening. His history reveals how insight and action are complemented by relationship to an ambiance, producing an infectious feeling tone of dynamic equipoise. The events of his life and his poetry form a bouquet of images that can pervade our own peaceward dreams. As peace seekers, our strongest motivation arises from seeds of our own planting, but we are encouraged onward by the mythic potency of images derived from the lives of those who have absorbed and suffused the atmosphere with peace.

Tagore's childhood pulsed with numinous potential. The house where he was born in 1861 was more like a minute city-state or a riverside Olympus than an ordinary family home. The sprawling building in Calcutta housed the child's parents, more than a dozen older siblings and all their spouses and progeny, many other kin, and a large retinue of servants.

Possibly the great talents of Debendranath, Tagore's father, also known as Maharshi, the wise one, included the premonition that his rebellious and impractical youngest son was destined to become the man Gandhi would call the "Sentinel of Asia," the founder of a school and university, a humanitarian reformer in the style of his grandfather, one of the most famous and celebrated men in the world during his lifetime, and the culminating poet of a 3,500-year-old tradition of poetry, as well as a man steeped in what Debendranath himself prized most dearly: a fountain of inner peace.

Surprisingly, Rabindranath Tagore suffered unusual deprivation in the midst of wealth and culture. He was raised amidst rare cultural attainment and wealth by poor and ignorant servants, who treated him abusively. Later he was to call it his days under "servocracy." To make sure the noble brat would cause no trouble, a servant in charge of him—himself little more than a boy—drew a chalk circle on the floor and guarded Rabindranath tight within that circle. Tagore remembered from those earliest days the theme that was to be found recurrently in his writing: imprisoned indoors in dingy light, he yearned for the freedom, greenery, and sunshine that he could spy through the window. The Maharshi's son, born for brightness, remained in shade.

The man who was to become one of the most widely educated men of the twentieth century, who was to receive the pinnacle of literary and intellectual honors, who was to become "the spiritual ambassador of India . . . her spokesman and the living symbol of her culture" could not be educated in school. After he reached thirteen, even his educationally obsessed family, father and older brothers, resigned themselves and gave up on him, and his formal schooling ended. He wrote:

> When I was very young I gave up learning and ran away from my lessons. That saved me, and I owe all that I

possess today to that courageous step . . . if I had cultivated a callous mind, and smothered this sensitivity under a pile of books, I would have lost this world . . . I have experienced the mystery of its being: its heart and soul . . . I know, really, that you do not dislike me because I know less mathematics than you; for you believe that I have attained the secret of existence in some other way—not through analysis but as a child who enters his mother's chamber. I have kept the child spirit. . . .

The spirit of rebellion in service of joy, depth of feeling, and autonomy is a precious precursor to a lifelong childhood in the garden of peace. The passive, complacent dotage often stereotyped onto seated mystics is opposite to Tagore who, like all peace-seekers, learned to protect his purity of heart. Peace is always young, its disciples buoyant, and its fields full of resilient refusals like daisies in rain. Tagore's defiance was a faith that kept him open for the next step.

When Tagore turned twelve, his father took him out of the family to Shantiniketan and to the Himalayas. Shantiniketan was a cottage Debendranath had built on a plot of uninhabited desert in rural Bengal. The name means "abode of peace." Maharshi Debendranath came here to meditate; now he brought his son here and let him roam free in open space for the first time in his life. Did this fulfillment of the boy's dream—to ramble in sunny nature with his father nearby—make an impression on Rabindranath? For the bulk of Rabindranath's life, Shantiniketan was to be his home, the locus of his creative achievements, the center of his school, and the site to which scientists and scholars, ambassadors of law and letters, would come from around the world to pay homage to him. All this occurred at the site his father consecrated as the center of his own quest for *shanti*, peace.

From Shantiniketan, father and son traveled for some three months, sojourning in the Himalayas, where Debendranath taught his son astronomy outdoors at night, as well as English and Sanskrit by day. Love of nature and peaceful language were layered into Rabindranath. Father was transmitting peace across generations by location, by example, by desert-mountain-word-and-star.

Young man Tagore pursued the life of the romantic poet and writer. He had transcendental experiences of a divine loving world in nature, and wrote volumes of clever, successful poetry. Once again it was his father, the Maharshi, who deepened his life, this time by making Rabindranath head of the family estates.

Torn from his idle literary life, Rabindranath assumed the responsibility of traveling among and managing the family's far-flung lands. Accounts, crops, the hardships and crises of the tenanted poor began to occupy his mind. This was how he came to know the rural people of Bengal, from whom his class and culture had previously kept him isolated. His main residence was a houseboat on the Padma, or Lotus River, as the Ganges was known in Bengal. The image of rivers and the life of their waters and shores became one of the hallmarks of Tagore's poetry, and his sympathies were always with those in pain. This was not a political position or a social philosophy, but a reflex of his being. Insight into suffering, and empathic engagement, became enrichments of his meditative training. Tagore's greatest pride was not in the literary honors he was to reap, but in the fact that boatmen and farmers loved and sang his songs.

Although Tagore had absorbed his grandfather's competence and humanism and his father's religiosity, he remained a poised nobleman, not yet a disciple and purveyor of peace. The dilemma of his children's education pushed him forward on the path.

His five growing children needed a school, but for Tagore to send his children to school would be like a nightingale shooing its fledglings off to visit a fox. What could he do?

Because I underwent this process when I was young, and remembered the torture of it, I tried to establish a school where boys [and soon after, girls, a radical breakthrough for India in 1901] might be free in spite of the school. Knowing something of the natural school which Nature supplies to all her creatures, I established my institution on a beautiful spot, far away from town, where the children had the greatest freedom possible. . . .

The Calcutta-born Rabindranath had his first taste of natural freedom at his father's Abode of Peace; and it was there, also, that he sat at the Maharshi's feet in those three unique, glorious months of intimacy with his pious, aloof father. So it was at *Shantiniketan* that Tagore began to teach children outdoors under trees. The basis of his school sprang up from something deep inside him . . . unity . . . harmony . . . sympathy . . . *peace.*

I had it in my mind to create an atmosphere; I felt this was more important than classroom teaching. The atmosphere was there; how could I create it? The birds sang to the awakening light of morning, the evening came with its own silence, and the stars brought the peace of night . . . I invited artists from the city to live at the school, and left them free to produce their own work . . . to include this ideal of unity in all the activities . . . educational . . . artistic, some in the shape of service to our neighbors by helping the reconstruc-tion of village life. . . . The children began to serve our neighbors . . . to be in constant touch with the life around them. . . . The highest education is that which does not merely give us information but makes our life in harmony with all existence.

Tagore's experiment with education based upon the mood of harmony was to grow into a major school and university that continues. Fulfilling his grandfather's administrative thrust and his father's vision for Shantiniketan, Tagore wove ancestral threads into an institution where peace was robust and three-dimensional. This is the voice of a poet who also wants to shape bricks and thatch, a visionary who thinks of peace as a basic life skill.

> I believe in a spiritual world—not as anything separate from this world—but as its innermost truth . . . Born in this great world, full of the mystery of the infinite, we cannot accept our existence as a momentary outburst of chance drifting on the current of matter toward an eternal nowhere . . . . In India we still cherish in our memory the tradition of the forest colonies of great teachers . . . they were to society what the sun is to planets . . . the students took the cattle to pasture, collected firewood, gathered fruit, cultivated kindness to all creatures and grew in their spirit with their own teachers' spiritual growth . . .
>
> This idea of education through sharing a life of high aspiration with one's master took possession of my mind. . . . All around our ashram is a vast open country. . . . Travelers coming up this road can see from a distance on the summit of undulating ground the spire of a temple and the top of a building, indicating the Shantiniketan ashram, among its *amalaki* groves and its avenue of stately *sal* trees.

It was at Shantiniketan that Rabindranath lived under the name of Gurudev, Revered Teacher, cultivating with his students harmony, unity: ". . . the lasting power of the Eternal in the passing moment of our life," all in an effort "to impart the breath of life to the complete man." The school had as its guiding spirit personal love and peace, for Tagore called Shantiniketan "the boat which carries the best cargo of my life," and "my tangible poem."

Shortly after the founding of the school, tragedy began to strike at Tagore, not once but repeatedly. His wife became ill, then died. Tagore believed that individual life was a gift in service of the infinite, and that personal grief was insignificant compared to the larger tasks of life. Through his wife's death, and all the suffering that was soon to confront him, he worked on, displaying no public grief. But here is the poem that followed her death.

> *In desperate hope I go and search for her in all the*
>   *corners of my room; I find her not.*
> *My house is small and what once has gone from it*
>   *can never be regained.*
> *But infinite is thy mansion, my lord, and seeking*
>   *her I have come to thy door.*
> *I stand under the golden canopy of thine evening*
>   *sky and I lift my eager eyes to thy face.*
> *I have come to the brink of eternity from which*
>   *nothing can vanish—no hope, no happiness,*
>   *no vision of a face seen through tears.*
> *Oh, dip my emptied life into that ocean, plunge it*
>   *into the deepest fullness. Let me for once*
>   *feel that lost sweet touch in the allness of*
>   *the universe.*

The special gift that Tagore increasingly cultivated was the capacity to feel every event enveloped within a vast and holding world, whose containing curve was lined with peace. In the events of his personal history, we hear about not only happenings, but the supreme poet of peace gradually internalizing his father's way and allowing it to expand, until peace became like oxygen, like sky, invisible and everywhere.

Tagore was now in charge of his children. His daughter fell ill with tuberculosis; they raced to the mountains, high altitudes being the only known treatment for tuberculosis in 1903, but her condition worsened, so they returned to Calcutta, where she died less than a year after her mother. The aged patriarch Debendranath died a year and a half later, and two years after that the youngest son, said to be

Rabindranath's favorite, died at age thirteen of cholera. For five months, Tagore didn't even return to Shantiniketan. Then he began the period of his greatest creations.

> *If the dark night of sorrow can make thy benign*
> *   light glow*
> *Let it be so*

Recurrent, personal anguish transformed Rabindranath Tagore from a benighted romantic into a universal poet. The poems and songs that he wrote after the period of serial personal loss reveal the struggle and the solutions to the questions demanded by his circumstances. His writing became not merely artful but relevant and revealing, filled with complex, wise innocence. The ambiance he had absorbed needed to be deepened, strengthened, to a peace more sustaining, such as we all need.

The poetry and song in which Tagore expressed his solitary frailty and his visionary faith in peace as an embracing reality catapulted him into a level of adoration and fame that was unequaled for any poet in human history. The lonely, moiling souls of the world heard in Tagore's grief and peace their own voice. Yet his work tumbled precipitously into obscurity after his death, and the manner in which this happened also reveals important features of Tagore's way of finding inner peace. Let's turn to his poetry and song lyrics to learn directly from his own words how he cultivated peace when eclipsed by mortality.

FOR RABINDRANATH TAGORE, inner peace began with the cultivation and elaboration of a sense of intimate, loving relatedness to a personalized divine presence. He gave this felt relationship centrality in every event in every moment. He permitted his daily experience to resonate between immediate facts and cosmic concern. Tagore interacted with a You everywhere, who was a person, but not merely a person; who had a pantheistic presence, but was not contained in pantheistic ideology. For Tagore, human ethical and spiritual ascension matter to eternal creation. God didn't exist as a separate old man in the sky, but there was a heartbeat evolving within every moment.

Tagore felt called by events in nature, in social history, and in his own psyche, to relate to eternity as if it contained a Person who mirrored his own loves and aspirations. Unlike the gods of organized religions, the You within Tagore's vision had no fixed form, shape, gender, no final spoken text. To be searching for Him through His presence and His elusiveness, His dramatic revelations and His absences, His personnness and His impersonalness, was the essential relationship-creating, mood-salving, peace-giving act. Tagore's openhearted quest, his unfinalized exploration, his continuous self-transformation in search of the expanding and enhancing Other, was his source of purpose and of dynamic peace. Every event was meaningful, but there was no final fixed meaning. In tumult, Tagore felt the creative agitation of divine foment. In loss, he felt the necessity for wider horizons. In fear and tyranny, he heard a drumbeat for sacrificial action. In death, he found a portal. The continuous change of costume and Person as the world unfolds revealed to Rabindranath an embracing "yes." Nothing was "wrong." Out of this intimate relatedness to all things flowed his calming sense of reassurance.

Tagore's search for divine presence in every tilt of fate wasn't one-way traffic. He felt that the divine presence was in its own search for each one of us as well. Tagore's psychological and poetic quest led him to feel that the You needed us. The world is continuously being created through the media of our search to understand and fulfill our relationship to the ultimate. The world evolves through our efforts to comprehend and express our response to its totality. This relational, interactive affirmation of life is epitomized in one of Tagore's most famous poems, "Balākā."

"Balākā" was written at the height of Tagore's worldly fame and poetic power. The title alone presents all the problems of translation from Bengali to English, since the word can mean either "crane" or "swan," but also has a Sanskrit connotation, "bird of the soul." The poet is standing near a river at dusk. The world is beautiful but impersonal, mute. Nature is wonderful, yet separate from the poet.

> *Suddenly I hear,*
> *In the vast emptiness of the evening sky*
> *The lightning flash of sounds . . .*
> *O Balākā*
> *Your wings drunk with the wine of wind*
> *And scattering peals of joyous laughter*
> *Awoke waves of wonder in the sky . . .*

The inchoate meditation of static nature is broken by the summons of motion: great birds in flight. The poet imagines that all nature is possessed of the same motile ecstasy: mountains awaken and yearn to become adventuring clouds; trees yearn to turn their leaves into wings. The flying wanderers have sympathetically aroused in each aspect of nature a yearning for the Beyond. Now poet and nature have the same essence.

> *O Balākā,*
> *Tonight you have opened for me the door of silence.*
> *Behind her veil in earth, sky, water,*
> *I hear the restless beating of wings.*

The poet realizes that all the components of nature are animated by the same principle. Grass is fluttering its wings; beneath the earth, opening seeds spread wings; the range of hills are wings outspread from land to land; the stars are pulsing in flight.

> *I hear the countless voices of the human heart*
> *Flying unseen,*
> *From the dim past to the dim unopened future,*
> *I hear within myself*
> *The fluttering of the homeless bird,*
> *Winging with countless other birds*
> *Night and day, through light and darkness*
> *From unknown shore to shore*
> *The void of the Universe is resounding with the*
>   *song of wings:*
> *"Not here, not here, somewhere far beyond."*

The migrating birds personify the restless longing of the human heart. This symbol itself would make Tagore a poet of agitation. But "Balākā" isn't a nature poem. The birds, the poet's restlessness, are particular manifestations of a universal, timeless vitality. Every human life is one *balākā* winging from an unknown to another unknown, in an undecipherable yet precisely articulated series of cosmic pulses. The restlessness of the individuals within nature expresses the spiritual urge to fly beyond corporeal fact. The migrating flocks, the flight of the heart, are journeying from tangible fixations toward the impalpable harmony of creation. In the beings of this world, birds and poets, the creation is seeking its own deepest self. Tagore experienced unity in diversity, commonality in difference, peace in motion. The poem creates an exquisite sensation of tantivy into an unknown yet welcoming sky. Peace is found by transcending the tangible and the visible.

THE INDIVIDUAL POEM, with its single revelation, does not capture the process by which Tagore arrived at his integrative, overarching feeling of harmony within change. He exposed this psychology of peace in his volumes of poems and song cycles, in which he leads the reader through his own psychological methodology, conveying practical guidance about peace-seeking life. His first translation into English of a book of song offerings—*Gitanjali*—transformed the literary world and his own life.

In the short books of lyric cycles, such as *Gitanjali* or *Crossing*, both of which Tagore himself translated into English, he describes how he lives within modes of understanding that continuously transmute discordant experience into peaceful song. Tagore's descriptions embody many aspects of the way of inner peace that I have traced through so many biographies in this book, but Tagore writes with commanding imagery and unique allusions, so that, upon reading him, we enter a world at once well-known yet magically new. Even though Tagore's song lyrics are written in the words of a fictionalized self, the recurrent emphases through many poems, and the depth of feeling, are evidence that Tagore must have *lived* the events that provoked the poems. The charmed prince of Indian culture and literature suffered the same sense of loneliness, rejection, anxiety, and dread as the rest of us. But Tagore utilized suffering. Instead of falling beneath it, he was animated by it. He transformed it into a deepening sense of peace.

In the imaginary poetic universe that Tagore created in *Crossing*, the speaker of the poems has a dynamic sense of return toward peace. Tagore often speaks as a female, a convention that he borrowed from medieval Indian religious poetic traditions, and which suited him because he wanted to claim as his own the attitudes associated with femininity in medieval India: patience, receipt, surrender. She may be a beggar, or a farm wife sitting at the wayside selling produce from a basket.

> *When the market is over and they return*
> *homewards through the dusk,*

> *I sit at the wayside to watch thee plying*
>   *thy boat,*
> *Crossing the dark water with the sunset*
>   *gleam upon thy sail;*
> *I see thy silent figure standing at the helm*
>   *and suddenly catch thy eyes gazing upon me;*
> *I leave my song; and cry to thee to take me across.*

At the close of an ordinary day, the farm wife, seated in the market, breaks convention and does not depart when her friends do. She perseveres in expectant waiting, and envisions a personal call from the unspeakable mystery of things. The image of crossing a river is a traditional Indian symbol for spiritual transcendence. A boatman—seductive and frightening—must be engaged. She opens herself without reserve. At the focal point of her gaze is an embodied reply, a man but not a man, an ambiguous magnetism. She doesn't know what awaits her, but she is ready to go. Not yet at peace, she opens to it wholeheartedly.

Tagore constantly repeats the theme of *dynamic readiness* as the first step to peace. "My eyes have lost their sleep in watching; yet if I do not meet thee still it is sweet to watch." "Now at my broken gate, I sit still and wait for your coming." This attitude of self-controlled attendance upon life's fruition is sometimes expressed as a holy idleness: "men and women hastened down the woodland path with their offerings of fresh flowers. But I lay on the grass in the shade and let them pass by. I think it was well that I was idle, for then my flowers were in bud." Superficial busyness blocks fallow ripening. A pregnant, earnest leisure is the pace of peace.

In other poems, readiness for new levels of realization is expressed in the image of pilgrimage, an active search, an intentional priority, for a deeper life: "The night is dark and thy pilgrim is blinded . . . this wayside becomes a terror to me . . . I pray for thy own morning light." Expectation and preparation can be metaphorized as a beggar's seeking: "I felt

I was poor, and from door to door went with my hunger."
Tagore once confessed in a letter to a close friend; "I carry
an infinite space of loneliness around my soul." Instead of
breaking under or trying to escape from that loneliness, he
activated it as a condition of attention and receptivity. In
Tagore's poetic psychology, the first step to inner peace is a
readiness, an expectant openness, a dynamic search to find a
world beyond mundane preoccupation.

Tagore's literary voice changes gender, age, social position, but along with dynamic yearning and waiting, further
pursues the classic stations of inner peace, such as the theme
of solitude. The mysterious boatman of the Far Shore appears
to the farm wife only after the market has closed and other
vendors have departed. "They walk away in their different
paths leaving me behind; if I am alone, still it is sweet to listen
for thy footsteps."

Along with solitude goes selectivity: "Let my song be
simple as waking in the morning, as the dripping of dew from
the leaves." In fact, despite family wealth, Tagore inhabited
austere cottages and donated his personal earnings to his
school at Shantiniketan. After his adolescence, he was never
free of the struggle for economic survival and the mundane
financial strains that tugged at Shantiniketan as they do on all
institutions. This did not complicate his life, but compelled
him to simplify it. Though born a rich kid, Rabindranath
shared with the rest of us the bipolar struggle to earn money
and preserve spiritual freedom at the same time.

The world of Tagore's search for peace is marked by an
attitude of holding, humble waiting and searching, simplicity
and solitude, endurance, and detachment from convention.
It is a world metaphorized as that of a young, poor girl in
a feudal patriarchy. Her external helplessness belies the fire
of hope and feminine passion that is destined to bear new
life. Her destitution charges her with courage and determination. She has nothing to lose. She sets forth on her road:

"It stretches its beckoning hand towards me; its silence calls me out of my home .... It leads me on I know not to what abandonment . . . I know not where its windings end."

We know that Tagore was a city boy who was released into nature during adolescence, and if he is nothing else as a poet, he is a nature poet. Seeking peace, he drenched himself in the outdoors: "I am a bee that has wallowed in the heart of thy golden dawn." His identification with natural scenes and moods was so complete that he felt nature spoke and acted on his behalf: "The earth is waiting . . . let me feel in her grass and meadow flowers the spread of my own salutation." Through nature, he himself greeted the secret serenity in the heart of things.

Borrowing from Indian poetic and devotional traditions, Tagore created a malleable, metaphorical relationship to the Other, to life, and to the world. In his varying experiences, the Other is always present yet always different in form, which is only a symbol for an undefinable possibility. Tagore can capture the qualities of his own peace by describing it as encountering and relating to Someone who is responsive and alive in the world beside him. The Other symbolizes the fulfillment of the quest upon which the seeker set out alone and vulnerable, yet called and faithful.

In union with a sense of perspective that places individual life within an eternal context, the pain of life can be seen in retrospect as having been a helpful provocation to a serious search, the way that sexuality is the necessary stimulus to mating and procreative fulfillment: "Thou hast done well, my lover, thou hast done well to send me thy fire of pain." Having placed himself within a greater whole, Tagore now finds the joy of *continuous relatedness to his highest values and ultimate concerns:* "There is a secret joy in the bosom of the night . . . the joy of the midnight forest in its hoarded bird-songs." The darkness is full of potential.

But his relationship to life, his deepest self, is never finalized or static. He is a *balākā*, a life in flight. His nimbus interactions play through all the vicissitudes of the emotional sky. He is like us, filled with conflict and turmoil. His peace isn't a monotone, but a song with verse and chorus. He may hide to evade unpleasant truths. He may be provoked by passion. He may fling himself into wild, dangerous love like a reckless adolescent girl.

> *You troubled my heart from ripples into*
> *waves, rocking the red lotus of love.*
> *You asked me to come out with you into*
> *the secret of life. . .*
> *Through the patter of rain I hear your nearing*
> *   footsteps . . .*
> *I walk to your side and put my hand into*
> *   yours, while*
> *your eyes burn and water*
> *drips from your hair.*

He may turn cautious and isolative, or may insult life and push it away. He may find himself stirred internally by dreams and moods. He may have the gall to chastise life like an Old Testament prophet, feeling that if there is an Other, that Other has an obligation: "That the bud has not bloomed in beauty in my life spreads sadness in the heart of creation." He may stamp and demand: "Much have you given to me, yet I ask for more—-Not for guidance to the door alone, but to the Master's hall; not only for the gift of love, but for the lover himself." There is no attitude or mood, no matter how earthy or impious, that is fundamentally damaging. Tagore rejects none of himself. He has no concept of sin. His own selfishness, stubbornness, blindness are aspects of his relationship that affirm the reality of that relationship. Real relationships with real people are full of mortal folly. Since the Relationship is also about reality, it, too, has room for—in fact, utilizes and thrives upon—the child in man, the girl in the father, the fool in the sage. Unlike religious relationships with God that strive for an ideal of holiness or obedience, Tagore's attunement to affirmation engaged him in a Relationship that grew, the more of him that it could contain. That life surrounded and held him no matter where he stood was proof to him that his existence was significant to Someone.

He may rebel and blame, yet find himself ironically blessed: "Rebelliously I put out the light in my house and your sky surprised me with its stars." He may feel awe at the real dimension of his life: "and I saw that we were playing unafraid in the silent courtyard of our King's palace." He may feel the entire world is related to him as a friend, a comrade, a playmate.

In this affirming sense of meaning and purpose for individual life in cosmic time, as personified by a Relationship, Tagore may feel confirmed in his worldliness and impiety when he imagines being told, "you kept all the doors open in your house .... With the wild crowd I came to you again and again unknown and unbidden. Had you kept shut your doors in wise seclusion, how could I have found my way into your house?" This last theme—*the refusal to cleave between mundane and sacred action*—is the core of Tagore's steadying gift. Because he felt no activity or person was intrinsically outcast, he lived saturated in a mothering, soothing presence. No niche was unnoticed, no potential lost; even what he failed to do had relational significance: "my melodies still unstruck are clinging to some lute-strings of thine, and they are not altogether lost." This way of knowing the world was the cornerstone of Tagore's sense of peace: "let me find my peace in thy presence."

I hope I have made it clear that the varying presence upon which Tagore's peace rested should not be misunderstood as a theological deity. It had no fixed name, form, doctrine, or church. It was a nurtured attitude, a felt relation, alive, real, yet elusive and ungraspable. It was a variable personification for each event and for All. Although Tagore did refer to the word "God" he was not conventionally religious. He broke away from the Hindu reform sect that his father had led and that he himself had briefly captained.

Just as the speaker in Tagore's spiritual songs changes from man to woman, from rich to poor, and just as the relationship with "Thee" is portrayed as varying from vassal to king, lover to lover, friend to comrade, the Other is also a person, an interaction, but not a known object. The Ultimate is another subjective, a "you" or a "thou," who is known at transitions and edges, by hints and intuitions: "I try to gaze at thy face and know not for certain if thou art seen." Peace is known through love, the measure of which is hope: "Why does this foolish heart recklessly launch its hope on the sea whose end it does not know?" As the quest begins in solitary waiting, the capacity to endure uncertainty continues to move the life of peace forward: "I know not if I have found him or I am seeking him everywhere, if it is a pang of bliss or of pain." Due to his receptivity and affirmative openness, Tagore repeatedly experiences himself as beneficiary of the simple, great gifts: the morning's golden goblet filled with light; the quenching water of life, and the moon and stars, lighting the lamps of the tropical night.

> *My guide comes with a lamp and beckons me.*
> *I ask his name.*
> *But I only see his light through the silence*
> *and feel his smile filling the darkness.*

Tagore's nameless peace giver can only be felt. The very elusiveness in the secret of being is what kindles human love. The fact that peace cannot be known by any other way than the heart is what is so evocative and commanding, for, according to Tagore, people love most deeply the invisible harmony and grace within things. To seek is a deeper love than to hold. The "Balākā" is animated by search, not by entrenchment. What we feel but can't know makes us sing. The nameless mystery, not the material fact, is what brings us moods of peace.

> *You hide yourself in your own glory, my*
>   *King.*
> *The sand-grain and the dew-drop are*
>   *more proudly apparent than yourself . . .*
> *You make room for us while standing*
>   *aside in silence; therefore love lights her*
>   *own lamp to seek you and comes to your*
>   *worship unbidden.*

Tagore's poetic universe may be intellectually unsettling to the rational thinker, for his equation has no fixed constant, and the poet, love, and the Presence are all polymorphous, suggestive, and transitional. Tagore's peaceful, yea-saying tone rests on an antecedent attitude: *reverence,* reverence as a preconception before any content. Tagore's world may be painful and his tone of voice querulous, but everything is wrapped and treasured. To absorb his teaching is to live every event with the conviction that it's a blessing. He reminds us to feel cradled and grateful.

In the deepening realization that his own reverence is itself the action of the very You that it seeks, Tagore finds silence, stillness, peace: "stand mute before him for a while gazing at his face; then leave thy house and go out with him in silence." The oracle to which Tagore ultimately listens is pure silence: "I have wandered in pursuit of voices that drew me yet led me nowhere. Now let me sit in peace and listen to thy words in the soul of my silence." Human insignificance, so shatteringly powerful to an observer of the stars like Tagore, is canceled by the knowledge that human love could not exist if the universe, of which humans are a part, weren't capable of love. The universe must certainly receive human love, because human love is only the name given to a small discrete unit of its own love. "Thou hast given me thy love, filling the world with thy gifts. . . . And I know that in return thou wilt receive from me a little flower of love."

Tagore's inner peace flowed from the only source of inner peace, the one spring where the river arises. The play of his poetic symbolism reveals not a religion, but a psychology. He transcended psychic pain, loss, confusion, despair, because he found a way to transform those states as they arose within him. Rather than rejecting, fighting, repressing them, he quickly affirmed and elevated his mental pain. Holding it aloft, he offered it back to the living universe with its pulsing heart—to the presence he felt on the other side of every experience. This did not lead to sticky-sweet caretaking. The universe is too vast for that. Inner peace is found in the fact that inevitable pain—for Tagore, the death of his wife and four children as he entered his mature years—can pull the individual back to consciousness of larger dimensions than private happiness.

Tagore's peace flowed from the knowledge that human pain is the method by which we sort out our ultimate meanings from among trivial ones. "Hold thy faith firm, my heart . . . . The day is near when thy burden will become thy gift, and thy sufferings will light up thy path." Sadness and pain are the bridges across which an individual moves toward divinely held peace: "The peace of sadness is in my heart like the brooding silence upon the master's lute before the music begins." The seeker of this unifying life must pass through suffering and pain, in order to understand his or her transience and his or her dependence upon larger forces: "incense never yields its perfume till it burns." Peace resides in the confirmation of a love and purpose for each person within a vast cosmic harmony, in the abiding presence of an entryway that opens to the ultimate from every mundane moment. "I gleaned sorrow while seeking for joy, but the sorrow which you sent to me has turned to joy . . . while I wandered from door to door, every step led me to your gate."

The result of Tagore's efforts was an outpost on the highest altitudes of spiritual integration: "Let thy love's sunshine kiss the peaks of my thoughts and linger in my life's valley, where the harvest ripens." "Stand in my lonely evening where my heart watches alone; fill her cup of solitude, and let me feel in me the infinity of thy love." "Let thy love . . . pass through my heart into all my movements . . . let me carry thy love in my life as a harp does its music."

EVEN THESE POETIC ECSTASIES don't capture Rabindranath Tagore's final vision of peace, which grew as he grew, as he read, thought, meditated, and experienced. His vision penetrates even one more veil.

Tagore's sense of peace rested upon his interaction with the You that is the presence, continuously interactive throughout life; and his own form of service to the You was poetry; but Tagore did not imagine that the universe was run by an anthropomorphic deity. Every image he created of the divine, every aspect of his relationship with the You, was, he felt, after all, the product of his own mind, his own projection. He didn't believe in these poetic symbols as external realities, but he utilized them to understand himself. Such heartfelt projective participation in the universe is necessary for fulfillment of the human heart, he felt. The metaphor of God as personlike was a way station by which he could feel with human feelings connection to higher truths. At the highest stages of peace, the You loses face, name, even "You" disappears. Peaceful, integrative, harmonious tranquillity remains. At last, Tagore passed beyond even the presence that had sustained him.

> *. . . life's stream touches the deep; and the world of forms comes to its nest in the beauty beyond all forms.*
> *My heart bends in worship like a dew laden flower, and I feel the flood of my life rushing to the endless.*

In this ultimate unison with being, there is no longer even "God" or "You"—just the formlessness beyond all mind and matter—*pure peace.*

Tagore cannot be correctly understood as either a theist or an atheist. His metaphors and attitudes cannot be extracted beyond his poetry. Although for a long period of years he referred to his "life-god doctrine" and claimed it was central to his thought, this "doctrine" was a protean cloud of sentiments, Hindu philosophy, Islamic poetic conventions—a descriptive term for an opus of art. Later, Tagore abandoned this term entirely, having outgrown the need for self-referential consistency. He donned and doffed philosophies, divinities, and similes with artistic license. He shattered categories, like a migrating gander, orienting himself by keeping his gaze on inner peace.

In his ultimate reverence for formless peace, he is closest to the Buddha.

"I have reached the brink of the shoreless sea to take my plunge and lose myself forever." In his final poetry, written as he was aged and bedridden, he described how he observed his bodily sensations objectively, like Thoreau dying, like Muir mountaineering, a calm and detached witness to the peace beyond his personal shores—similar to the Buddha's Vipassana meditation. At the borderland of life and death, Tagore passed beyond the island of his body into the sea.

I saw, in the twilight of lagging consciousness,
My body floating down an ink-black stream
With its mass of feelings, with its varied
  emotion . . .
Its outlines dimmed . . .
As shadow, as particles,
  my body
Fused with endless night.

For Tagore, peace was a realization that initially used divine imagery, but ultimately penetrated beyond conscious ideas and forms to a fusion with transcendent, indescribable peace. Through his varying images and practices he found malleable renewal of life in reference to formless peace beyond self.

Chapter 23

PEACE IS
PARTICIPATION

AMONG THOSE WHO PASSED through the cloud chamber of existence and left a track of inner peace to hover behind them and to guide those who follow, none left a more exquisite trace or lived a more complete life than Rabindranath Tagore. His life is exemplary of a life of inner peace and participation. He mastered and manifested the intricate rhythm of solitude alternating with service in an atmosphere of dynamic harmony. He participated in every sphere, an energetic and active life with a broad sweep of interests that brought him into contact with a world fellowship, a bold life of competence and engagement. Yet his residual vapor unambiguously condenses into peace.

The peace that Tagore basked in did not transform him into a sedative sage. Out of this peace emerged a whirlwind. The goal of peace was to catalyze a fearless plunge into creative action. For Tagore, the true measure of the depth of peace was the amount of giving it stirred. Sublimated ferocity, a sword of nonviolence, flashed out of Tagore's inner peace.

Tagore's sublime tranquility inspired poems that have been accused of being saccharine, but his complete poetic vision wraps the whole human emotional landscape into a unity. Rage and terror, held in nets of harmony and love, energize heraldic struggle. He courted the storm to capture its force. His peace, like migrating swans drunk with joy of the wind, was filled with the animation of unstoppable life. Struggle, pain, tenacity, endurance are not antithetical to peace; they are the streams that flow out from its spring. "Who is awake all alone in this sleeping earth? . . . in the depth of the pain of my being?" Pain is creative force. Peace is as deep as the emotion it can circle and contain. Such an elastic peace can't be punctured by vibrant and committed daily life.

From Tagore's example we can discern a general principle important to all of us. The service that springs out of peace is not to be mistaken for do-gooding. It isn't an action to be measured by external criteria. True peaceful service can be recognized neither when it is participating in group protest nor when it is aloof. It can't be affirmed by anyone else's approval. It will not follow the straight lines laid out by a profession or by noble political or social movements. It is far from denominational missionary fervor, or from political jostling by those who need to preach to others to hide their own brokenness.

The service that springs from peace is the idiosyncratic, particular fruition of a seed that has found its nourishing soil. It is the overflow of a well that has struck the underground source. It has its own interior origin, and its own rhythm of growth or dormancy. It is independent of someone else's measurable accomplishment, since its origins and intentions are in eternity. Yet to the person who has touched down into it and in whom it wells up with fulminant pressure, it is unstoppable. It bursts open the seed case. It floods the walkway. It turns firm ground to morass. It destroys what was built so carefully with prudence and, without offering reassurance or goal, it commands setting forth in an unknown direction, like Tagore's adolescent girl. Under the power of such a call, a person disappoints friends and confounds well-wishers, who spy in his or her clumsy forays something benighted or neurotic. We can't name it even for ourselves, but as soon as we stop or attempt to tame it, it surges through us again, and we come to know it only as a particular direction that we remember once naïvely courting. It kindles motion that fills us like sap, and our leaves open, and the sky comes nearer, and the winds of life turn what had been personal gyrations into the rustle and music of foliage in the canopy of life.

Tagore combined in his worldview the passive supplicant, bowed down, that has been stereotyped as "Eastern" or "mystical" or "feminine," alongside the active, political, and forceful. This fusion, or completeness, is one element of the intimate adoration that his best writing provokes in so many readers. He makes us feel whole and understood in both our turmoil and our elevation. Tagore's ability to connect us to peace at the very moment we feel most bereft of it makes his work saving, integrating, and animating. He evokes a peace that can be stretched and tightened but never broken.

There was no greater admirer of Gurudev's songs than Gandhiji. In the horrible days of the partition of India and Pakistan, when Gandhi's twin life works of an independent, unified India attained through nonviolence both smoldered in ruins about him, and when he set off alone—banishing all his followers—barefoot through the violence-torn villages of Noakhali, observers reported that the aged, bony, heavy-hearted ascetic took along with him his most reliable talisman of peace: his memorized repertoire of Tagore's songs.

THE PEACE THAT TAGORE CULTIVATED AND EX-PRESSED led this son of the Himalayan Maharshi to far-flung participation on a world stage. In his view, the most authentic outcome measure of peace was action on behalf of undivided humanity. Women, children, rural poor, and conquered peoples captured his sympathies, but men and conquerors were included in his embrace. His peace sprang from and strove for a seamless world. The second half of Tagore's life is emblematic of the practical, political, esthetic relevance of one man's depth of inner peace. His apparently personal, interior quest provided him the power to address the problems of millions. His fertile remove ultimately enabled him to have an extraordinary engagement in the eternal play of peace and perplexity in history.

Tagore was a member of a race considered too inferior to rule itself; and he wrote in a language as obscure to the English speaking world today as it was at the turn of the twentieth century. Then, on an inspiration that he could never explain, he translated some of his songs into English and carried them by ship to England, where they stirred reverential, almost disbelieving awe among the leading intellectuals of the age, like Yeats. Before the close of the same year, Rabindranath Tagore became the first non-European to win the Nobel Prize for Literature (1913). For the next quarter of a century, the honors and adoration were to flow at an unparalleled level, as he spread peace to a congregation that covered the world.

The activities of Tagore's mature and late years occurred on a canvas so broad that they fill many chapters of his biographies. Like the *balākā* he was, he flew the mighty arc of the homeless bird. Here I can give only a highlighted, impressionistic outline.

Tagore was honored with knighthood of the British Empire. Many of his books still can be found in local libraries today bearing the author's name, *Sir* Rabindranath Tagore. After British-led Indian troops massacred hundreds of unarmed civilians at Jallianwalla Bagh in the Punjab in 1919, Tagore renounced his knighthood, saying he was thereby intending to be "giving voice to the protest of the millions of my countrymen, surprised into a dumb anguish of terror. The time has come when badges of honour make our shame glaring . . . and I for my part wish to stand, shorn of all special distinctions." This moral rejection of a membership intended to be above politics embittered both the British government and many of his closest British friends, and left him the subject of continuous political repression for the rest of his life. The defiant boyhood truant still cultivated his purity, now in a socially potent way.

In an era before airplanes, Tagore covered the globe making personal contacts with readers and with intellectuals worldwide. The excitement attending upon his tours was never again equaled by any artists until the Beatles. He toured America several times, and lectured at Harvard, the University of Chicago, and scores of other universities and cities. He toured Europe multiple times, where in countries like Germany and Denmark crowds ". . . worshiped the ground he trod . . ." and millions of copies of his books were translated and sold. His 1926 tour through Norway, Sweden, Denmark, Germany, Hungary, Yugoslavia, Bulgaria, Turkey, and Greece was described as ". . . an emotional wave that rolled from one end of Europe to the other." Tagore's privately cultivated inner peace had become an intoxicating nectar imbibed by millions. He had princely receptions, and was greeted as a prophet. He visited Japan on several occasions. Initially adored as the liberator of Asian poetry from European constrictions, he later assailed the Japanese with fearless public defiance, overlooking the politeness expected of a guest, because of his abhorrence of growing Japanese militarization in the 1920s and 1930s. He visited post-Revolutionary Russia, where he praised economic progress for rural peoples but forcefully criticized the suppression of individual liberty. Given characteristic adulation by the Shah of Persia and wildly enthusiastic crowds greeting him as the poet of Asia speaking free of imperialism, he was still courted by England's great intellectuals, and, in 1930 gave the Hibbert Lectures at Oxford reserved for "distinguished philosophers."

As the aging, gray-bearded, long-haired, robed, six-foot three-inch Gurudev swept over the planet again and again during the teens, twenties, and thirties of this century, he was ironically acclaimed as a flowery mystic at the same time that he was fomenting recurrent confrontation on political immediacies. The poet of peace touched individual hearts at the same time that he was attacking imperialism, militarism, and racism. In between his world tours, he could be found at Shantiniketan, writing seasonal rituals for children, or alone in his own sparse quarters, writing, writing, writing. The most fiery anti-British nationalists, like Subhas Chandra Bose, came to Shantiniketan to bow down before Rabindranath to gain the poet's blessing.

As Tagore approached death in his early eighties, he continued to function as moral spokesman, teacher, and poet of peace. During his final years, he remained prolific. His last poetry continued to mix active political awareness of the European Theatre of 1940 and 1941 with sublime references from the Upanishads and open-minded questions about life's ultimate meanings. The last word in the last poem in his last translated volume—written shortly before he lapsed into a coma and died was "peace."

THE DEPTH OF TAGORE'S inner peace gave birth to a poetic voice uninhibited and unreserved. He exudes faith without a trace of prevarication. Tagore calls us to open widely to our ultimate capacities. He chastises not merely the cynical, but even the tentative. Many modern readers recoil from his call to soar toward infinite possibility. Tagore threatens intellectual, self-protective caution. He leaves no room for sophisticated aloofness. He stretches our wings; he urges flight. His writing provides a trail of light where mere attainments like genius or Nobel Prizes are transcended. He speaks for orphans and girls and the terminally ill. He provokes us readers, as he provoked the British government, the Japanese militants, the American materialists, the Soviet anti-individualists, the Gandhian pastoralists. His writing stimulates inspiration in some of us but defensive envy and ridicule in others. His personal and literary residue is unabashed boyish devotion to honesty, love, beauty, like an adolescent who is millions of years old. He can't be winked down to apostasy. He constantly dares us to ascend. Modern readers who can't dream of roofless peace recoil to a chary cynicism. Some twenty-first-century readers need to be supercilious toward this shameless heraldic poet, who crisscrossed earth lofted on song. Tagore's peace is based on arms-outstretched welcoming. To him, the world with all its shattering vicissitudes was greeted as his *Guest.* "Guests of my life . . . . after you had taken your leave I found God's footprints on my floor."

Tagore's literary reputation in the West has declined so precipitously (though not in India, where he continues to reign as *The Poet*) because his faith is embarrassing in an era of doubt, his spirituality is threatening in a materialistic society, his praise of sacrifice is incomprehensible to hedonists, his effusiveness chastises pragmatic reserve, and his love affair with death and beyond is incomprehensible to people who have mistaken technology for science and hypothesis for conclusion, and who therefore cannot envision any world other than that of their own material senses. Like all classics, however, his great works, revealing a psychology for living, continue to speak to thousands of individuals. Fresh translations of his poetry and prose continue to appear.

If you read him, you will find yourself inspired to follow all the stages of inner peace: to enshrine peace as your goal, to pursue it in a dynamic, accepting, changing way, to cultivate a modicum of simplicity, to drink in the beauty of rivers and mountains, to study wisdom in the word, to confront your suffering as a gift, and to see your life objectively in the light of cosmic time and personal death, to seek solitude, and to emerge social, scientific, educated, and inspired by personal relationship with the formless. Tagore's devotees will be school teachers and social workers and organic farmers whose actions take root in a presence from eternity whose essence is peace. Eschewing any division between the worldly and the mystical, Tagore said that he slept and dreamed that life was love; but he woke and saw that life was action; then he acted, and realized that action was love.

It is very rare that history emits a man at once so brilliant, so moral, so personally impeccable and warmly engaged, embodying virtue heaped upon reason, and sonorous with poetry, who transcended mundane concerns and brought to bear upon duration the expanse of infinite hope, at the same time that he was planning school lessons or giving public talks. In the scope of his accomplishments and his attention to the ordinary, Tagore's achievements confirm our own jobs, families, politics and bereavements as the best and only soil of our sapling peace. Tagore's life story reveals that inner peace is stillness but not stasis. He reminds us that inside the babble of our daily chores, invitations and caretaking, live the greatest poems and the wingbeats of wild swans.

PART IX

Chapter *24*

PEACE IS PURITY

THE NUCLEUS OF INNER PEACE is purity of heart and mind. When you say, "I want inner peace," you mean that you want to be able to live with what's inside you, to be at ease in the depths of yourself; and that integrated positivity, without cracks or seams, is called "purity."

To illustrate what is meant by purity, I'll tell you of an experience I had about twenty years ago while my wife and I were young travelers in India. One evening we arrived at a Hindu temple in a Himalayan valley through which flowed a tributary of the holy Ganges. The temple was jammed with salty peasants from the austere uplands of terraced rice paddies, and inside, a priest was slowly, methodically, rhythmically smashing a huge bronze gong, which resonated with deafening intensity. We entered and sat on the floor amidst the throng of silenced and transfixed hill-farm families. The gong pulsed so loudly that it shattered our minds, cutting down our thoughts to stubble. This was the evening meditation for the villagers and for the pilgrims who were wandering upward into the sacred mountains. The gong scythed out all troubling thoughts and feelings. Everyone on the temple floor was temporarily relieved of worry, distraction, or confusion, and our minds were of necessity emptied and focused by the monotonic sound. The long day, with its labor, uncertainty, ill-health, quarrels, and bare feet could end in forgetful focus. Anger and dread were driven underground.

The gong's ear-splitting intrusion into our beings dissolved inner tension and layered a zone of mental silence over our lives. This seemed like an understandable way to end a choiceless and chilly autumn day in a poor and rocky life.

This gong unforgettably illustrated the principle underlying many kinds of meditation, including hypnotic drumming or repetition of a mantra. Calm is induced by the repression of mental activity through the creation of one fixed vibration. Silent meditation functions differently, with different goals and methods, suited to different individuals or different karmic situations.

Where living conditions are more optimistic and there can be more hope for deepened calm, silent meditation can function in the opposite way from meditation with a gong. Meditation without a gong, a mantra, or a mental picture permits distress to rise up, rather than be squelched, and the meditator, instead of inducing forgetful trance, is mirrored in the silence of his or her own mind. In silent, wordless, imageless meditation, the files of one's own memory, thought, and action are exposed to internal illumination. This sort of meditation can froth with distress that cannot be alleviated merely by driving the demons back underground with amnestic cymbals, but only by changing one's entire life. By changing how you live, the residue of your thoughts and feelings as you perceive them in your meditation will be sweetened. Then, what you say, do, think, and feel, when it rises back up in your silent mind, won't need to be squelched. This kind of meditation induces a dialogue, a feedback loop, between active life and meditation, so that life becomes entrained behind awareness and calm. This is what is meant by "purity": cultivating a way of life that you can live with.

Silent meditation isn't a way of forgetting but a way of being unable to forget, an instant replay of your own game. Through silent meditation, we cultivate purity not because we want to avoid hell in some afterlife, but because we want to avoid watching ourselves stumble awkwardly across the internal silent screen. A lifelong commitment to this sort of self-awareness naturally purifies life, deleting whatever is incompatible with silent, tranquil peace. The more rigorously we immerse ourselves in ourselves, the nicer a person we're going to want to be. Purity means being able to relax with who we really are. By this I don't mean mere self-acceptance, but self-transformation, so that wherever we penetrate we find no hindrance or harm. We stop shocking ourselves. Meditation focused on purification isn't something we do to overcome our day, but what we do to guide our day toward sustainable peace of heart.

Inner peace built on purity isn't just psychological; it's a positive circle of action, reflection, and purification: actions that help, purification of states of mind that hurt. When we live with the ramifications of our thoughts, when our view is unsheltered from the effects of our deeds, we will spontaneously want to feel as if light could shine through us from any direction. Deep meditation is built over the realization that what harms us harms others, and that what helps us helps others. Every thought and act that separates us will also bring disharmony in its wake.

Purity is freedom from anger, fear, and passion, the narcissistic emotions. Conversely, love, compassion, sympathetic joy, and equanimity—all pure moments—are boundary-crossers, unifiers, so that purity is always selfless and universal in reach. Purity means egoless, non-self-referential life. Physically, there may be a center of the universe somewhere in the axis of the Milky Way, but meditation reveals that the transformative center of the world will well up inside of us in any pure moment.

If you think back through the many approaches to inner peace discussed in the preceding eight parts of this book, you will see that they are all aspects of, or avenues toward, purity. A dynamic focus on peace, a selective life, a thoughtful, informed, compassionate, and natural life that appreciates the catalytic role of sorrow and the ameliorating beneficence of social service and a realistic perspective, are all spokes on a wheel whose hub is purity of heart. No matter where we start—even if it is opposite to someone else's starting place on the wheel—if peace is our goal, we want to deepen our gongless purity. Meditation based on purity is exposing rather than soothing, and it elucidates where real, external lifestyle changes can be reflected to shine internally as peace of mind. It is unambiguously ethical. It stresses insight rather than amnesia.

Meditation that focuses on the direct purification of the mind is called Vipassana meditation, and it provides access to the deepest peace. "Vipassana" means "insight" in an ancient Indian language, Pāli, in which the Buddha's teaching is preserved, and Vipassana is the meditation technique that the Buddha taught and practiced. Vipassana isn't Buddhism—the organized religion that congealed around the Buddha's teaching after his death—but is a depth psychology, a systematic transmission of objectively observable truths. Although Vipassana has been preserved by the Buddhist community, it is in itself a nonsectarian method of self-observation that can be practiced by anyone, regardless of previous religion or lack thereof.

The Buddha himself emphasized that Vipassana was not a discovery unique to him, but a rediscovery of the teaching of all the Buddhas, which can be taken to mean, in a Western historical sense, that Vipassana can be rediscovered by anyone who seeks eternal peace. As I have commented from time to time throughout this book, elements of Vipassana seemed to well up spontaneously in the lives of Henry Thoreau, John Muir, Mohandas Gandhi, and Rabindranath Tagore, and subtler traces of it can probably be discovered in your own life because it is a natural process. But the specificity of Vipassana as the Buddha taught it shouldn't be confused with the pied personal texture of its fragments within particular people. Elements of Vipassana recur in lives that don't exemplify or complete it. The Buddha's teaching of Vipassana was complete and free of unnecessary extras. Vipassana as the Buddha taught it is exactly and only the path to Nibbāna.

Nibbāna is unshakable inner peace, absolute purity that is defined by what it isn't: not desire, not fear, not anger. It is freedom from wish or fantasy, pure reality unimpeded by egocentric blinders. It is insight into the cause of suffering, and release from suffering. The Pāli language roots of the word "Nibbāna" are variously taken to mean "no arrow," meaning no higher goal to be reached in life; or "no wind," meaning beyond all turmoil and change.

Nibbāna can also be defined as the culmination of mental purity—that is, the elimination of all contaminating wishes, anxieties, and viewpoints. It is the extinction of craving and aversion, the peace of impersonal perspective, eternal peace realized in this moment.

Cultivation of mental purity to the highest level of perfection is the Nibbāna the Buddha attained, and the goal of the path he taught. Those peace-seekers of various backgrounds who never heard of Buddha nor Nibbāna, or who chose different nomenclature for their quest, or who didn't get quite as far, all concur on this quintessential role of purity. When shaggy, wild, unemployed John Muir was wandering in the Sierra wilderness, refusing job offers from Harvard and the Boston Academy of Sciences, his goal was not merely to study geology and natural history, but to "keep your mind untrammeled and pure." Gandhi declared, "True beauty consists in purity of heart."

Divisive mental states, like self-appropriation, hatred, and anxiety, shatter mental harmony. Those attributes of the mind that are free of negativity and that are affiliative, healing, helping, are called "pure" because they produce both interpersonal bonds and inner peace. What the Nearings cultivated in their garden, what Thoreau reported in his journal, what Tagore lived and sang, were attempts to purify themselves, to unite rather than to divide. The path to Nibbāna is only a rigorous delineation of common sense: cultivate a peace-giving mind and abandon all that harms us and others.

The laws of nature are simple: the peace of a pure heart comes from doing what helps oneself and others, and from avoiding what harms oneself and others, both in action and in thought. Ethics and harmony are the same thing.

Purity understood in this way has nothing to do with the moralistic condemnation with which the term has come to be associated in colloquial English, with its historical links to religious intolerance. Purity in the context that Muir and Gandhi understood, and as it is taught in the Vipassana tradition, is less like excision and more like distillation. From real insight into our own well-being, we let go of irritants that we no longer misconstrue as pleasure.

The process of mental purification can be analogized to the skies two nights after the full moon. Darkness has already established its kingdom. Stars mottle the sky. Slowly the moon ascends above the top of the distant pines, casting around and ahead of itself a continuously changing light that enamels the visible world. The spreading sheen absorbs both darkness and individual starlight, until the world is visible in a new light that equally eliminates the golden stars and their black interstices. A single penetrating focus has revealed that in heaven everything can be seen clearly.

This metaphor is very different from that of filth evicted by goodness, or sin expunged by external redemption. Purity is based on the natural process of change. It isn't a consequence of rejection but of neutral, observing light that abolishes nothing but illuminates everything. There is no need to judge and ostracize, the negativity of which would contradict purity itself. Instead, purity expands its presence by a growing glow of insight.

HOW CAN SUCH A SPIRITUAL IDEAL really be approached by an average sweating mortal? The Vipassana tradition is alive and well today, accepting ordinary people from all walks of life. Having been such a student myself many times, and having been a volunteer to guide hundreds of students through such experiences, I'd like to take you into the minds of a group of people attending their first ten-day Vipassana retreat.

A person who applied to take a Vipassana meditation course would receive a packet of preliminary information describing a codified, concentrated training in a common-sense approach to equanimity via mental purification. The prospective student would have to stay for ten days, temporarily subsuming themselves to a regulated schedule starting at 4 a.m. and ending at 9 p.m., and this commitment would propel forward their cherished aspirations toward inner peace.

Arriving at the Vipassana Meditation Center at Shelburne, Massachusetts (one of dozens of centers found throughout the world),* the new students have some idea what to expect, having read the introductory information from the dhamma. org website or from the packet that arrived in the mail. They are white, black, or brown, employed or a mother, she or he, an Ivy League dean or an unemployed member of Alcoholics Anonymous. They may have a diffuse intuition as to why they have come, or a particular goal they hope to attain (which they may find themselves dramatically revising).

As they walk the dandelion-spangled grass while waiting for the course to begin, they may be surprised to find themselves reexperiencing the mild Richter-scale of summer-camp homesickness that they haven't felt for ten or thirty years—after all, married or single, with four grown children or a young doctor-in-demand, they have come here alone, to take a step backward from surface distractions and turn their attention within.

Around them on the small campus of tents, cabins, and buildings, there is a hubbub of unpacking, old friends meeting, families departing—the exciting loneliness of a green, rural train station accepting passengers on a hopeful departure, rumbling with new beginnings.

They meet fellow students here or there as they register or unpack, and feel intimidated or leery or warmly surprised by the elderly grandmother from New York whose doctor recommended the course to her, or by the local carpenter who is back for the fourth consecutive year. Slowly the anticipated time stretches through the afternoon; suddenly in the evening they are seated in a row on the floor of a silent hall. A window shade rises in the house of their mind, and they are alone and can begin to live with themselves in a private moonlight.

Their Vipassana course will be ten days in the atmosphere of noble silence: ten days free of telephone, conversation,

---

*For more information about Vipassana centers, see Notes.

books and mail, ten days of unpunctured solitude in supportive, kindred company. It will also be ten days of safety under the guidance of volunteer teachers who have spent decades or more practicing the technique themselves under the same course guidelines and conditions, inheriting a tradition stemming from an unimpeachable eruption of mental purity in human history. The hall where they are seated with fifty or a hundred other people has an atmosphere of ruddered, communal listening to directions that derive from a successful historical apogee. Absorbing the opening formalities, the students find they are listening as if to a voice from within themselves.

The students are asked to internalize the emanations of quiet, determined truth-seeking by three acts of mental sanctuary. First, they "take refuge in the Buddha," meaning in the capacity of a human being to be peaceful, selfless, free of bondage to conditions of historical accident, a seeker of universal truth. Enlightenment, personified by the Buddha, is incipient in anyone. The Buddha isn't a historical person or a religious leader, but a personification of the seed of purity in everyone. Next, they "take refuge in the Dhamma," meaning in the order and coherence of the universe, the lawfulness of physics and psychology that enables a path to exist, a teaching to be conveyed. The students will aspire to follow truth, not comfort and illusion. Third, the students "take refuge in the Saṅgha," meaning in the humanness of their enterprise, the person-to-person inspiration, guidance, and friendship of those who have had the glimpse to those who are in shadows. Alone in silence, the students are also in wise, caretaking company.

Now that they have girded themselves in safekeeping of their own best wishes, they are ready for another mental step: commitment to precepts, to behavior that expresses the goal. This step, like every step, is directly targeted, logical, consistent. Before the airplane flies, it is pointed on the runway. Before meditation, there is a facilitory position to take: "I will not kill, steal, lie, become intoxicated, or commit sexual misconduct." Peace is based on a kind and caretaking life. This is a school of self-responsible self-restraint.

Meditation begins that evening in the half-lit hall. The students are directed to focus their attention on breath passing in and out of their nostrils, a quiet, invisible touch of their own life, a subtle, sometimes elusive focus for a mind more used to data processing, diagnosis, or diapers. The students doze and wake, oversoothed into somnolence by the sudden dimming of daily clamor.

That night they sleep exhausted, or they anxiously lie rigid over sleep all night, and arise at 4 a.m. to begin three days of reminders, explanations, and their own solitary repetitive effort to master a cascading and slippery mind.

From within, as the students try to focus on the bare sensation of breath at their nostrils, they find themselves bombarded by the lives they have lived: memories, wishes, fantasies, and plans, sluicing past the diaphanous gate of their effort to concentrate on the soft fact of breath. At times the students seem to be drowning in reminders: to call their accountant when they get home, to buy a new sofa, and to write to their father. The students almost cry, feeling asthmatic with frustration of mental dyscontrol that has underlain consciousness all their life but has never been exposed before. No one can do what the student is asked and wants to do: concentrate on bare breath. All of their previous concentration all of their life was dependent upon glaring stimuli to attract and hold attention. In life, we all concentrate by using a loud gong of stimulation to command our focus. But subtle breath slips from our attention like sand grains grasped in hand. Our students find they have ridden a fantasy jet into passionate liaisons or into lotteries of excess time and cash.

Their daydreams are florid and for hours unstoppable, like a rock dislodged and ricocheting down a precipice.

After a day, or two, the students realize they *have* concentrated. It happened for mere seconds even on that first dim evening when they had taken their vows. It happens again in the muffled predawn hours when they feel too tired to worry or fabricate. It happens again and again as the first three days unroll. Sometimes our students concentrate unbroken for thirty seconds, and not again for an hour. Sometimes they concentrate a few seconds at a time, on and off, for half a day. Then again, tidal waves of memory sweep over them. Old wounds, harsh words, rejections, humiliations, successes, triumphs, epiphanies, are left exposed by the undertow of the racing mentation. The students wallow in them; then, reminded by the near yet seemingly distant lifesaver thrown out by the teacher's voice, they effortfully restore their concentration. Long runs, *samādhi*, happen.

Of course, these people have concentrated before, most of their lives in fact. Maybe as a medical student memorizing anatomy, or as a ninety-word-per-minute typist, or as a mother watching her rambunctious son in a playground pronged with swings and curbs, they have concentrated on achieving a goal. But this *samādhi* is different. When it lances through the imagery of mind, and holds only the touch of breath in its purview, one, two, sixty moments, a clear, pure tranquility dawns. All other concentrated calm is based upon external stimuli or pictorial fantasy: "Tomorrow I will be on the beach," "When my boyfriend visits, I can relax," "When my son really marries that girl who is so good for him, then I'll grow old happily." But the calm of concentration on bare breath is situationless; it contains no "if" or "when"; it has no picture. Sometimes a marquee of lights, or a moonglow, sometimes only the ripple of respiration's tickle, suffuses the mind. Tranquility is possible, incredible. Based on observation, it is actualizable but unobservable, like fresh air. It emerges from effort, from a wrestling match with self. Then it coasts in frictionless ease, contentless freedom. Only after it has dissolved again can the student feel tranquility absent once more under the tangled arms and brass band of mental life.

Our students are now anchored in moral orientation of their refuges and vows, and increasingly, if intermittently, concentrated in mental mastery for three days, and are ready to practice Vipassana meditation per se.

He or she "dwells observing the phenomena of arising and passing away in the body. . . . This awareness develops to the extent that there is mere understanding and mere observation and s/he dwells detached and does not cling to anything in the world of mind and matter." In that one sentence, Buddha described Vipassana. Today, as thousands of years ago, it is taught as a gradual training, a step-by-step comprehensible technique. Taking almost a week to be accurately taught and initially experienced, it can be summarized as direct, serene awareness of the vibratory totality of the sensations of mind and body, in their ephemeral, impersonal, yet lawful nature.

The students learn to concentrate not merely on a focal point of breath, but gradually, by practiced expansion of locales and then simultaneous regions, they eventually gain the capacity to be aware of all the sensations in their body—scalp, forehead, eyes, nostrils, sinuses, head, mouth, face, chest, heart, lungs, abdomen, etc. Meditation becomes the sweeping motion of awareness flowing through the entire structure of the body, a scanning alertness in which the object of concentration is the totality of the subject themselves. They observe the mass of themselves flickering in its constituent particles. They feel as if they can observe their entire body as a "dot matrix" person.

But why this focus on the body? Doesn't the inner light spring from the mind? The Buddha himself taught: "Mind comes first, mind matters most." We feel ourselves to be primarily our thoughts, our feelings, our psyche. How can a technique be deep, be other than a tranquilizing gimmick, if it continuously requires turning concentration away from psyche to soma? What does this meditation on breath and body have to do with mental purification and inner peace?

For the mind to be plumbed, it must be observed at the juncture where it is coterminous with the body. As self-observers, we cannot observe our mind alone. It buries us. It subsumes our objective, observing powers under its own urgent theater of imagery. The cinematographic reels of the mind are seemingly endless and dominant. We *are* them—so it feels. We believe in them, are captured by them, live them out. Yet the elaborate drama of our mind in which we always star, that screen where we take up most of the space, is predicated on a brief package of body.

There are many levels to reality. Our skillful preoccupation with mundane details has its own proper role. Everyone must competently wend their way through a complex world where ability, labor, and pragmatism corral their fair domain of food, shelter, friendship, knowledge, and affection. But inner peace is the pollen of absolute reality. Ultimately, the visible, tangible universe is a shifting flow of matter in ceaselessly transforming aggregations. The final fact is change. Deep meditation leading toward abiding peace must descend beyond the useful but ephemeral thoughts of transient personality, to the eternal truths at the basis of all personalities at all times.

Vipassana is a submarine-based observation of change. It carries our bare, honest observation to the depth of the sense of self. Every thought, dream, mental picture is a product of the body that contains it. A biochemical reaction underlies every flicker of the mind. The mind is juice squeezed from change. Neurotransmitters, complex biochemicals streaming across synapses in the dendritic microforests of the brain, enable our moods and our mentations. Psychiatrists prescribe medicines that regulate these chemicals to elevate depression, compress mania, or salve schizophrenic horror. No one can think with his head chopped off. The "I am" who inhabits our thoughts and feelings is a product of the possibilities of the biology, chemistry, and physics of our bodies. As we think, we change our chemistry. Chronic thought-patterns change our bodies, ulcerate our duodenums, break our hearts, or restore our vitality. Mind and body are two sides of a coin.

But mind alone can convey the illusion of "I am" that obliterates the reality of ceaseless transformation in every atom, every body, every galaxy. Mind unpinned from its body dreams it is free of flux. Uprooted from the truth of ceaseless transformation, mind elaborates the illusions that alienate it from integrative harmony with the facts of the world.

We have no difficulty in becoming aware of our mind. It floods us: it spawns epics and anecdotes and vacation plans. We all dwell in the captivity of our own melodrama. No one who has not spent whole days sealed alone inside her own head can know the fantasia of multiscreen ideation that will not stop for a moment. How can this self-entranced mind gain a more embracing and enduring perspective?

The only way the human mind can experience truth is when that truth is felt directly in the bodily basis of "self." To stand outside ourselves and view our lives with the "cosmic long view," we must penetrate ourselves within and find the multitudes of galaxies swirling in our bones. We can only stare at the heavens. We live and die in our hearts; we can directly experience our own sensations. Transforming self-knowledge derives from the inner journey. Purity, transcendence of imaginary and divisive selfhood, is the outcome of the experience of ineluctable change throughout the dream of the self. When the bodily basis of the self dissolves into the impersonal flows of universal matter, one drop of purity glistens in the mind. Purity is a direct product of experiencing ultimate reality of change in every particle of one's own body-mind. In a moment of sweeping, penetrating meditation, the students may experience themselves as they might if they observed themselves from a helicopter for a hundred years: as a passing cloud.

As the meditators learn to sit still, observing arising and passing away in the body, merely observing without reacting, they are again reflooded, this time not only by mental contents as they were while concentrating on breath, but also by somatic clouds and suns previously unknown. At times they will find Vipassana a paradox. Having come to it for inner peace, they temporarily find themselves more beset than ever before. After moments of stellar clarity, mental hullabaloo returns. An ancient loss buried twenty years ago rises up and screams, "You'll never be able to forget me!" A wish unfulfilled dances tantalizingly hour after hour: "How can you live without me? When you leave this course you must change your life to have me. You will never, never feel satisfied unless you have me."

One student runs to the teacher, confused, upset: "I must be doing something wrong. I can't concentrate. My back feels like it has a hot iron ramrod in the muscles beside my spine. I can't sleep at night. But I fall asleep as soon as I try to meditate! Instead of transcending desire, I am becoming a furnace of passion." He is incredulous when the teacher laughs and reassures him that he is right on target! His honesty, self-insight, and deepened appreciation of the human dilemma are all signs of progress. Having tasted a drop of purity, he is now consciously aware of the self-attachments that are its antithesis and would keep him from it.

Another student's unbroken penetration of meditative mindfulness into the bodily sensate self has unshelved reactions in the dusty library of her unconsciousness. Piles of her past conditionings are stirred from where they moldered in the unexplored archives of body-sensation-based mind. Her awareness of buried sensations brings up awareness of their repressed mental contents that are the two sides of the same coin. Not just her brain her whole body is filled with memory and desire.

Modulated by vows, buffered by tradition, teacher, and technique, the students' archaic reaction patterns rise and transpire from the surface of mind, neither driving action, because the students are sitting still in the sanctuary of their vows, nor able to hide any longer in unawareness. Systematic, penetrating awareness of body-mind in mere observation and dispassion peels off old snakeskins of old "selves."

As the days crawl past through the thick broth of loneliness and confusion, then alternately flash forward in exhilarating insights, breakthroughs and discoveries, the meditators are reminded by a persevering teacher's voice to return to awareness of the reality of sensate bodily life, observing its instantaneous, incessant changes with a balanced mind. The moon of the students' own clarity slowly absorbs the excited flashes of stars and shines light down into the black hours. The new meditators learn to ride the transformations of themselves. The students can balance above the surges and urges inside themselves, like a horseback rider, like a surfer, learning detached self-humor within the whirlwind. Now our new meditators can recognize the way thoughts rise out of their body, and sensations change with thoughts. They are developing freedom from the compulsions of animal life. They are exercising new mental organs, new spiritual muscles. They can watch themselves change, body and mind, like the earth in its seasons, like historical eras in the geography of time, and yet know the poise of being meteorologist and historian of themselves. They experience peace as they have never known it before—peace based upon detachment from the undulating reality of change.

From under the cover of their blinding ignorance they see the rising of the qualities of a purified mind. Why harbor and rationalize so much hatred or fear, all based on transient scenarios? Fantasies of a permanently happy self in the confines of terrestrial life are tossed off like childish daydreams. They realize that clinging to fairy tales about themselves is the source of their suffering. They recognize that all living beings suffer the same core anguish that they have. They feel called to release others as much as they have been released. Sorrowing for the ignorant bodies everywhere clinging to their transitory, illusory selves, they find their own self-pity uncoiling into love. Every one, every thing is an orphan, an exile, a friend. Their detachment is from themselves, not from others, toward whom they yearn to reach with the wand of their own insight: truth brings peace.

Within the pain of change, loss, dissolution, is the liberation of serenity and its generous light. When ceaseless change is realized to be the ultimate fact of every moment, you know you are reborn into freedom a thousand times a day. The even mind, without demand, is objective, realistic, clean. Muddy mind is a product of its own self-referential expectations, projections, confusions. Purity is awareness and equanimity. The path to Nibbāna is simply peace walking toward deeper, more unshakeable peace. The students have understood that suffering is caused by their self-obsessed mental drama; and for moments, hours, days of the course, they have now felt free. For intermittent hours, or for whole days, they have come to thrive in Vipassana, aware of but not reacting to sensations of pleasure and pain, mentally stepping aside to watch objectively, free of personal craving or distaste. They have experienced peace that is simultaneously intimate and animated, yet so deep that it makes normal relaxation with a book, or normal vacations, seem like a hubbub. They have climbed up the foothills to get a glimpse of liberation. They leave the ten-day course with a sense of having worked incredibly hard and having experienced a quality of peace that is unique, profound, and inspiring.

Will they really leave their course benighted, loving, self-less, and wise after ten days? To some extent. One week of pure Vipassana meditation hasn't made them Buddha, and their friends and family will recognize them only too easily on their return. But the life they only imagined so shortly before, they have now begun to live. One smudge is wiped from the window glass. One moon has risen in an interior heaven. Who can see far enough to predict where a ray of light will halt? These new meditators are on the Path.

Hopefully, they will see their Vipassana meditation course as a first step. They may start and end the rest of their days with meditation upon reality as it is. They may return to sharpen their insights in more courses. They may progress to where they can help others learn.

For their meditation to actually change their lives, and not be just an interlude, they'll have to realize that meditation isn't sitting still. It is the cultivation of a permeating perspective. Practiced sitting, it can grow until it accompanies the active mind in its daily tasks. A life of meditation saturates work, family, leisure, and friendship, until the round of existence turns increasingly frictionless on the hub of purity and equanimity.

Chapter 25

A Personal Experience
of Vipassana
Meditation

I TOOK MY FIRST Vipassana meditation course in 1974 under the guidance of Mr. Goenka. The motives that led me to the course are extensive enough for a full-length autobiography, some unique to me, many common human themes. Among other things, I was born at the end of World War II (two days, in fact, after the bombing of Hiroshima), that destroyer of naïve beliefs. I grew up on a planet contorted by Holocaust and crusted with thousands of nuclear warheads, many pointed at me. By the time I got to college and then on through all the years of my professional training, the Vietnam war was raging. Therefore, my young adulthood was spent figuring out how to avoid being murdered by the most powerful and avowedly humane government in the world.

I escaped better than those men who were actually killed or broken by the war, but I experienced a pervasive alienation. I had a very good reason to distrust authorities and so-called civilization—Nazi Europe, imperialist Japan, and narcissistic America. I saw corruption and compromise everywhere. To merely pick up my degree and move into suburbia was unthinkable. I intuited both a goodness to life I couldn't locate in any of my surroundings, and also a moldiness in what was held up to me as wholesome. I thought of these reactions as products of my time, though now I realize that these feelings occur to many people in all times. War and dismay are always with us.

Not all of my motivations were based on the conditions of my historical moment. I was a romantic, wanted to travel, and had already been induced by Thoreau and the Indian civilization course at the University of Chicago to meander through the great classic texts of Indian literature. Among their arcane and exotic diverticulae was a clear center of hopefulness and well-being, and a radical perspective of time that gave emotional valence to the scientific worldview.

More important than either dismay or ecstasies on my mind at that time, though less clearly articulated, was already the realization of time, change, loss, death, and the illusion of individualistic reference. As a child I had leafed through ancient history books and watched the changing shapes of the empires of the Medes and the Persians, learned how agriculture grew and Mesopotamia faded, and I had realized I was standing at the precipice with an infinite vertigo. Given reality, what could possibly be the point of life . . . of *my* life?

In those days, Vipassana wasn't being taught in the West. I made several trips to India and returned with the technique half-learned. I didn't know where it fit into my life, but I saw it as something honest, free, and useful. I could own it myself, practice it without being swallowed by a religion or being wafted away in a pointless vacuum of career and convention. It got me up early in the morning, and reminded me there was more to life, but it also revealed me to myself in ways I didn't always like. I briefly drifted over to Zen but came back to Vipassana for two reasons. I could understand it. It was taught in a logical, coherent way—no paradox or blind faith or mysticism. It was taught by Mr. Goenka with a patience and pragmatism that my frustrations and worldliness required. And its living traditions were sober, guru-free, no financial or sexual scandals.

I became increasingly committed and serious because every time I "sat" I felt I got something out of it. I never had any mystical or unusual experiences. I both experienced my mind-body, and was able to get some distance from it. I kept returning for ten-day courses, and practicing with increasing devotion in between. By now I've lived half a lifetime this way, and am archeological proof that meditation isn't "Eastern thought."

Vipassana as a way of life has walked me past every component of inner peace. Obviously, to maintain these practices and foci, I have to live a consciously and carefully selective life. With two professions, family, house, cars, quarterly tax installments and Macintosh computer, we aren't living a Shaker-style, nineteenth century, agrarian, celibate life; yet our days are polished in a careful gloss that enables us to slide right through the distractions of television, movies, "talk of kings, courtesans and highwaymen," and return to meditation, mutual listening, and vigorous outdoor joys. I'm no Shaker, but hopefully they would recognize my focalized enthusiasm. I've had to accept my path not as fast and easy, but as one of mental disruption and return, a millionfold dynamism. Rather than constricting my life into either a religious or a scientific mold, meditation became the bridge that led me to explore the religious literature of the world, discovering common psychological truths and opening me into dialogues with religious people whose worldviews I had never previously appreciated, but with whom I now could find common points of reference, based upon personal experience rather than theology. Ethics, concentration, and wisdom are part of every religion. The prose-poetry of Mr.

Goenka's chanting and discourses during meditation courses carried language inside of me to a new depth. It was from this absorption of linguistic vibration while meditating that I could experientially realize the deeper role of language in transforming human life, my life.

Vipassana practice has deepened my appreciation of nature, not as an esthetic picture placed in front of me for my personal pleasure, but as a community of kindred, evolving lives. Vipassana meditation centers are magnets of friendship with flowers, trees, and stars.

Sorrow, humility, perspective, and service are the running water that rotates the mill wheel of meditation. During a life of annual meditation courses and twice-daily sittings, I have witnessed the arising and passing of innumerable scenarios of happiness and dread, the entire mythic imagery of my life and its origins in generations who lived, struggled, and died, and its goals of attainments, successes, and pleasures. These pictures and perceptions of my life are all reasonable, but transient, ultimately parochial and insubstantial, like a sparrow dreaming of seeds. I have felt fathomless sorrow for my own cornered, doomed, bodily life, hardly noticeable in its brief plummet through the Grand Canyon of time. At the same time, I've been made aware of how attached I remain—in spite of the antecedent insights—to my own happiness, my health, my life. Humility is a mild term for the paradoxical realizations of perspective, and of how far I must yet progress to fully immerse myself in the great freedom that those realizations can ultimately bring. Perspective, sorrow, and humility are a snowstorm in which I'm traveling. Service is my as-yet-to-be-tested skill in building a shelter of fir boughs and a fire, and inviting in all the snowshoers, deer, and ghosts for a hot cup of harmless, universal friendship. I can find shelter only by providing it, in the blizzard of moment-by-moment immediacy: psychiatrist, writer, father, husband, friend, servant of meditation.

While meditation is often associated with solitary re-move, it is also intrinsically familial, since its goal is to make everyone's aura hospitable. The stability, order, and calm of our household may be the greatest gift we have gotten from Vipassana. Overcommitted to the quilt of daily life, we also always return to quiet, self-observation, and equanimity. This turning and returning to meditation tens of thousands of times has sewn for us a lifestyle handstitched and a perfect fit for us, ironically because its essence is to adhere to a truth outside of ourselves. This atmosphere of pause and perspective has also created an appropriate locus for group sittings.

For the deepest closeness, a marriage must contain enough distance and differentiation for authentic meeting to occur. The practice of an annual meditation course has contributed to our autonomy, and buffered us against the fusion that can lead to overdependence and loss of self-responsibility. We are never closer than when we are apart because one of us is sitting a "long course." Then, when the domestic partner stops the ongoing routine of pet feeding, food shopping, childcare, and professional obligations, to meditate morning and evening, we can feel our Other, hidden in deep meditation far away, yet exquisitely close. It is true for all people that our bonds to others are as deep as the wellsprings we have discovered in ourselves. Reverence and love are rivers that flow in the immaterial caverns of the universe. When we dip into them, we touch everyone who has also been to their shores. Not only my wife, but many, many Others from the past, present, and future, are meditating with me, with us, every day.

MEDITATION IS BASED ON THE IRONY, or on the mul-tiplicity of perspectives, that the more we pursue universal truth, the deeper we plunge into our karma, our unique, idiosyncratic, fingerprint personality. Tens of thousands of hours, every day, weeks or a month at a time, I have self-observed the questions: "What puts me at peace?" "What distresses me?" Real meditation is simply education, learning to modulate turmoil through insight into equipoise. In psychiatry, unfortunately, where once a value was given to resonate and vaulted self-knowledge resulting in inward containment, and where a psychiatrist was once expected to dispense time for reflection, poise, and resilience, today in contrast many psychiatrists pride themselves on their frantic, faddish conformity in dispensing elixirs at fifteen-minute intervals. Of course, I too dispense medication to palliate suffering, and understand some mental illnesses as having biogenetic roots, but people also suffer or grow from realization of one simple, basic, psychological law: whatever brings concord and gladness and unites others, will bring peace to your heart. The peace we yearn for is within, like the pericardium, a thin but powerful tissue that enfolds the heart. Every human heart is already enfolded in the capacity to feel peace as the direct result of loving-kindness, compassion, and truthfulness.

I am not liberated from ordinary irritations and moods. The world seems increasingly, not decreasingly, sad to me. The only way we usually can walk forward is to wear blinders like old cart-horses in heavy auto traffic. Millions murdered in Iraq. Millions drowned in Bangladesh. Unending warfare in the Sudan, the Middle East, Afghanistan. Stockpiles of nuclear weapons. America's cities unsafe at night, filled with cocaine and an ongoing race war of crime and violence. Yet, meditation has removed, not expanded, my blinders. It changed my life from one of hopelessness, or blind hope, to contentless hope. Every time I meditate I feel I can draw up and away, free for a moment or two, able to see that all fear or grief is just my own self-pity. When I'm not clutching myself, there is only possibility. Who can say what the meaning of this teeming, death-dogged world is? When I judge it, that's only my own ignorance and arrogance asserting its dominance. Again and again I know I can contact a pure moment in myself when negativity is absent and I know I am a beam moving through the universe toward an absolute goodness that will draw at least a few others behind me in tow. The suffering in the world seems more enormous than ever to me, but so does the opening between the clouds. The more clearly I see the vastness of ignorance, the more clearly I see the path out of it and the stronger my motivation to persevere in meditation.

I used to ponder about Nibbāna. Would I attain it, would I not? Fortunately, I've been able to let go of the question. Every medical student wonders . . . someday . . . will I win the Nobel prize? But after a while, you have to forget it. You can't do research with your life and feel, "Only if I've found a cure for cancer will my life be worthwhile." The suspense and frustration would crush you. So you have to think, "Pursuing knowledge is intrinsically worthwhile. Great discoveries are often built up on the knowledge of lesser ones. Even if I make only minor contributions, they will have some value when they are tallied with the whole. Or even if my work goes down a blind alley and an entirely different direction proves fertile, my life still will have been meaningful. I inspired others. I challenged them. I grew and developed as a person. My modest results represent a fragment of truth, too. You need a critical mass of scientists working on a problem before even the genius can have a breakthrough. Science always happens in community."

In the same way, Nibbāna is the goal of Vipassana, yet whether I will or won't obtain it is irrelevant. I'm walking in the direction of truth; I don't need to impose a time limit and I don't know how far I will walk before I die. I'll still be meditating as I die. My whole life is aimed at expelling my own ignorance, living as peacefully and constructively as I can. I feel now I couldn't live any other way. It's my temperament, or "rebirth karma," the impulse of my personality. I've caught fire from a few meditator friends, and I hope a few others will catch fire from me.

Vipassana can sound solitary and impersonal, but it's always a part of a community of teaching, learning, practicing together. It's a continuity bigger than those who are carrying it forward today. From the upper level of a meditation pagoda in India, I once watched students far beneath me flowing slowly down the central aisle of the campus grounds, their white clothes rippling in wind, and I realized they were current droplets in a river that has been, and will be, flowing for thousands of years. This effort of awareness and equanimity—in what historical era, on what planet, in which galaxy, would it be less than precious? Through Vipassana I feel part of the flow of truth and peace.

MEDITATION IS NOT ONLY A PERSONAL ACTIVITY. It is an entryway into wider participation, expanding identification. It moves in two directions, spiraling outward like planetary rings, at the same time that it drills downward. Both of these aspects of the practice are activated, whether one meditates morning and evening during daily life, or during meditation courses.

For example, the deeper one goes into oneself, the more one spontaneously finds thoughts to be swirling outward in gratitude toward those who teach. As I sit, working my way out of the web of self-preoccupation, out pops the image of Mr. Goenka, who went traveling around, dispensing meditation for free, making it available at no cost to people he never knew, like me. Without an attitude like his, the tradition wouldn't exist because there's no profit in it. It has to spread out of sheer spirit. There is no Vipassana technique without this human, personal giving and receiving. The more I penetrate my own meditation, the more I find phosphorescence from his orbit.

Returning to daily meditation, I find that some of my hour gets spent digging down into daydreams or trivial plans—maybe making the time to contemplate details of life is itself worthwhile. Some of the time passes in reveries from when I was thirteen, or how I hope to spend my August vacation—knowing how I feel about events is a valuable use of time, too. But some of that time the drilling stops, and I hover out, just aware. My body is a flickering, flowing ocean of eddies, currents, stagnant pools, impenetrable darkness and sparkling lights, an essenceless, changing collection of energies temporarily held in the same shoreline, and all my thoughts and daydreams are the whales and sharks and krill passing through. That flowing world passes by, but I'm observing, objectively seeing myself from a dimension beyond myself. My head is above water. I can see reality without drowning in it. When I can hold it in clear awareness like that, I feel I could also turn and glimpse the far shore, beyond the whole ocean.

Courses are different from daily practice. The turmoil is greater, and so is the peace, each axis amplified. They're not a vacation; they're an experiential laboratory. I remember them and work with them all year. Unlike the hour-long meditations of daily life, the unbroken immersion in meditation during a course can raise into consciousness storms of reactions that can hardly be recognized as oneself. In panicky moments I've tested the skill of my longtime friends and co-meditators who now serve as assistant teachers, and who have adeptly encouraged me to cross terrain of inner life that I wouldn't have been able to cross on my own, and who have said to me, "We'll do anything we can to help you." And in the silence and solitude of my meditation cell in India, I've been beset by passions like demons in a painting by Bosch.

But courses also provide weeks of unbroken tranquility in which my heart never accelerates, and my awareness sharpens so much that I have felt more alive in a five-minute walk with my eyes downcast between my cell and my room, than I typically feel in an entire mundane day of phone calls, forms, and files. Ironically, the less we do, and the less excited we get, the more that life's deepest feelings, like children and mountains, swell to their fullest in us. The equanimity I have developed during meditation courses has provided me a reference point that is distinct from calm or happiness, and that feels absolute, as if I had opened a door to my room and discovered I was on a balcony looking over and beyond all time.

Then my mind can sweep out among reverie and reflection to envision every helping hand that has ever been extended to me. There have been princesses, wizards, and teachers who, in the guise of relatives, professors, and authors, have appeared on my path and opened doors that can never again block me. Gratitude isn't merely an extra, an outflow of meditation. The deep peace of meditation gushes up from the realization that an infinite series of events have crystallized into this moment of equanimity in me. A long history, on many stages, with a changing, numerous cast, is contained within this moment's peace. My peace in this or any moment is the principle of peace, guided, purified, manifesting now in me. Any individual's equanimity is always a product of the same laws of peace, whose shafts enter and illuminate us. All peace is an inheritance; every moment of equanimity glows from the same invisible gift.

Meditation has made me aware of other modes of knowing that complete the human dimension: receiving vibrations in direct awareness.

This important feature of truth and peace was humorously symbolized to me by my dog, Sita, who lived to be sixteen years old, spending her last years deaf and blind. You could clap your hands next to her ear, yell her name, or hurtle your hand menacingly toward her eyes without raising a whisker on her. Nevertheless, she would sit outside our Vermont cabin, near her birthplace, hardly hobbling a few steps from the front door—though in the past she had intrepidly terrierized the surrounding woods and their denizens—and on her ancient perch she would sit bolt upright, alert as a gopher, surveying the world. Her nose would point out and wave slowly here and there like a conductor's wand. She remained entranced by the world through her doggy nose, receiving news bulletins that to me were inaudible, invisible, and unsniffable.

There are many messages arriving daily whose envelopes we have yet to open. There is a truth we have yet to sniff out. Merely because we haven't smelled what is wafting toward us doesn't mean there's nothing there, and it may take some Homeric canine to remind us that we have been attuned to only one of the many sagas unfolding around us. We have yet to receive the full import of the world in its totality. Beyond our death, beyond our era, beyond the self-enfolding curves of our ellipsoid universe, may lie a message, a springtime, an unglimpsable Nibbāna, whose existence would confirm our intuitions and efforts if we could tune our receptors to the vibration it emits.

I won't limit myself to the scientific worldview, or to religious attestations; I want a viewpoint that reveals to me both everything my dog was smelling, and everything beyond the senses themselves. The earth we perch on is a front stoop among illimitable realities. The Nibbāna of eternal peace beyond all time, all things, all change, may open up to us if we patiently keep sniffing for it, even as we grow old and blind.

When you really experience ceaseless change, change throughout every particle of your body, in the brain that holds your thoughts, beliefs, feelings, throughout everything you call yourself, then you know the limits of your ideas. Your religion, your science, your nihilism, are all thoughts, beliefs, passing clouds of particles in the box of one little mammal's head. Every future—next minute, next year, next eon—will itself be only a present that will change into something else. The realization within yourself, through direct awareness of sensations, of the fluidity and impermanence of every particle of your being, and of the universe itself, eradicates all fantasies. Instead, insight into this truth leads you into the present moment, immediate and unadorned, which changes.

To the extent that I can cultivate and maintain this awareness, I feel liberated and am living the truth, which is peace. In that moment I am free from fear, free from yearning, purified of myself. There is the simple truth of the moment, changing into the next moment, in infinite series, forever. There are no ideas, no constrictions, no knowledge in absolute truth, which has no final form. In such a moment, a person is a solution through which truth and peace pass.

For me, my freedom is occasional, partial, like a view of a distant shore seen by a swimmer over a wavy sea, and after one upward thrust and glimpse, I once again begin to splash and struggle in the drama of myself.

"Peace" as a word is not as specific as "Nibbāna," which means the total purification of mind resulting in complete egolessness and unshakable equanimity. Not everyone will want to follow Vipassana, the path to Nibbāna. Those who don't can still grow in peace by focusing on it as a goal, selecting for serenity, tuning up to wise words, empathizing with all beings, attaining sorrow, humility, and perspective, as I have discussed in this book. People who follow Vipassana exactly as it is taught, adding nothing, subtracting nothing, will find, if they persevere, that all the other aspects of peace will have been incorporated into their lives. The apparently separate steps of peace will all be hooked up behind the engine of Vipassana.

Initially we seek peace for personal, self-serving reasons. This is only sane: we want to suffer less. As we find more peace in our hearts—even though it is intermittent, even though so much of our lives remains a struggle within the illusory daydream of our selves, even though our purity is partial and the Nibbāna of total purity and ineluctable peace remains "lifetimes away"—our goals change. Ultimately, the goal isn't to contain peace but to transmit it, isn't to have peace but to *be* peace. The goal of the peaceful life is to be a vehicle of love, compassion, joy, and peace, not directed at any single target, without any circumference, just flowing out and penetrating whatever it encounters. That is why I'm writing this chapter, this book, holed up alone in a cabin among singing vireos, thunderstorms, and mice in the walls chewing on my transient insulation.

Inner peace is a form of falling in love, an ongoing romance with human potential that cynics find foolish. Peace derives from the affectional capacity of the mammal who is raised by love instead of by instinct. Take that love and shoot it like an arrow beyond mere personal romances, beyond everything you see and know, beyond any hope that can fail, beyond history, earth, and space. Peace is for fools who can fall in love with a world freed of self-reference, a world beyond what will happen to us.

PART X

Chapter 26

OUR INNER PEACE
IS EARTH'S FRONTIER

CULTIVATING INNER PEACE is the most important action we can take to help planet Earth, on whose back we all ride, whose breath we breathe, whose plants provide our food, and whose properly intense sunlight is the source of energy for the molecules that form our body. Rather than solipsistic disinterest, the cultivation of inner peace activates our fundamental human calling: to overcome our predatory egotism—which is the source of war, overpopulation, and environmental destruction—and to reorganize our lives around the deepest gratifications we can feel: love, sympathetic joy, compassion, and peace of heart and mind.

When you walk the path of peace, whether you take one step or a lifelong pilgrimage, you are revolutionizing human nature away from requisition, appropriation and consumption, toward gratitude, reverence and appreciation. Everywhere you look you will see life-sustaining gifts. All your possessions, even your thoughts, will appear to be a loan of precious heirlooms. Mythical saints and angels will seem to you to be rumor and gossamer when compared to the people you live with and love, whose bodies are molecules shaped by earth, plant, and sun, whose minds are the product of eons of human evolution, and who float around you in aquamarine companionship and care. Your own life and death will feel like tides.

Inner peace in humanity is earth's frontier, a new interior landscape where evolution can be released from the crumble and decay of old ways, and where people can begin to build a world of well-being based on introspection and illumination. Yet the old ways are too much with us.

Today we quaver before the onslaught of a fatal plague of people. There are too many bodies, consuming too much, too aggressively. Population expansion, resource depletion, and warfare are products of materialist lives lived for what they produce and get. Our future rests on the evolution of psychic, emotional, interior life. We need to develop a human community based on gratification and on meaning attained through internal states of being. Western society today is marked by a frenzy of daytime self-promotion followed by electronic pacification in the evening. Yet, with our relative comfort and wealth, we have the chance to cultivate an internal light. Peace is a pure octave within the growing traffic jam.

Inner peace enables heightened perspective, as if viewing from a great altitude. From outer space, astronauts have photographed the earth as a small sphere, the urgent turbulence of which is barely visible as transient wisps of atmosphere. This physical portrait of earth from a far remove implies that dispassionate equipoise is the proportional response to the ephemeral clouds of history. But we can't base our actions on an intellectual, visual portrayal of reality, because as soon as we close the cover of our book of planet Earth as seen from satellite photos, we are instantly caught again in our personal melodrama, forgetting the whole. We sigh philosophically that we are all riders on the earth together, then bolt our doors for safety before bed.

Inner peace, gradually accreted in the chambers of the heart, culminates in a felt, applicable, enduring warmth. We can go beyond mere reenvisioning of the earth outside our domiciles, and feel our own heartbeats in flannel.

AS YOU GROW IN INNER PEACE, your relationship to the world will change. Plants and animals will become your beloved and intimate neighbors. You will love them, not just with sentimental patronizing, as with household pets, but you will experience all beings in an essentially new way. Let's take an excursion into the woods, where you'll be able to feel what I mean.

In the forest at dawn in May, the volume of birdsong is loud and penetrating. A scientific naturalist could separate this flood tide of diffuse chanting into the voices of each individual avian species. In spite of the overlap, the concatenation, the apparent confusion, the practiced listener can discern the repetitive, circular lilt of the vireo as it cascades down from the top of tall maples. The multitextured flute of the wood thrush unrolls and retreats into low shadows. The brief cantata of the hermit thrush, the bleary waterfall of the veery, each stake out auditory zones of turf, discrete sound counties among the opaque green lattice of spring foliage. Listening with empirical knowledge enables us to partition a wall of tangled stimuli into recognizable, coherent signals.

There is another way to listen. Listen to the flood. Throughout the forest in every direction, waves of life are rippling. Just as the oceans cover the seafloor over three fifths of the earth, an ocean of life force is rippling through the atmosphere, and as the planet rotates and the sun's rays slowly and continuously sweep over section by section of the earth's surface, singing rises up at the hint of light, and saturates the atmosphere. In spite of air pollution, in spite of the hordes of humankind deforesting and spilling oil into the oceans, in spite of depletion of the ozone layer and paving over of cropland and the desertification of nations, a great chorus resounds in the forest and fields and suburbs and even the cities. Daily in repeating series of dawns, the earth is ringed by this paean of billions of dawn-risers.

If we listen even less discretely and ornithologically, and more holistically, we can hear the dawn chorus traveling across and around the planet, rising and falling in response to sunlight, the baton of a solar conductor. This planetary chorale has endured for an epoch so vast it is inconceivable. Even scientific quantification cannot enable the human mind to grasp it. Time becomes mere words when we try to breathe meaning into these facts' the first birds evolved from their reptilian ancestors about 150 million years ago. About 10 million years ago, after 140 million years of evolution, bird-life peaked in numbers and diversity that exceed those we see and hear today. The music has slowly shifted, as species have declined or evolved, but the chorus has never missed its appearance on some part of the globe daily, hourly, minute-by-minute as the moving finger of morning glides around the planet. With northern and southern hemispheres and diverse climates and environments, for millions of years the planet has never been naked of birdsong. When only crows are squawking in wintry New England, Latino and Australian birds maintain the unbroken avian songtide. In terms of the duration of our own lives, the chorus in the forest is eternal. It arose in a dawn of dawns, and has yet to succumb to any sunset.

Like the ocean of water, the ocean of song is formed by the aggregation of individual drops—birds, birds everywhere, hidden in the shadows of tropical lianas or in the gnarled roots of oaks or nested in tundra grass. Scientists believe that birdsong reflects territoriality; males sing to designate an area where they control food collection, and this regulates food supply, viability of offspring, and population density. Birds may be singing to competitors of their own or closely related species. The sense one gets while listening in the dawn forest, that the songs are grappling, may be literally true. The songs may serve as swords. Although motivated by separation, they collide and intersect. The aggregate action produces a weave, a tapestry of synergistic interconnection in which all elements are subsumed into an overarching, spreading unity. There are billions of birds singing, but there is a uniform ocean of song. Each bird may sing from knowledge in its genetic code, mixed with the possibility of spontaneous or conditioned variation, but the song of the forest itself flows from a deep spring that gushes from the archaic effulgence of life.

Woodland birds differ from orchard and lawn birds. Instead of proclaiming themselves from a prominent perch the way a cardinal or robin or mockingbird will do, from the top of a suburban rosebush—the woodland species sing from hidden niches in dense foliage. Suddenly, when darkness has barely paled, their notes pour forth from nowhere, until a tapestry of song is woven around you, a web of invisible beauty that appears to have no locus or origin. Their music seems to arise out of the intangible shadows that antedate the physical world. Unlike other beings—a horse with its steaming aroma, for example—hermit thrushes and their kin evoke the disembodied. Their song of secrets lures us beyond the visible world.

Is it territoriality? Is it joy? Do we people only hear it as joyful based upon an evolutionarily induced delusion of our own? Those people who imagined joy, projected their own joy as they listened to birdsong, were more likely to survive and generate offspring, because of the greater fullness of life they felt? Scientifically, birds sing for adaptive reasons; "joy" is an anthropomorphic projection. The austere factuality of the scientific worldview has been shared by all radically honest truth-seekers. The Buddha taught that we should understand mental and physical life as the flow of nutriment, an impersonal, mechanical process. Out of a bird is born a bird that is driven to consume nutriment; its bodily mass grows; it mates to form more birds that are driven to consume nutriment and grow, and so on, inexorably. The process of the tangible world has no comprehensible origin, no end, no purpose we can spy. Science shuns teleology, and cannot answer the question: What is the goal of life on earth?

The flow of nutriment is singing, across the world, across the ages, it greets the dawn with something we cannot objectively call joy, each individual bird arising and singing and vanishing again, while the genetically guided flow of nutriment replaces the individual, and the music rotates above our planet. The resonation of this ageless voice is apprehended by another form of the flow of nutriment, men and women, who feel in it a kindred spirit to their own love and awe and terror at the mystery of the arising and vanishing of their own life-flow. We sense in our cousin birdsong a clue to our deeper nature.

Each person's body-and-mind is a temporary vessel, a brief crest on an ocean wave, a transient aggregation of nutrients. Out of the forces of evolution, genetics, history, and environment, our body-and-mind swirls up nutrients like a passing whirlwind, holds them in human form for a while like an upright local tornado, then slows, dissipates, disappears. During its residence, the individual spins in interconnections with people, place, time. Like a drop in the ocean, a bird in the forest, each person contributes to a greater hum than we can fully hear.

The human body-mind can imagine and anticipate its own dissolution. To the extent we struggle against the universal law of cessation, that much suffering will arise from the yearning for durability. We are a passing twister. Individual life is merely a temporary vortex. The irony of human fate is to suffer more loss the more we cling to our own life.

But there is a higher sphere. It is only through taking form that the formless sings. Birds draw up something unexpected from another aspect of reality, and this deeper expression can be felt in the emotional power of birdsong, which derives from its earnestness and absoluteness. The veery or the wood thrush *must* sing music that is an essential outpouring of the singer, rather than mere entertainment. The song derives not from the will of the singer, but from the same source as the singer. The singer was born to sing, and is a conduit for messages from beyond its elemental self.

The Buddha, who dared stare life in the face and see his own body and mind as the flow of nutriment, was also a singer. Frequently at the end of a prose discourse, the Buddha broke into verse. Even his prose, as preserved in the Pāli Canon, is sonorous and uses language in its rhythmic and suggestive dimensions. Within the physical, material matrix of life, song arises to convey a dimension that exceeds materiality, and this is why the passing human tornado hears in the birdsong of the forest an expression of its own capacity to transcend the flow of nutriment. The Buddha taught that beyond, within, the mental-physical flow of nutriment is the Unborn, Uncreated. In birdsong, we can hear echoed our own grateful acclaim for life, for the possibility of expressing the eternal within the temporal.

Each individual birdsong is a mere biological function. The more we isolate the individual voice, the more minimal is its message. We can hear another realm only when we relinquish isolating thought and perception; and when we stop identifying ourselves as our minds and bodies, there is an internal dawn. The material realm of the flow-of-nutriment does not explain the whole song. On the flood tide of the tranquility of nondistinction comes an endless possibility.

Dawn is everywhere, all the time, and all beings are our kin. When I absorb the song of the thrushes with the same rapt attention that it is delivered, I realize they are my companions, my fellow mortals, the composers of sacred songs that best express my peaceful heart.

A rickety wooden chair on a cobweb-festooned screened porch to a cabin in the forest is where the world most expertly tunes me to the rapture of sympathetic joy with all lives.

THE LIFE OF INNER PEACE not only increases my personal well-being, but it also diminishes my human-centered fortifi-cations, and makes me a receptive participant in common suf-fering and joy with many forms of life. In addition to racism or sexism, our era suffers from "species-ism," as if, because we pollute the air with Chevrolets, that makes us superior to ospreys and spruces, and grants us the right to decide how long or how many of these chattel of ours will live or die. In an era soon to arrive on our planet, our contemporary attitude toward plants and animals will be regarded in the same way as we now view the self-appointed tyrannous attitude of white slave owners toward their African slaves.

There are no better friends in peace than trees. Let us wander for a moment among these great beings, not just to label the characteristics of their leaf patterns as if we were in a science class, or to slaughter them for sticks like buffalo hunters and redwood-choppers, but to encounter and learn from them a deeper lesson about peace—trees, who hold our avian singers in their limbs and who build the shadow worlds of woods. The Buddha attained enlightenment meditating under a tree, and in his talks and lectures, he repeatedly advised us to meditate under trees. Tree worship penetrates into contemporary religions through such symbols as the

Christmas tree, the Hebrew tree of life, the Christian cross, and the *bodhi* tree.

Trees are at the source of our life. We are all beholden to, and products of, the green. We eat the green whose molecules become us, and we breathe the green. We breathe the breath of our mother leaves who nurse us. We are all saprophytes, sucking on the life of plants. We inhale the life-gift of leaves. Our bodies run on the sugar energy, and our minds are lit by the breath of green plants.

Among green plants—algae, grass, herbs, shrubs—trees stand out. They are the source of life in upright, elevated form. Addressing trees, Rabindranath Tagore wrote, "O Tree, O silent solemn tree, it was you who first joined patience to valor and showed how power can incarnate itself in peace."

Trees create an environment. They provide shade. They hold soil in place. They are the source of food for insects and lemurs and orange-and-coconut-eating people. In the immediate environment of every tree there is an aura, a vibration of life reaching up and out over earth and atmosphere to form the canopy of life.

Trees reveal their history in form. Every bend their branches make reaching for the sunlight-source of life congeals their past into motile shapes. Branches that break off leave bowls and knots so that their absence is visible. Old New England maple trees with their gnarled, knotted trunks and arching limbs personify the struggle, perseverance, triumph, and doom of all of us. Vast, thousand-rooted banyans in India create a microcosm that demonstrates manyness in unity, the proliferative spirit of life, the shaded hospitality of the world, and its mortal limit.

Trees are in constant motion. A squirrel shakes a limb as it jumps. Birds flip leaves as they fly into their nests. Raindrops strike a xylophonic patina on leaflets. Most of all, the wind constantly waves and ripples among the fluctuance of leaves. Trees stand in deep earth, but they wave and flutter halfway to heaven, earth-born but sky-bound. They reach. As the sky flies over them, their leaves undulate under it, generating noise that is soothing, constrained, varying, and oceanlike in its rocking, peaceful promise, harnessing the wind to make music.

A peaceful person with an open heart can feel a tree's experience. Free of pretension, free of pain, their rough bosoms manifest determination, strength, and endurance. They beautify the first layer of the atmosphere. They house birdsong. They die without complaint, and donate their bodies to the next generation. They do not quiver, flee, imagine, or pray.

Life is a flow of nutriment that commences with the oxygen and glucose created by green plants, and that assumes shapes and forms—baboons and whales and accountants—all dependent on the flow, all eating and breathing from the collective pool, all in constant transformation and flux. The cycle begins in unconsciousness and ends in death. Our bodies crave, demand oxygen and food. A moment of deprivation produces agony. Deprivation is always imminent. There is a relentless scramble, born in ignorance, punished by pain, ending in death—a scramble for breath and food. Restless desperation is intrinsic to ignorant life. All pleasure and relaxation is a temporary interlude purchased by a previous or pending scramble after sustenance. We feast on the deaths of wheat and carrots.

Born in ignorance and craving, unable to consciously know our purpose, we flow from birth to the unknown death that we cannot even dare to think about. Attempting to elevate ourselves through culture, civilization, and exalted thought, we build Auschwitz and the killing fields of Cambodia. A lust for security and self-assertion lurks in every collective human act.

We must face this aspect of truth to be liberated from it, by plunging into another dimension. Under the *bodhi* tree a man attained enlightenment. This is a metaphor for another aspect of the flow of nutriment: it can lead beyond itself, lifting a person beyond passion, greed, and autistic delusion, to find freedom, to feel and teach peace.

The tree is found at the commencement of the ignorant flow of nutriment, and sheltering the culminating path of wisdom. Preserving, befriending, living among trees is an association that elevates.

Thoreau and Muir gave homage to trees, and Tagore spoke directly to them.

> *I take refuge in you. Initiate me into the fellowship*
> *of tranquility, that I may hear the profound*
> *message of silence.*
> *I bend my head, burdened with anxious thoughts,*
> *and touch the dust in your soothing shade.*

Our bodies, our minds, are gifts. Our food, our breath, have all been donated to us. Reverence and gratitude make dust the proper crown of poets. Befriending trees, preserving them, planting them, meditating in their company, are all expressions of the peace-bound heart. We have protectors and friends whose leaves are already humming hymns of peace.

Chapter 27

A GREAT CRY
ON EARTH

THE PRACTICES FROM WHICH INNER PEACE DERIVES,
and which it in turn furthers, transcend material reality without rejecting it. To find inner peace, a person must be turned
completely around. A challenge is set before us by the radical
perception of "the flow of nutriment," which means: Is there
anything more to your life than the tumbling on of animal
instinct—"the male collects food, and the female lays eggs"?

Unconscious, ignorant human life today is more destructive than the glaciers that scraped earth bare. The conquest
of infectious illness—through the discovery of the germ
theory and the creation of modern hygiene, vaccination,
antibiotics, and other forms of technology—was the most
transformative event in the history of our planet. It eased
the suffering of billions of humankind across generations,
lessened mortality as well as pain, and created the population
explosion. Now the locust plague of humanity is consuming
the earth. Adding almost a billion to our population almost
every decade, there is no end in sight to the aggregation of
biomass in human bodies, males collecting food, females lay-
ing eggs, eating up every continent, every wild animal, every

open space. Someone likened human population growth to a giant zucchini in the garden that no one will pick and that just keeps growing.

Born out of thoughtless urgent procreative squirming, each body craves, demands, seeks, destroys in order to sustain itself. Where the population exceeds materials, as is true in Bangladesh, suffering is immediate and manifest. In America, there seems to be plenty. So reasonable people feel free to have three or four children, each of whom owns more by the age of eight or ten than a Bengali villager will own throughout his entire life. American children learn to compete, to achieve, to win, to get, to own, to consume . . . so their own children can get into a good college and get a head start in getting and consuming for their own children. Lest anyone interfere with the flow of raw materials necessary to maintain this cycle, the force of nuclear megatonnage stands ready.

Human life on earth is following the same laws that govern all unconscious procreation. Amoebas in a drop of water increase at the same rate as we are now doing . . . until at some critical mass, all nutrient is subsumed into biomass, toxic wastes increase, and extinction occurs. The drop once again becomes pure, sterile, dead. Natural population growth in an enclosed sphere like a drop, like planet Earth, inexorably grows toward a self-annihilating population holocaust.

The spontaneous direction of human life has produced a self-limiting expansion. The material basis of life is threatened by its own growth. Political discussions do not address this problem, but are characterized by avoidance and perseveration of symbolic power struggles. Yet what we face and what we must do has never been dearer. Science, literate communication, widespread education, historical and cultural research, all coalesce to give people the opportunity to understand their own impact upon the world and to direct the force of existence toward personal and communal enhancement.

But conscious selection for well-being for our drop of earth requires both an accurate picture of life and a satisfying and appropriate response. We require actions that empower each one of us to participate in collective reorientation.

The deepest value that inner peace brings within an individual exceeds the enhancing perspective and the ethical empathy that it bestows on that one person. Inner peace springs from cultural potential, reaches its farthest orbit in attained persons, and then radiates down through the social atmosphere, influencing the direction of society. Inner peace is the adaptive response of each individual heart that listens to the whole earth.

With a handful of simple facts we can comprehend our plight and clarify the social and ecological implications of personal peace.

A population deluge is flooding the earth. The number of human mammals never grew as high as one billion until the early nineteenth century. That it took us one or two million years to expand our population to one billion is not surprising, considering the magnitude of "one billion." To count to one billion would take ninety-five years! If we counted only once with every breath, day and night, without stopping for food or sleep, from birth to death, we would never even reach one billion. Such a vast herd of noses could accumulate only over eons. Yet to grow from one billion to two billion took only about one hundred years. Given a huge breeding population, not only the absolute numbers, but the rate of growth dramatically increased. By 1975, less than fifty years from the addition of the second billion, not one, but two billion people had been added to the earth's population for a total of four billion. The doubling time of the herd had shrunk to less than half the previous doubling time, and the absolute numbers exceeded human breath, time, or thought. Is it any coincidence that vast, impersonal killing began, and warfare became a matter of megadeath?

Because the base number is so gigantic, the population deluge is accelerating. If a billion children stood on each other's shoulders, they would tower past the moon. One billion children are now being added to the world approximately every ten years. One hundred million children swell the ranks every year. All the new people are children. All are helpless, dependent, needing parental time, food, clothing, schooling, and a corner of a room. Few will have more than a corner.

Because the base population is bigger and the doubling time is shorter, this increase in population does not just continue. It is snowballing. Today's population of nearly six billion is expected to double in about forty years (somewhat more than a billion each decade), to twelve billion. Where will they stand? What beach will they go to in the summer? Where will they take a quiet walk? Where will their feces be amassed? How will they be fed? Who will govern them, and by what methods? If every fertile couple in the world were to become a conscious, responsible reproducer, and there were to be no more than two children per couple on the average, given our current size and rate of growth, the population would stabilize at ten billion people. But if population continues its current real trend, there will in fact be sixteen billion people by the year 2100.

A great cry is hidden in the earth. The diverse forms of life that evolved over hundreds of millions of planetary years are being trampled. The flow of nutriment is drying up evolutionary diversity and is sweeping in a tidal wave of human biomass. What can all these bodies want and mean?

No wonder your personal life has speeded up its competitive pace. Billions of people want what you have, the cotton in your shirt, the water in your sink. In another decade, Mexico City alone will have thirty million people. Who will feed them? What political system will administer justice in a maze? By what means will Americans dare seal their border to the tens of millions of immigrants and refugees from Latin America, where seven out of ten people will soon live in urban slums? In fewer than forty years, the cities of India alone will house a nation much more populous than all of Europe today. In the twentieth century, India's population tripled, and is expected to double its monumental size again within the next thirty-five years, so that India will soon have as many people as did the whole world at the beginning of the last century. Where will solitude, deep thought, communion with nature, steal into a human community so compressed? John Muir tried to rescue Yosemite Valley by creating a National park there, but Yosemite has become like a loaf of bread in time of famine. Since seventy-five percent of Americans live in cities, and increasingly seek soothing rural vacations, two and a half million people visit Yosemite Valley annually. A typical summer day in Yosemite National Park was described by Ranger Starr Jenkins.

> . . . a fair-sized city—40,000 to 60,000 people—complete with smog, crime, juvenile delinquency, parking problems, traffic snarls, rush hours, gang warfare, slums, and urban sprawl . . . Bicycles, motorcycles, cars, stores, gas stations . . .

The furry mammals which were religious totems to humankind for hundreds of thousands of years—and which remain kin to children, who learn to name them before they learn to name familiar objects of their own culture, hugging stuffed effigies of their paleo-dream cousins—will all be delimited to rare and encircled survivorship in parks and preserves. Even when the dinosaurs were eliminated, not as many forms of life died out as are being exterminated today. The lords of fomenting and primeval lands, like caribou herds and polar bears and rhinoceros and elephants are all being murdered, evicted, eliminated. If elephants do not vanish entirely from Africa, due to environmental degradation and ivory hunting by desperately poor men, then they will be huddled as precious pets in big outdoor zoos, their lordship gone, their majestic statement of earthly imagination reduced to a lugubrious artifact. That they emerged as a solution to existence, a realization of the determined surge of being, will be a lost memory of an era of history smothered by the monoculture of people.

The sentimental designation of "endangered species" is outmoded. A tidal wave of predation, a spreading eruption of human hands and mouths, is dominating the plains, ravines and mountains, eating the large fleshbearing whales and elephants, and stamping out the stems of green.

If these ecological facts, statistics and descriptions seem severe or exaggerated to readers in America, it is because our society and pattern of life have protected us. The gaunt, restless millions that the facts portend are already here in agonized throngs. The evening news cushions us by leaping from issue to issue, focusing on the "developed" world, panning the camera across the faces of individual heroes or villains. The most significant form of denial utilized today is the belief that expanding population is a local problem in our own New York or Jakarta or Amherst, Massachusetts. The "local problem" is ubiquitous. The suburbanization of Connecticut is part of the same phenomenon as the gangs of childhood prostitute-thieves in Bogotá. They represent the unconscious expansion of human life without any other goal than food, warmth, and reproduction. Life with conscious direction is not yet represented by any civilization.

WHAT CAN WE DO? We like to imagine that our life has principle because we practice medicine or pursue socially responsible business or have sympathy for the poor. But how does this reverse the wave of blind physical accumulation that underlies our existence?

We need an entire reorientation to life. "Doing good" within the human community is meaningless when the community is itself lurching pointlessly forward. As long as we feel entitled to destroy, we are destructive. Our focus upon domination, however, can be turned around toward the harmony that internally peaceful people naturally extend toward people, birds, trees, and all other beings.

Can we imagine any purpose to a continuously expanding population of people? Will the world be more "meaningful" in the year 2100, when it has sixteen billion people, than it does today with six billion? Will there be any wild animals left, any open space left, any personal freedom left? Will political harmony prevail among the hungry, teeming, nuclear-armed tribal nations? If more life isn't better, is there any good to life at all? Are we the artifacts of physics and chance, as many scientists believe? Are we other than siphons of food material, machines of activity, protoplasm dividing? How do we differ from amoebas in a drop?

I watched a bird fly into the wide-open north door of a garage. In front of it, there was a small south window. The bird flew straight toward the window and banged into the glass. Hour after hour it fluttered up against the glass of the south window, seeking to fly toward the light it saw but could not reach.

Inner peace reverses our flight, turning us around to view the open door by which we came. Our revolution must certainly be inward-directed. The missing link between ecological knowledge and social activation of it is a psychological step. How can we alternatively produce the satisfaction that humankind currently extracts from procreation, consumption, and aggregate destruction? I place my hope on the cornerstone of inner peace.

"There are a thousand hacking at the branches of evil to one who is striking at the root," wrote Thoreau, but "there is nowhere recorded a simple and irrepressible satisfaction with the gift of life. . . . All health and success does me good, however far off."

Restrained lifestyle and inner joy, sought by each person starting with themselves alone, are the commandments of history. Containment and meditation are the angels who will intervene for us. Peace is the countercontagion. Enough honest souls anchored in the depths of themselves can form a stabilizing ballast to save us all from the hurricanes of humanity. And it is "the well-ordered heart that can mitigate the whirlwind."

People contain an invisible wavelength that grows out of the feeling of "enough!" It is not exotic nor esoteric, for it is found in every person, more or less developed. Peace ascends through the aperture of psychic fullness. Energy to pursue high values, mindfulness of the ephemeral sensations of every moment, thoughtful inquiry beyond complacency— these are the seeds of enlightenment. Concentration, calm, joy based on perspective rather than acquisition—these are seeds of enlightenment. Equanimity in all circumstances is the culmination of inner peace—the radiance of sufficiency.

Inner peace is not one particular belief system with guidelines and formulae for saving the world from the famine, violence, and confinement that current population growth augers. It is not justified merely as a social movement, so that if enough people practice it, then one day the world will be peaceful, wise, and saved. Instead, it offers a direction to those who take it. May we not hope that many will?

Whenever a man or a woman sits down contented and contained, aware of the transiency of body, mind, and self, finding liberating guidance from the inner quest, there, it seems to me, another step in evolution has been taken. Reptiles developed wings, but it was birds who made the atmosphere vibrate with song. Algae photosynthesize, but it was a tree that sheltered the quest for universal love and light. Human peacefulness can arrest the flow of nutriment, and initiate the flow of equable beneficence.

It is not necessary or desirable that every man and woman splash in the current of events. Only rudderless souls change their direction with the evening news. The quest for wisdom, serenity, and joy remains a private sanctuary and a group hope. Here is a durable, ever-relevant orientation. We don't need more steeples and turrets; we need deep wells of peace. The multitudes of small, apparently private personal decisions made by men and women are the crucibles of the earth.

AN OPULENCE OF NATURE endures around us. Even in the crowded Northeast United States, along the edges and seams of the old wildness, within the past twenty-four hours alone I saw a bald eagle lift its hulk and fly over my son's and my canoe; two mother turkeys with their bobbling horde of pinheaded young strutted in front of my car, and a doe grazed under the ancient apple tree in front of my cabin, her fawn racing up after her out of the woods on stick legs like a kid late for the school bus. Eagle, turkey, and deer are all resurrected species, once exterminated by New Englanders but later restored by conscious environmental love and planning. Our friends will rejoin us if we let them. There is a vibrant life yet to be lived in a world full of meditation centers, rivers, and furry company. The surge of population is also producing a complex problem-solving tool: the transpersonal mind. I am throwing myself into that current as hard as I can.

Nineteenth-century inventions were typified by individual breakthroughs, as when solitary Edison invented the light bulb, but the computer typifies not just new technology but a new style of working on solutions. We don't know the name of a person who invented the computer. No one invented the computer. It is still being invented as it was at the start by hundreds of thousands of multinational persons, groups, corporations, and tinkerers, working competitively, synergistically, through the addition of thousands of breakthroughs in rapid sequence and continuous redefinition.

Solutions that no one can imagine still exist. No one could imagine the multiple directions taken by computer technology. No one in the nineteenth century could have imagined our twenty-first century world. Jules Verne's brilliant prognostications of submarines and flying machines only reveal the shortfall of any one person's imagination. From the Holocaust to the moon walk, our world has been beyond imagination, and the same is true for the future, for better or for worse. But our expanding world will certainly be increasingly interconnected and interdependent, economically and through transportation and communication. We have become one people on one planet not through philosophy, religion, or enlightenment, but through the biology of food and the physics of space. That people contemplate global problems is a radical change presaging global solutions.

The cumulative aggregation of problem-solving thought exceeds not merely the capacity but even the wishful dreams of any one individual mind. I know that I can never know what can be known. We may still design a technology not only of information but of reverence and appreciation. The future may be better than our most fanciful hope. No amoeba could imagine a dinosaur; no dinosaur could conjure in its imagination the image of a human being. Dark forecasts measure only the constriction of individual thought. The world is never as narrow and small as one person's mind. Realizing the population blight we face shouldn't intimidate you; on the contrary, it should free you to feel there is nothing more important than to live *now* for inner peace. All of us are answering together Earth's question as we pursue our most cherished promptings.

Chapter 28

WE ARE
EVERYWHERE

COSMIC MAGIC, stewing slowly over a few billion years, transformed the dead elements of planet Earth into the incandescent human mind. This mind travels in its collective galleon across the ocean of time. The transgenerational length of this voyage is guided by those who can detach themselves from their personal transience long enough to glimpse the orienting point of inner light. Humanity navigates by people whose astrolabe points toward an eternal interior star. Hope enters the human community through those who "see the farthest and have the most faith."

Solutions to the new, crowded, interconnected era will not be just technological but spiritual. They will embrace sorrow for what each individual life is not, for without conscious awareness of the sorrow that is intrinsic to individuality, there will be no possible solution to group self-aggrandizing aggression and the plagues of externalizing blame that have characterized organized religions and nation-states. I prefer to meet people covered with tears rather than those holding a fistful of complaints.

Every young man and woman knows that love consists of barely punctuated silence. Silence makes way for great forces. Let us bring our silence to bear on the war of opinions and actions. Our footsteps are compressing the earth, our alimentary canals consuming and despoiling it; our vast collectivity is roasting it. Let us have better of less. Let us migrate like birds to the places where our songs—with their admittedly selfish territoriality—interweave with dawn itself.

The great sages have yet to be born.

The heavens we see above us reveal our neuronal capacity of perception. A more spangled constellation still rotates within. The complexity of our group vision has yet to be tapped. In the heart and mind, new scriptures beyond the limit of words remain suspended in orbit.

I have written this book in the hope that humanity can turn toward inner peace, living simply but with energy and devotion; having fewer children and raising them to fulfill their potential as creative, loving, poised people; eating and consuming selectively; crossing over their fear of sorrow and loneliness; vibrating in the renewal of ennobling words; aware in every moment that personal life is a temporary emergence, and steering this brief passage toward the ethical eternal. Once, it seemed naïve to imagine that the majority of adults would be able to read and write. To imagine humankind living toward inner peace may also become a self-fulfilling prophecy.

Just as we are taught to temper our self-serving aggression in preschool, in the same way we can develop a refined and elevating esthetic in our relation to earth. Every time we turn on the tap, buy food, drive our cars, or plan our careers, we could have in mind the whole, as already today we might sensitively weigh how our personal decisions will impact on our child's future or our spouse's mood. With harmony in every ripple of thought, we may heal our world as we prune ourselves in daily interpersonal engagement.

What I had hoped to be the greatest source of salvation for me—unspoiled nature—has been a recurrent source of suffering based upon my ignorant insistence that the world operate as I want it to work. What an era we live in! How clarifying! Everything I call "nature" is being destroyed. The God-in-nature is certainly pulling a trick on us relictual nineteenth century naturalists. Either he's checked out, leaving his estate to vandals, or he has a new scheme, to turn earth into a replica of Hoboken.

Maybe the anguish will be embodied in a new existence, the way Auschwitz led to Israel. Maybe all the dead whales and elephants and redwoods and bisons and rhinoceros, maybe the dead waters and dead skies, will cry out in new voices in new births that will be heard, and a new harmony and order will arise from the ashes.

Maybe people will adjust to a scraped, polluted earth the way people by the millions have already adjusted to New York and Tokyo and Calcutta and Ethiopia and Madagascar and Haiti. Maybe the giant sloth will cough his last Pleistocene laugh.

I'd like to see some more people sit still. I'd like to see internal joy replace external manipulation as the primary form of play. I'd like to see eternal peace accepted by all of humanity to be as real as personal death. Then everyone will know that inner peace is older than birdsong, more realistic than politics. I'd like to see childbearing become a rare, precious act, as treasured and uncommon as one's own birth and death should be.

My cabin, engulfed by spires of June grass and cupped in maternal enclaves of overlush forest, is still so beautiful, a haunt for scarlet tanagers, chestnut-sided warblers, and indigo buntings. I still dwell among Earth's babble of diversity in modes of being, in Earth's lush and secret spaces, in her silent folds, among her creative mammalian kaleidoscope.

I'm taking care to instill myself in the wisdom that erases suffering, by not stifling my life-pain, but, in full awareness, detaching myself from it. Maybe these hard-won new vibrations will help extinguish the fires of consumption on our planet; and if they don't help (for expecting them to would only be more suffering), then they will move one person toward liberation from infancy of mind. Suffering is an old story; wisdom is a new adventure, quite remarkable if we are truly descended through trilobites and lemurs. We have only just begun.

The spirits of those who live and speak for inner peace lead us to a vanishing point. Studying them is like watching deer that graze and suddenly fade into the foliage. Even if we are strong enough to yank free and traipse after peaceful exemplars, their trail evaporates. True leaders cannot be imitated. In the solitary field of personal decision, conscious life begins. The direction for our species is not set by the bellowing and shoving of premiers and captains, but where the vacuum of peacefulness sets off a deep, irresistible current. Our truest leaders have no names. They are everywhere. We are everywhere.

BILLIONS OF PEOPLE QUIETLY LIVE OUT some or much of what constitutes the path to peace. Inner peace is like the water molecule, which has a subtle charge called a "dipole moment" that enables it to bend and turn when pressed into microscopic creases and cracks in stone. Even when water molecules cannot flow, they can rotate. With cosmic patience, water wears down the rocky mantle of the earth into sand and life-bearing soil. Because of the ache it satisfies in the human heart, peace is a pervasive, illimitable force.

Individual citizens have a dipole moment that will turn the world. Destruction is public and vast like storms sweeping down the street, but peace starts in private crevasses, at the heart, within.

On the mythic day of Armageddon, when the world is destroyed and every sinner stands naked and unsupported in the void to face fate in accordance with his or her deeds, I imagine the tribunal judging us won't consist of winged angels or horned devils, but will be a black-capped chickadee, a lynx, and a birch tree. They will know as clearly as you and I do that one predator species has cut down every virgin forest, killed as many plants and animals as he could get away with, spoiled every source of fresh water, and fouled every ocean of the planet. Who can you and I bring forward as our character witnesses? Right now, I am cultivating friendship with black bears, a woodlot in Vermont, and a Canadian river. I'm not saving nature: I'm letting nature save *me.* The redpolls who fly south from the Arctic in winter to eat thistle outside my kitchen windows are missionaries to the savage that I am. I am letting them convert me. I offer them food so they will fly and sing on my behalf in a peaceful world.

Whether humankind U-turns away from dysplastic growth toward peace or not, I have—and you have—the option to live the best possible life. Inner peace is already within you, waiting to be opened. Cultivating inner peace will make you happier and more resilient and practical, able to face the difficulties of your personal death and human communal confusion head-on. It will open you to realizations that exceed the pragmatic, so that you will enter the stream of peace that is always invisibly flowing in and around you. Engaged in the world most helpfully, you will become an internal habitue of a place beyond the wind, the abode of peace.

I dream that some evening at 8 p.m., the whole world will sit down to meditate on the transient sensations of their body, with an accompanying peaceful awareness of the illusory nature of individuality, and as 8 p.m. travels east to west around the globe, a vibration of human harmony will follow the path of the fading sun. I may not be there, the particles of my eyelids and bones long since dispersed and reaggregated into other forms that grew, then passed away; and the thoughts of my mind long since absorbed by ongoing generations the way that children soak up affection from watchful eyes. The trace of my own meditation will still be felt, the way that rivulets of rain leave pathways, and you will have received that rain, and will be meditating with the birds, the trees, and the earth.

Then your quiet will hold your greatest power, your stillness will become your most important action, and your inner peace will be the simple great gift you will transmit.

Notes

PREFACE (pp. xvii-xxii)

"Ask, and it shall be given"   Luke 11:9-10.

Paul R. Fleischman, *The Healing Spirit: Explorations in Religion and Psychotherapy,* New York : Paragon House, 1990; and *Spiritual Aspects of Psychiatric Practice,* Cleveland, SC : Bonne Chance Press, 1993.

INTRODUCTION (pp. 1-15)

The poetry quoted in the Introduction comes from *You Can Never Speak Up Too Often For the Love of All Things*, by Paul R. Fleischman, M.D., Pariyatti Press, Onalaska, WA, 2004, and from *Tides of Renewal*, by Paul R. Fleischman, M.D., a forthcoming collection of poetry.

Tapas first appeared in *Insight,* Fall, 2001.

CHAPTER 2 (pp. 32-39)

E. Jones, *The Life and Work of Sigmund Freud,* 3 vols. New York: Basic Books, 1953, 1955, 1957.

"In the morning, I bathe" H.D. Thoreau, *Walden.* New York:

Mentor Books, 1942, p. 198, "The Pond in Winter."

J. Mascaró, trans., *Bhagavad Gita.* London: Penguin Books, 1962, particularly pp. 80, 89.

E. Odum, *Ecology.* New York: Holt, Rinehart, Winston, 1963.

J. Mascaró, trans., *The Dhammapada.* London: Penguin Books, 1973, particularly p. 64.

"... *troubles were overcome*" *The Times* (London), 24 March, 1987.
The London Times published The *Times* (London), 12 March, 1966
"*The sun shall be no more thy light*" Isaiah 60:19.

CHAPTER 3 (pp. 43-49)
"*I no longer perceived colors*" Quoted in J. G. Ravin, "Monet's cataracts,"
    JAMA 254 (3):394.
"*You can still do it*" Quoted in Metropolitan Museum of Art,
Monet's Years at Giverny: Beyond Impressionism. New York: Harry N.
    Abrams, Inc., 1978, p. 32.
"*I am terribly sad*" Quoted in J. G. Ravin, op. cit., pp. 398, 399.

CHAPTER 4 (pp. 50-59)
The quotes of the Nearings in this chapter come from the following
    sources:
H. Nearing and S. Nearing, "Our search for the good life," *Country
    Journal* (November 1976), p. 64.
H. Nearing and S. Nearing, *Living the Good Life.* New York: Schocken
    Books, 1970, particularly pp. xv, xvi, xviii,.20, 43, 45, 183, 184,
    187, 197.
H. Nearing and S. Nearing, *Continuing the Good Life.* New York:
    Schocken Books, 1979, particularly pp. 2, 4, 11, 16, 182, 184. D.
    McCaig, "Helen Nearing," *Country Journal* (January/February
    1990), p. 58.
See also:
"... *what it means to begin.*" M. Buber, *The Knowledge of Man,* M.
    Friedman, ed. New York: Harper Torch Books, 1965, p. 7.

CHAPTER 5 (pp. 63-65)
"*unencumbered by baggage*" C. G. Valles, *Unencumbered by Baggage:
    Father Anthony DeMello; A Prophet for Our Times.* Anand, India:
    Gujarat Sahitya Prakash, 1988.
"*Bravery deals not so much*" H.D. Thoreau, quoted in R. D.
Richardson, *Henry Thoreau: A Life of the Mind.* Berkeley: University
    of California Press, 1986, p. 69.

CHAPTER 6 (pp. 66-73)
"*a long talk with the Indians*" J. Muir, "Discovery of Glacier Bay,"
    Wilderness Essays. Salt Lake City: Peregrine Smith, UT 1980, p. 23.

CHAPTER 8 (pp. 85-93)

The quotes about Shakers in this chapter come from the following
    sources:

"A Broadside of Shaker History and Belief," on display as a poster at
    Hancock Shaker Village, Hancock, MA.

F. Morse, *The Story of the Shakers.* Woodstock, VT: Countryman Press,
    1986, pp. 7, 14, 16, 33, 40, 63, 84, 86, 88.

C. Newman, "The Shakers' Brief Eternity," *National Geographic* 176
    (3):304, 319, 321.

L. Riddle, "Shaker Village Buoyed Up by New Blood," *The New York
    Times,* 28 August, 1988, p. 43.

See also:

". . an island unto yourself." W. Hart, *The Art of Living.* San Francisco:
    Harper & Row, 1987, pp. 15 and 23.

". . . the artist, the human being." Quoted in R. D. Richardson, *Henry
    Thoreau: A Life of the Mind.* Berkeley: University of California
    Press, 1986, frontispiece.

CHAPTER 9 (pp. 97-98)

"In the beginning" John 1:1.

CHAPTER 10 (pp. 99-106)

"By seeking truth I have discovered" R.A. Mitchell, *The Buddha: His
    Life Retold.* New York: Paragon House, 1989, p. 137.

"carried Leaves of Grass *around Concord like a red flag"* R. D.
    Richardson, *Henry Thoreau: A Life of the Mind.* Berkeley:
    University of California Press, 1986, p. 348.

"He speaks the truth " Nyanatiloka, *The Word of the Buddha,* llth ed.
    Kandy, Sri Lanka: Buddhist Pub. Soc., 1967, pp. 50-51.

". . . nothing remarkable about him" L. Fischer, *The Life of Mahatma
    Gandhi.* New York: Collier Books, 1950, pp. 370-380, 355.

CHAPTER 11 (pp. 107-118)

All quotes of Walt Whitman's poetry come from:

W. Whitman, *Leaves of Grass.* New York: New American Library, 1960,
    particularly pp. 49, 50, 52, 74-77, 89, 90, 91, 93, 95, 136, 138, 142,
    144, 269, 416; W. Whitman, *Leaves of Grass, the first*

(1855) Edition, M. Cowley, ed. New York: Penguin Books, 1959, pp.
    9, 29, 30, 55, 82, 85, 138; and W. Whitman, *Leaves of Grass and
    Selected Prose,* Mod. Lib. Ed., J. Kouwenhoven, ed., New York:
    Random House, 1950, pp. 552, 640, 759.

Biographical and critical quotations about Whitman come from:

M. Bucke, *Cosmic Consciousness.* New York: Causeway Books, 1974, p. 182.

J. Kaplan, *Walt Whitman: A Life.* New York: Bantam Books, *1982,* pp. 13, 17, 24, 171,229, 230, 249.

B. Perry, *Walt Whitman.* New York and London: Chelsea House, 1981, pp. 96, 276.

P. Zweig, *Walt Whitman: The Making of the Poet.* New York: Basic Books, 1984, p. 10.

See also:

H. D. Thoreau, "Reading," in *Walden.* New York: Mentor Books, 1942.

CHAPTER 12 (pp. 119-126)

L. Fischer, *The Life of Mahatma Gandhi.* New York: Collier Books, 1950, p. 94.

M. K. Gandhi, *An Autobiography.* Ahmedabad: Navajivan Publishing House, 1927, pp. 65, 102, 119, 224.

V. Mehta, "Mahatma Gandhi and His Apostles," *The New Yorker* (10 May, 1976), pp. 45-50.

H. D. Thoreau, "Sounds," in *Walden.* New York: Mentor Books, 1942.

CHAPTERS 13 AND 14 (pp. 129-144)

Quotations from John Muir can be found in:

J. Muir, *Stickeen.* Berkeley: Heyday Books, 1981.

J. Muir, *The Mountains of California.* New York: Dorset Press, 1988.
J. Muir, *Wilderness Essays,* Salt Lake City: Peregrine Smith, 1980.

M. P. Cohen, "Origins and Early Outings: A History of the Club's Birth and Its Early Wilderness Travels," in *The Sierra Club: A Guide,* 1989, p. 9.

J. Muir, *The Story of My Boyhood and Youth.* Boston: Houghton-Mifflin, 1913, pp. 2, 25-26.

Biographical information and quotations can be found in:

L. M. Wolfe, *Son of the Wilderness: The Life of John Muir.* New York: Knopf, 1945.

CHAPTER 15 (pp. 145-155)

"the patron saint of ecology" L. White, "The Historical Roots of Our Ecological Crisis," *Science* 155 (1967): 1203-1207.

the Theragāthā V.F. Gunarama, *The Message of the Saints: Thera- Theri-Gatha.* Kandy, Sri Lanka: Buddhist Pub. Soc., 1969.

Quotes of Thoreau can be found in:

H. D. Thoreau, *The Portable Thoreau,* C. Bode, ed. New York: Viking Press, 1947.

H. D. Thoreau, "Spring," in *Walden.* New York: Mentor Books, 1942.

H. D. Thoreau, *The Journal of Henry Thoreau,* 14 vols. B. Torrey and
F. A. Allen, eds. Boston: Houghton-Mifflin, 1906.

H. D. Thoreau, *The Maine Woods,* J. J. Moldenhauer, ed. Princeton NJ:
Princeton Univ. Press, 1972.

For biographical information as well as direct quotes from Thoreau, see:

R. Fields, *How the Swans Came to the Lake: A Narrative History of
Buddhism in America.* Boulder, CO: Shambala, 1981, p. 64.

W. Harding, *The Days of Henry Thoreau: A Biography.* New York:
Dover, 1962; the chorus of quotes describing Thoreau's death
come from pp. 454-468.

R. D. Richardson, *Henry Thoreau: A Life of the Mind.* Berkeley:
University of California Press, 1986.

"Every morning was a cheerful invitation" The quotes in this passage
come in order from the following:

H. D. Thoreau, *Walden,* op. cit., pp. 64, 65; W. Harding, *The Days of
Henry Thoreau,* op. cit., p. 198; "Walking," in *The Portable Thoreau,* op. cit., pp. 594, 630; H. D. Thoreau, *Walden,* op. cit., pp.
92, 93; "Life Without Principle," in *The Portable Thoreau,* op. cit.,
pp. 646, 469.

See also:

"Civilization, in the real sense" L. Fischer, quoted in *The Life of Mahatma
Gandhi.* New York Collier Books, 1950, pp. 305, 309 (quote).

CHAPTER 16 (pp. 156-158)

"Cherish the forest depths" Last Days of the Buddha, Mahā-Parinibbāna
Sutta. Kandy, Sri Lanka: Buddhist Pub. Soc., 1974, Wheel 67/68/69,
p. 5.

"Now I see the secret" W. Whitman, *Leaves of Grass.* New York: New
American Library, 1955, p. 138.

CHAPTER 17 (pp. 161-171)

D. Berrigan, *To Dwell in Peace: An Autobiography.* San Francisco: Harper
& Row, 1987. For the subsequent quotes, see pp. 81, 95, 248.

CHAPTER 19 (pp. 179-184)

"Once there was" D.G. Mukerji, *Rama: Hero of India.* New York: E.
P. Dutton & Co., 1930. Contains one version of this widely told
myth.

CHAPTER 20 (pp. 187-197)

"like a phantasm, a fantasy" N. Senzaki, *Like a Dream, Like a Fantasy: The Zen Writings and Translations of Nyogen Senzaki, E.* Shimano, ed. Tokyo: Japan Pub., 1978. For subsequent quotes, see pp. 30, 46, 47, 31, 42, 35, 38, 39, 41.

"Buddhist monk is celibate" P. Reps, ed., *Zen Flesh, Zen Bones: A Collection of Zen and Pre-Zen Writings.* Garden City, NY: Anchor Doubleday, undated. For this and subsequent quotes, see pp. 4, 85, 51-52.

"Friends in Dhamma be satisfied" Slightly varying texts appear in R. Fields, *How Swans Came to the Lake.* Boulder, CO: Shambala, 1981, p. 218; and in N. Senzaki, op. cit., p. 8.

CHAPTERS 22 AND 23 (pp. 215-246)

For background on Rabindranath Tagore, see the following:

H. Banerjee, *Rabindranath Tagore.* New Delhi: Pub. Div., Min. of Information and Broadcasting, Govt. of India, 1971.

K. Kripalani, *Rabindranath Tagore: A Biography.* London and New York: Oxford Univ. Press, 1962.

P. K. Mukherji, *Life of Tagore.* Thompson, CT: Inter Culture Associates, 1975.

V. S. Naravane, *An Introduction to Rabindranath Tagore.* Columbia, MI: South Asia Books, 1978.

R. Tagore, *My Reminiscences.* New York: Macmillan, 1917.

"The spiritual ambassador. . . symbol of her culture . . ." H. Banerjee, op. cit., pp. 141-142.

"'When I was very young. . . I have kept the child spirit. . . " Quoted in A. Chakravarty, *A Tagore Reader.* Boston: Beacon Press, 1966, p. 206.

"Because I underwent this process. . . the greatest freedom possible . . ." Quoted in A. Chakravarty, op. cit., p. 215.

"I had it in my mind . . . harmony with all existence." Quoted in   A. Chakravarty, op. cit., pp. 215, 216, 219.

"I believe in a spiritual world . . . stately sal trees," Quoted in A. Chakravarty, op. cit., pp. 221-223.

". . . the lasting power of the Eternal . . . my tangible poem," Quoted in V. S. Naravane, *An Introduction to Rabindranath Tagore,* op. cit., pp. 150, 159, 162, 164, 165.

"In desperate hope I go . . . the allness of the universe." R. Tagore, *Gitanjali,* with an introduction by W. B. Yeats. New York: Macmillan, 1913, poem 87.

"If the dark night of sorrow . . . let it be so." Quoted in H. Banerjee, *Rabindranath Tagore,* op. cit., p. 84.

"Suddenly I hear" For the quotes from *Balākā*, I used two translations: A. Bose, trans., *A Flight of Swans: Poems from Balākā,* by Rabindranath Tagore. London: John Murray, 1955, pp. 1-3; and L. Ray, trans., *One Hundred and One Poems by Rabindranath Tagore.* New York: Asia Pub. House, 1966, pp. 100-101.

In the imaginary poetic universe All the quotes following come from R. Tagore, *Lover's Girl and Crossing.* Delhi, Bombay, Madras, and Calcutta: MacMillan Co. of India, 1918, except where otherwise noted.

"I saw, in the twilight" R. Tagore, *Selected Poems,* W. Radice, trans. Middlesex, England: Penguin Books, 1985, p. 107.

*"giving voice to the protest"*Quoted in K. Kripalani, *Rabindranath Tagore,* op. cit., p. 266.

". . . worshipped the ground he trod . . . one end of Europe to the other." H. Banerjee, *Rabindranath Tagore,* op. cit., pp. 124, 130.

"Guests of my life . . . God's footprints on my floor, " Quoted in R. Tagore, *Lover's Gift and Crossing,* op. cit.

CHAPTER 24 (pp. 249-267)

"keep your mind untrammeled" Quoted in L. M. Wolfe, *Son of the Wilderness: The Life of John Muir.* New York: Knopf, 1945, p. 154.

"True beauty" Quoted in L. Fischer, *The Life of Mahatma Gandhi.* New York: Collier Books, 1950, p. 300.

"He or she dwells observing" *Mahā-satipaṭṭhāna Sutta,* Seattle: Vipassana Research Publications, 1995.

A person who wants to locate a Vipassana course, taught for free by volunteers who themselves received the technique for free and who cultivated it for a lifetime, can find information and course schedules at **www.dhamma.org.**

Courses are conducted worldwide. Meditation centers, run on a donation basis, dot the globe from India and the rest of Asia through Australia and New Zealand, to Europe, America, and elsewhere, and courses are run outside of centers, too. More than one hundred thousand people a year currently attend them.

CHAPTER 26 (pp. 285-295)

"I take refuge in you" R. Tagore, *One Hundred and One Poems,* V. S. Naravone, trans. New York: Asia Pub. House, 1966, p. 116.

CHAPTER 27 (pp. 296-306)

"the male collects" K. Uchiyama, *The Zen Teaching of "Homeless" Kodo.* Kyoto, Japan: Kyoto Soto Zen Center, 1990, p. 23.

To count to one billion D.M. Schwartz, *How Much Is a Million?* New York: Lothrop, Lee & Shepard, 1985.

". . . a fair sized city . . . stores, gas stations . . ."Zero Population Growth Reporter, October 1989, p. 3.

"There are a thousand hacking" H.D. Thoreau, *Walden.* New York: Mentor Books, 1942, pp. 56-58.

"the well-ordered heart" D. Berrigan, *To Dwell in Peace: An Autobiography.* San Francisco: Harper & Row, 1987, p. 173.

Index

About the Author

PAUL FLEISCHMAN, M.D., a practicing psychiatrist, was awarded the Oskar Pfister Award of the American Psychiatric Association in 1993 for his outstanding contributions to the field of psychiatry and religion. A Phi Beta Kappa graduate of the University of Chicago and a member of the Alpha Omega Alpha medical honors society, he received his M.D. from the Albert Einstein College of Medicine and trained in psychiatry at Yale University. Dr. Fleischman has been a psychiatric consultant to hospitals, colleges, and clinics, and has been a Williamson lecturer in medicine and religion at the University of Kansas, special guest lecturer at Smith College Chapel, as well as a keynote speaker at medical schools, psychiatric societies, churches, synagogues, retreat centers, and colleges. His professional papers have appeared in the *Yale Review, Nature, Landscape, American Journal of Psychiatry,* and numerous other professional journals. He is the author of *The Healing Spirit, Spiritual Aspects of Psychiatric Practice, Karma and Chaos* and *The Buddha Taught Nonviolence, Not Pacifism.* His recent focus has been on poetry. Forthcoming collections are: *You Can Never Speak Up Too Often for the Love of All Things* and *Tides of Renewal.*

Dr. Fleischman lives in Amherst, Massachusetts, with his wife, children's book author and teacher, Susan Fleischman.

ABOUT PARIYATTI

Pariyatti is dedicated to providing affordable access to authentic teachings of the Buddha about the Dhamma theory (*pariyatti*) and practice (*paṭipatti*) of Vipassana meditation. A 501(c)(3) non-profit charitable organization since 2002, Pariyatti is sustained by contributions from individuals who appreciate and want to share the incalculable value of the Dhamma teachings. We invite you to visit www.pariyatti.org to learn about our programs, services, and ways to support publishing and other undertakings.

Pariyatti Publishing Imprints

Vipassana Research Publications (focus on Vipassana as taught by S.N. Goenka in the tradition of Sayagyi U Ba Khin)

BPS Pariyatti Editions (selected titles from the Buddhist Publication Society, co-published by Pariyatti in the Americas)

Pariyatti Digital Editions (audio and video titles, including discourses)

Pariyatti Press (classic titles returned to print and inspirational writing by contemporary authors)

Pariyatti enriches the world by

- disseminating the words of the Buddha,
- providing sustenance for the seeker's journey,
- illuminating the meditator's path.

www.ingramcontent.com/pod-product-compliance
Lightning Source LLC
Chambersburg PA
CBHW021043090426
42738CB00006B/155